# Military Justice
## Is to Justice
### as Military Music
## Is to Music

*Books by Robert Sherrill:* The Accidental President

Gothic Politics in the Deep South

The Drugstore Liberal
   (*with Harry Ernst*)

Military Justice Is to Justice
as Military Music Is to Music

# Military Justice

HARPER COLOPHON BOOKS
Harper & Row, Publishers
New York, Evanston, and London

# Is to Justice

## as Military Music

## Is to Music

*Revised Edition*

*by Robert Sherrill*

Portions of this book have appeared, in different form, in the following publications: the *New York Times, The Nation, Pageant* and *Playboy.*

*First* HARPER COLOPHON *edition, revised 1970, published by Harper & Row, Publishers, Inc.*

SBN 06-090230-2

To
Willie Morris
Ronnie Dugger
Robert Hatch
Tom Congdon

# Contents

# Acknowledgments

Much of the research was made possible through traveling assignments from James Goode of *Playboy* and Harvey Shapiro of the *New York Times Magazine*. For auxiliary assignments that added important basic information on military penal defects, my thanks to Carey McWilliams of *The Nation* and to Dave Sendler of *Pageant*. I absolutely could not have done without the advice of several attorneys whose work on behalf of harried servicemen has been great: Charles Morgan, Jr., Reber Boult, Terence Hallinan, David Lowe, Paul Halvonik, and Edward Sherman; but of course any legal stupidities are my own and not theirs. My thanks also to all the servicemen, ex-servicemen, deserters and drifting AWOL malcontents who patiently unloaded details at our meetings from coast to coast; among the former officers who helped, my special thanks to Dr. Larry McNamee, who refused to accept the Pendleton way of life as being man's highest expression of humanity. Carl Rogers of the Servicemen's Link to Peace unfailingly kept me up with the latest confrontation. Dr. Paul Nelson was a real friend in tapping the Library of Congress for necessary research. And Mary, Brooke, Peter and Charlie were always right in there raising hell when the moment called for it.

Military Justice
Is to Justice
as Military Music
Is to Music

# 1. Citizens First, Soldiers Second

I T IS ONE OF THE IRONIES of patriotism that a man who is called to the military service of his country may anticipate not only the possibility of giving up his life but also the certainty of giving up his liberties.

Historically, the man in uniform has been viewed as the property of his commanding officer, to be fed, clothed, rewarded and punished as the commander believed appropriate for the preparation for war and the waging of it. The serviceman has had to bend his personal life to what even such a libertarian as Chief Justice Warren tolerantly viewed as the "military necessity" for absolute discipline, order and conformity. If the serviceman does not bend, his commander—with the approval of the federal government—can break him at will.

Such arbitrary jurisdiction, of course, cannot be exercised in a manner consistent with the guarantees of the Constitution. From the beginning of our country, the Bill of Rights has had little or no relevance to the code of justice governing the military. But in the last twenty years critical legal questions have been raised as to whether or not the military can safely be left to hold this kind of total power over a largely conscript army. The challenge to the old system is coming not from Congress, which set up the system in the first place, nor from the U.S. Supreme Court, which has steadily condoned the old tyrannies. The challenges are coming from many of the conscript servicemen themselves and from their militant attorneys.

One of the favorite sayings of those in the latter category, the GI underground—you read it in their newspapers, you hear it from their attorneys—is an old quote attributed to Clemenceau: "Military justice is to justice as military music is to music." As epigrams go, this one is unusually accurate. Both military music and military justice have purposes narrower than music and justice; one is supposed to keep "the boys" pepped up, the other is intended to keep them tamed down. But neither John Philip Sousa nor the Uniform Code of Military Justice is what it used to be, in its effects on the men in the ranks.

Some of the young draftees are asking why they should not be permitted to publish and distribute their own newspapers, even if the papers are filled—as, indeed, they are—with the bitterest of criticisms of U.S. foreign and military policies. Some ask why they cannot, as can the West German soldier, join unions that would negotiate with the government over working and living conditions. They want to know why they should not be permitted to march in peace parades and attend peace rallies. Considering themselves citizens first and soldiers second, they ask why it is that rights that other citizens take for granted—the rights to petition, to assemble, to speak freely, to publish at will—somehow cease to apply when a man puts on a uniform to defend those rights. They are also asking why a man, because he wears a uniform, should take unjust punishment without protest.

But more than inquiring, many of the dissident servicemen are acting. A shocked and angry Pentagon has watched its field commanders defied by servicemen like Captain Howard Levy, who went to jail rather than support the Vietnam war by training Green Berets for it; Second Lieutenant Henry Howe, who also went to jail for speaking his mind against this nation's policy in Vietnam; the "Fort Jackson Eight," who risked court-martial by refusing to end their rally against the war; the "Presidio 27," who finally would take no more abuse from their prison keepers.

The poles are quite distinct. At one end, the men who run the military system maintain that they must continue to have total domination over the lives of their personnel or the armed services will fall apart. At the other limit, many of the servicemen and their lawyers insist that they will accept no compromise, agree to no reform short of doing away with the military system of justice and delivering the servicemen to the jurisdiction of the civilian courts.

What follows are accounts of some of the court-martial and prison confrontations—not a detached, scholarly analysis of them but an effort to experience through them the ordeal of military justice, for whatever common-sense conclusions can be drawn. In their cumulative effect, these encounters are finally beginning to force the courts and Congress to deal with the overriding question of whether the Constitution should not be applied to the life of the American serviceman. At the same time, they are making it clear that the problem has grown to such dimensions that it will never again respond to half-answers and patchwork reform.

# 2. The Presidio "Mutiny"

ONE OF THE STRANGEST and certainly one of the most notorious displays of military justice in modern times occurred after twenty-seven young soldiers imprisoned in an Army stockade in San Francisco broke formation at the work line-up on the morning of October 14, 1968, sang songs and demanded to see the press, to see lawyers and to have an audience with the stockade commandant.

The Army base at which this happened is the Presidio, an old fort built on what is now one of the most valuable pieces of real estate on the West Coast. Its grounds abut the southern end of the Golden Gate Bridge. The air is usually sweet and cool. Much of the architecture in the neighborhood is Frontier Victorian, a style with a plain, restrained charm. It is not the place one would expect bitter confrontations. It is certainly not the place one would expect to encounter mutiny. But for the crime of breaking ranks and regrouping as a discordant chorus, the twenty-seven, whose average age was nineteen, were charged with mutiny, the rarest and most serious charge that can be drawn from the Military Code of Justice. By being singled out historically in this fashion they became celebrated as "The Presidio 27." Twenty-two were convicted of mutiny and two of disobeying an order, the other three having escaped prison and fled to Canada before their courts-martial could be held.

To bring about the convictions, the Army spent about half a million dollars for investigators, court costs, attorney salaries, public relations campaigns and travel. Not one but three preliminary hearings were held. The courts-martial themselves were scattered all over the calendar—from January, 1969, to June, 1969—and over the West Coast—three at the Presidio in San Francisco, one at Fort Irwin, California, one at Fort Ord, California, and one at Fort Lewis, Washington.

Depending upon one's bias, the prosecution of the Presidio "mutineers" will be seen as a courageous and proper response by the Army to the growing dissidence among draftees, or as the most heavy-handed kind of suppression of legitimate complaint. Those who side with the soldiers will doubtless agree with one of their defense attorneys that "the whole incident was an effort, misguided, perhaps foolish, to appeal, to beseech the properly constituted authorities to recognize that grievances existed and that those grievances had a real basis in fact"—sadistic prison guards, inferior food and quarters. Those who agree with the Army will find it easy to follow the logic of one of its prosecutors, Captain Dean Flippo, when he argued that it didn't matter if the protest was peaceful and it didn't matter if the men had grievances. "It is the attack on the system," he said, "not the method of the attack that is important in determining whether there is a mutiny. This was an attack on the system by these twenty-seven men. That is all we're concerned about."

The Presidio stockade was built two generations ago as a bank—it still uses some of the wiring originally installed for the burglar alarm. It is a dismal place. Paul Halvonik, an American Civil Liberties Union lawyer in San Francisco who has had clients in every major jail and prison in California, rated the Presidio in this manner: "San Quentin death row is a nice place to be if you don't want to live. At least they give you good food. The main line isn't so good as death row, but it's better than a county jail. Presidio stockade is worse than a county jail."

For persons who have not experienced the Lysol hospitality of any prison, the question of course still hangs: How bad is worse? At the time of the sit-down there were 140 prisoners at the Presidio, of whom 120 were imprisoned in space meant to hold 88. There was one toilet for about every thirty-five prisoners because not all of the toilets had seats and some were stopped up and unusable. Much of the time there was no toilet paper. The clogged toilets backed up into the shower rooms, the floors of which were some-times two or three inches under water. Human feces floated in the water, so it was sometimes best to wear one's boots while taking a shower. Prisoners had to buy their own soap, and if a prisoner ran out in the middle of the week, he couldn't have another bar until the next week. If he lost his toothbrush, he couldn't get another until the following month. Prisoners in segregated cells were sometimes not permitted to bathe or brush their teeth for a week. The barracks were crowded and prisoners lying on the top tier of the bunk beds were suffocatingly close to the ceiling. Once there was a fire in a segregation cell and prisoners on the top floor of the stockade found themselves locked in. On the day of the sit-down, as on other days, the stockade was short of food. There were only fifty-four drinking cups for the whole prison population. Recrea-tion consisted of one movie a week, chosen by the chaplain. The prison library, which closed at 4 P.M., before the men came back from work, was in the basement and accessible only by making one's way around garbage cans; the books were ancient ones, on such subjects as mysticism and military history. Families could visit prisoners, but it was against the rules, for example, for an inmate father to hold his baby. Everywhere were filth and the smell of human waste. And, of course, there were rats.

But the men who sat down in the prison yard that fine October morning in 1968 had deeper worries than arise from poor living conditions. There was an atmosphere of brutality about the Presidio stockade that made them panicky.

An official Presidio press release claimed that "prisoners live a more comfortable life than the regular soldier who performs his duties properly." Then why the fifty-two suicide attempts in 1968? Colonel Harry J. Lee, provost marshal for the Sixth Army, had a reply: "There have been no suicides nor has there been a bonafide suicide attempt at the stockade in the memory of personnel now serving at the facility since at least June, 1966." The Army does not call them suicide attempts; it calls them "gestures." Private Roy Pulley, one of the protesters, told how one gesture struck him: "I was lying on my side on the bunk reading one night, and this guy across the room was sitting on his bunk. He tied something around his arm to make the veins swell up so he could cut them better. And when he cut them, the blood flew about twenty feet—hit me right in the back of the neck."

A total of six gestures was made by Ricky Lee Dodd. On one occasion he cut his wrists when he was imprisoned in solitary. He was taken to the hospital, where the wrists were sewn up and bandaged, and he was returned to the stockade. This time he removed the gauze from his wrists and hanged himself. When he arrived back at the hospital he was pronounced dead, but he was revived. He had previously attempted suicide by slashing and hanging. After one of those earlier attempts, a guard had handed him a razor blade with the cheerful encouragement, "If you want to try again, here we go." After another, a guard had squirted him with urine from a water pistol.

One prisoner who slit his throat was taken to the hospital, stitched up and returned the same day to the isolation cell, where he had no toilet and had to sleep on an iron grating.

Twenty-one prisoners had attempted suicide in the three months prior to the mutiny—a total of thirty-three attempts. These included twelve cuttings of wrists, arms and chest; a throat cutting;

and eight dosings of lye, detergent, oven cleaner, shampoo, metal polish and something identified only as "poison."

The men who ran the Presidio paid little attention to these gestures. As Lieutenant Colonel John Ford, Presidio provost general, put it, they felt these prisoners were "just trying to get medical discharges."*

Every stockade has its isolation cells. (Some stockades are so crowded these days that two or three men will share "isolation.") The Presidio has five such cells; two were painted black before the prisoners demonstrated (since then they have been repainted gray, and Presidio officers pretend they were never painted black) and three painted white. Estimates of the dimensions of these "boxes," as they are called, vary somewhat, the prisoners claiming that they are 5½ to 6 feet long and 4½ feet wide. The Army claims that the boxes are 6 feet long and 5 feet wide. But even if the Army's measurements are accurate, the cells have less than the minimum space required by the Army's own regulations (8 feet long and 6 feet wide).

The isolation cells have no toilets; to go to the bathroom, one must persuade a guard to give escort, and frequently the guards prefer to ignore these requests. The white cells have no furniture but a bunk; the black cells have no furniture at all. The tops of these five adjoining cells are covered with wire screening. One light above this screen throws a feeble glow over the five cells, inadequate for reading the Bible, which is the only reading material permitted in isolation.

The isolation cells are frequently used to confine psychotic prisoners; prisoners who attempt suicide are always sent to the box. One of the insane inmates best remembered by former guards was a young man they nicknamed "Penis" because he sat around

* At one of the mutiny trials Captain Emmitt Yeary accused Colonel Ford of ordering the burning of five photographs, taken by a sympathetic guard at the time of the demonstration, showing conditions in the segregation cells and the latrines and also a bulletin-board roster that revealed the extent of the overcrowding of the stockade.

in his isolation cell all day moaning, "I want my penis, I want my penis." He played with himself, urinated on the floor and rolled in it, defecated on the floor and then smeared the excrement in his hair and over his face. He also used feces for writing and finger-painting on the walls and floor. Some of the guards, to tease him, would climb onto the mesh roof over his cell while he was trying to sleep and would jump up and down and scream to awaken him. He spent two weeks in solitary this way before they carried him off to the ward for psychotics at Letterman General Hospital.

The smearing of themselves with feces and urine is quite common among mentally unbalanced prisoners who are forced to spend any length of time in solitary. Prisoners tell of several others who did this, including one boy who tried to hang himself, was cut down and sent briefly to the hospital and then returned to the box, where he doused himself in excrement repeatedly for a week before the doctor thought it was time to send him to the hospital.

Stephen Rowland, one of the protesters, and perhaps one of the best educated of the lot (he had done some pre-med work at the University of Missouri before entering the Army), added these items to the history of the stockade: "A man went into an epileptic fit, and the guards kicked him. On at least three occasions men cut their wrists and were put in the box overnight without treatment. I was inducing vomiting in a suicidal prisoner who had ingested poison one night when the sergeant, apparently drunk, came up and forcibly interfered with my work. On two other occasions I found guards trying their best to help a poison ingestion case but doing the wrong things—they don't know what to do even when they intend no harm. In one of these instances the turnkey delayed calling the ambulance for at least ten minutes after being informed that the prisoner had ingested chrome polish."

In February, 1968, a soldier named Harman L. Jones was taken to solitary confinement. Witnesses said he was hysterical, scream-ing that he was supposed to go to the hospital. Jones had kidney and prostate trouble. In his words, "My testes hurt and I dripped."

But the guards had grown tired of releasing him from the barracks prison room to go to the toilet; so they put him in solitary and gave him a can and a roll of toilet paper. In his hysteria and anger, Jones threw the can and toilet paper outside, tore his clothes and urinated on the floor several times. Guards hosed out the cell, hosed Jones down as well, opened the windows (February can be very chilly on the San Francisco waterfront), and he was left for three days and nights without clothes or bedding.

The next day an Army doctor came, and, without asking Jones how he was, wrote "OK" on Jones' clipboard and left. "Later on that day," said a soldier confined in the solitary box next to Jones, "the guards came in and took all of us except Jones out of segregation to the TV room. On the way out, Sergeant Porter came in with three husky men. We were permitted to smoke, talk and watch TV. In general, the guards were surprisingly and unusually nice to us. We could hear Jones yelling and screaming. When we were put back in our boxes, Jones was sitting in a strait jacket in a different box. His lip was puffed up and his forehead and eyes were bruised. Jones later told me that the guards had rubbed his face in his own excrement. We were then made to clean up Jones' mess."

After the other segregation prisoners were taken from their boxes to watch television, the guards had gone in to see Jones. "Several of the guards spit in my face," Jones said. "Other guards grabbed me by the leg, tripped me. A guard got a rag off the floor, dipped it in urine and feces and rubbed it in my face and hair. I was so mad I was crying. I told Sergeant Porter he should have killed me, and he said he could arrange that, too. Then I was taken out of the box and put back on the other side. Sergeant Porter said something was going to happen to me and nobody would know. I was scared and wanted to commit suicide, so I ate paint off the wall. A guard saw me eating the paint. Then I was put in a strait jacket and taken to Letterman General Hospital. I saw a woman doctor there. While in the hospital I was in irons. And at the hospital while my stomach was being pumped a big guard was twisting my leg irons and laughing."

Things were bad enough before the "mutiny," but after it the prisoners, especially those involved in the sit-down, were treated even more harshly. Attorneys for the defendants sent five affidavits to Sixth Army Commanding General Stanley Larsen describing the new harassments, including beatings and slappings, but they got no responses. Some of the defendants were held in the Marine prison on nearby Treasure Island, and the treatment they received was apparently even worse. Private Lawrence Zaino, twenty, of Toledo, Ohio, couldn't take it. At the end of one day at the trial, when he saw the MPs approaching to return him to Treasure Island, he began shaking and mumbling, "It's true what I said about the brig, but they don't believe me. I'm sorry for what I did, but they don't believe me, but it's true." Just as the guards reached him, he tried to lift a chair to hit them, but he was shaking so hard he couldn't. He was in such bad shape his trial had to be postponed. The attorney for Private Ricky Lee Dodd said that his client's prescription glasses had been intentionally smashed by Marine guards and then he was harassed for not saluting an officer—though Dodd's eyesight was so bad without glasses that he couldn't see the officer at the other side of the room.*

The threat of Marine Corps treatment was often used to keep Army dissidents in line. Marine guards have special techniques of punishment, and sometimes guards from Treasure Island came over to the Presidio to show the Army guards how to do it. One day a Presidio prisoner called an Army guard "Uncle Tom"; a few hours later three Marine guards showed up and took over for the

---

* The response of the military judge to these accounts was: "I have sat here now and listened to this, and from past experience I don't see how it is possible for you to make a statement that all these accused here are being mistreated in this fashion." When the attorneys continued to press their accusations of brutality, the judge responded coolly: "Well, gentlemen, I don't know what you want me to do. I can't go out there and personally supervise."

occasion. As another prisoner related in a sworn statement, "You could hear screams from the man all over the stockade. Later he said he had been held by two Marines while the other grabbed and twisted his testicles and then hit him several times in the stomach." He told also of the occasion when six Army guards went into the box to get Private Richard Gentile, a veteran of twelve months in Vietnam who was in the stockade because he had marched in a peace parade: "A guard held up leg irons and said, 'If you don't come out, I'll beat your head with these.' The door to seg [the segregation cell] was open and five guards jumped Gentile, and after he was handcuffed and put into leg irons, he was beaten until he was bloody and almost unconscious. Then four of the guards carried him to a truck and sent him to Treasure Island, 'where the Marines can really take care of you.' " It was treatment of this sort that prompted Gentile to make two gestures: he drank a can of chrome polish, and he slit his arm from wrist to elbow, a wound that required forty-four stitches.

It was fear, well-founded fear, of physical abuse of the kind common to stockades, and fear even of being killed by the guards, that provoked the twenty-seven prisoners at the Presidio to demonstrate. In the words of Dr. Joseph Katz of Stanford University, a noted behavioral psychologist: "They were making an appeal to authority. They were reacting to survival needs. It was a cry for help that appeared very defiant. It was a cry of despair."

The demonstrators felt desperate because they had found it almost impossible to get the officers who had jurisdiction over stockade life to give serious attention to their complaints. The normal procedure for lodging complaints with post authorities was to file a 510 Form. Every 510 Form was supposed to be placed in a prisoner's dossier after it had been received by the proper authority and acted upon or rejected. But the forms had a strange way of disappearing. In Ricky Lee Dodd's dossier there were, at the time of the sit-down, less than a dozen 510s, whereas since he had entered the stockade he had filed (he estimated) between 250 and

300 complaints and requests on the proper forms, through the proper channels.

The desperation of the prisoners was also related to the quality of the personnel who ran the stockade. The three men with the most direct influence over the lives of the prisoners—Captain Robert Lamont, the correctional officer in charge of the stockade; Thomas Woodring, Lamont's top sergeant; and Miguel Angel Morales, sergeant of the guards—were hardly the sort to inspire feelings of security.

Captain Lamont was a twenty-five-year-old bachelor who at the time of the trouble had been in the Army two and a half years and at the Presidio for six months. Before the Presidio assignment, his only experience at prison supervision had been three months as assistant correctional officer at Fort Bliss, Texas. He had no formal training in correctional work. At one of the preliminary hearings, Lamont could not testify as to how many square feet per man the regulations called for; he could not testify how many toilets were in working order on the day of the trouble; he could not testify as to whether or not the stockade was under "emergency crowding conditions" on the day that he testified—all these being practical matters on which one might expect an officer running a stockade to be informed.

Sergeant Woodring, who had previously worked as a guard in civilian jails and for ten years as a Los Angeles policeman and sheriff's deputy, apparently held considerable influence with Lamont. A black prisoner testified that Woodring and Lamont tried to talk the Negro inmates into "a deal" by which they would get special treatment for "policing" the whites. Playing prisoners off against each other this way was reportedly a technique of the custodians.

Private Roy Pulley, who weighed about 145 pounds, claimed that Woodring, who weighed about 210, ordered him into a back room. "He followed me in [Pulley's affidavit reads] and closed the door. Then Sergeant Brown stood outside, blocking the door and

peeking in, while Sergeant Woodring proceeded to push me around
the room. I grabbed him by the tie and shoulder and tried to hold
him off. Sergeant Woodring was pushing and swearing at me all
the time, attempting to provoke me into fighting back. Eventually
he knocked me down and sat on my stomach, pinning my right
arm with his knee. He grabbed my fingers and slowly and methodically he twisted my fingers until one of them was broken. He
twisted for at least a full minute while raving at me. In the
meantime I was crying and screaming for help and asking him to
stop. . . . After my return from the hospital I was shoved in the
black box." Pulley's hand showed the effects of the mangling for
several months.

Other prisoners told of Woodring's drinking. The closest he
came to denying this was to say, "To my knowledge, no complaints have been made about me drinking on duty." Woodring's
assistant, Sergeant Morales, testified as best he could for Woodring: "I have heard of him working intoxicated but I have never
seen it. I have heard of it twice. I have never heard that he gets
mean when he gets drunk." If Woodring sometimes came to work
intoxicated, he apparently wasn't the only one. The prisoners said
the guards were frequently under the influence of LSD, marijuana
and liquor.

As for Morales, he had his own special technique for instilling
fear in new prisoners; he would tell them, "I'm so tough I shot a
Vietnamese woman in the belly, just like that, pow!" Later in court
he swore that this killing "was just a lot of b.s."; but he never told
the prisoners he was pretending.

No evidence was ever offered to indicate that Lamont, Woodring and Morales were dangerous men. Some prisoners complained
of being pushed around and beaten by Woodring, but a bully is not
necessarily a killer. Nobody ever said he felt his life was en-
dangered by even the meanest of the three. The prisoners' fear
apparently came from the belief that neither Lamont nor Woodring nor any of the other prison noncoms would protect them from

a group of wild and menacing guards who carried shotguns. And, further, the prisoners were apparently convinced that these men who ran the prison would do nothing to end the nightmare of roaches, rats, floating feces and segregation cells that was literally driving some prisoners out of their minds. So they decided to take their appeal to the public through the drama of the sit-down.

The immediate cause of the "mutiny" was the death of Richard Bunch.

Bunch had joined the Army when he was seventeen years old, with his parents' waiver. They hadn't wanted to let him go. "We didn't think he was exposed to elements in life that others his age maybe had been," his mother explains. "You know, to violence. I didn't think he was equipped to handle violence if he were to come up against it. This is what we feared for him. His life had been simple. He'd had no great problems to cope with. His main problem in life was how to get around Dad to do what he wanted.

"The big factor in his wanting to enlist was his very best friend was drafted. He'd been pressuring us for about a year to let him go. His dad was very unwilling, but you know how the Army's glamorized."

Perhaps because he was very young and very small—he stood five foot four and weighed 130 pounds—he had left his home in Dayton, Ohio, full of enthusiasm for the he-man world he was entering. But he didn't get the special training he had hoped for, and what he had thought would be a test of manhood turned out to be only a test of patience. It was the old, old story of the disenchantment of a young man who has taken the Army recruiting posters too literally. When the disenchantment hit, in January, 1968, he went AWOL, drifting from Fort Lewis, Washington, to the Haight-Ashbury district of San Francisco and taking up residence in a hotel room with four or five other youngsters. Soon Bunch was a familiar sight in that area, running around in paratrooper boots, passing himself off as a Vietnam veteran heaped with glory. He began taking heavy and frequent doses of LSD and amphetamines and eventually began to show clear signs of derangement.

In May he went home to Dayton. When he stepped through the front door, his mother remembers, "He had on this terrible outfit. He had on this wild, purple shirt, satinlike it was, and these dirty, dirty, filthy jeans. They were just all filthy, and Richard was never that type of person that went dirty, and his nails were grown out real long and he had this mustache. His sister took him to his grandmother's in Tennessee because if he stayed at home, the FBI would catch him. He left his dirty jeans, but he took this stupid-looking shirt."

Bunch had no stories to tell his mother about the Army. Instead, he was full of elaborate accounts of the new talents and strengths he had developed while on drugs. He was, he assured his mother, immortal. He had died, he said, and been reincarnated as a warlock. He had the power to kill people at a glance and the power to walk through walls. (Later, in the Presidio stockade, he would often attempt to prove this power by walking into a wall.) Sometimes he would interrupt his mumblings to get a piece of paper, draw a line on it and announce to the room, "I stand here."

Mrs. Bunch tried to get her son into a hospital, but none would take him because he was a soldier who was absent without leave— let the Army take care of him. So she finally phoned the Army hospital; they sent over the MPs, who took him instead to the county jail. Again Mrs. Bunch tried to get medical treatment for her son. Everybody passed the buck. Finally he was transferred to Fort Meade, Maryland, where he was put in the stockade. The assistant adjutant at Fort Meade wrote Mrs. Bunch promising that her son would get psychiatric treatment. The promise was promptly forgotten by the Army. When Mrs. Bunch produced the letter of promise later, the Army dismissed it as a "form letter."

Bunch's parents never saw him again. "We got a letter from

Fort Meade saying he was in the stockade, but I don't know how long he was there. The Army hasn't told us. We wrote him letters and the letters were sent back to us. We were never told his whereabouts until they came down to the house and told us that Richard had died."

Bunch had wanted to die. Later they found notes he had written: "One click and it's over. . . . All right America I'll pay. . . . If you can't give me love, at least do me the favor of complete annihilation." His mental condition was known to the Army. Psychiatrists at the Presidio had examined him and had diagnosed him as a manic-depressive; but he was sent back to the stockade. On October 10 Bunch had asked another prisoner the best way to kill himself. This prisoner later testified he had answered, "Tell a guard you're going to run away from a work detail and he'll shoot you."

Suicide by proxy is not supposed to be easy in the Army. But there was reason for the prisoners at the Presidio stockade to think that running away might be suicidal. For one thing, the guards who went out on work details with the prisoners were armed, even though all the prisoners were minimum-security men and therefore, according to regulations, should not have been guarded with guns. These guards loved to play with the shotguns they carried and point them at the prisoners and threaten to "blow your fucking heads off." Not long before the Bunch slaying, one of the guards had accidentally discharged a shotgun and had blown a hole in the roof of a building next to the stockade just as the prisoners were falling in for work. The sergeant in charge of the shotgun guards as much as admitted his men were careless, if not trigger-happy. He himself, he said, wouldn't like to work with their gun muzzles right behind him, only five or six feet away, as the prisoners had to do. Army regulations require that stockade guards be specially trained for confinement work, but only one guard at the Presidio had had such instruction. And some of the guards seemed clearly unstable. One had reportedly been transferred to the Presidio from another base when his commanding officer became uneasy about him; the soldier, a Jew, had said he had dreams that he was a Nazi.

On the morning of October 11, Bunch said he didn't want to go to work; he said he was afraid he would be killed. (Apparently he was momentarily afraid of his own suicidal impulses.) Prisoners say the guards took Bunch's religious medallion from his neck and told him they wouldn't give it back unless he went to work. The work detail to which they assigned him was in the street near the base hospital. About ten o'clock, the other prisoners in the detail overheard Bunch taunting the guard.

"What would you do if I ran?" he asked.

"You'll have to run to find out," the guard answered.

"All right," said Bunch, "please aim for my head."

And he went down the street, first walking, then skipping, then jogging, not really trying to get away. The shotgun blast caught him in the back when he had gone only twenty or thirty feet. Bunch was hit with what one California Congressman described as "not No. 7 shot, which we use for pheasant, or No. 6 shot, which we use for duck, but No. 4 shot, which can down a thirty-pound goose, a Canadian honker, with one pellet." Army regulations require that a guard fire only as a last resort and then aim for the legs, but this blast hit Bunch in the heart, lungs, spleen and kidney, and left a hole in his back four inches wide. The Army later claimed that something was wrong with the gun and that it discharged higher than aimed. Three prisoners working nearby said they had not heard the guard call out the required warning.

After killing Bunch, the guard whirled around and pointed at another prisoner and yelled, "Hit the ground, hit the ground or I'll shoot you, too!" Then, in terrified reaction, the guard cried, "My God, I shot him. Why did I do that?"

After an investigation, Major General Lawrence J. Fuller, Acting Judge Advocate General of the Army, wrote Mrs. Bunch that, "based on all available evidence, it was determined that the guard who fired the shot acted justifiably in the performance of his duties."

Bunch's death threw the stockade into bedlam. Prisoners wept, refused to eat, broke windows, overturned bunks. A couple of the prisoners tried to start a fire to burn down the stockade. There was talk of murdering a guard in retaliation. Iron rungs from bunks were readied for use as weapons. Several of the guards, in turn, threw prisoners down the stairs. It was a minor riot, but the Army, frightened for the moment, made little of it and punished the offenders only by putting a few of them in solitary.

The stockade commandant, Captain Lamont, was not an experienced or a sensitive man, but even he realized that something was horribly wrong and likely to get worse. That same afternoon, he summoned the prisoners and read them Article 94, the mutiny article, from the Uniform Code of Military Justice. But Lamont did nothing else to quiet their anxieties. He seemed strangely indifferent to the rebellious mood that others, in retrospect, said was very apparent.

The night of Sunday, October 13, some of the prisoners—nobody can now recall exactly how many were in on the planning—decided that the next morning, at the 7:30 formation, they would hold a sit-down demonstration and, when Lamont showed up, read a list of grievances. The planners were sure they would get a 90 percent turnout. Earlier, nearly a hundred prisoners had signed a letter to one man's Congressman. This, to the planners, suggested solidarity and dedication to the fight.

But when muster was called at 7:30 the next morning, only twenty-eight of the prisoners fell out of line and went into a huddle. One man, perhaps because the number was much lower than he had expected, quickly rejoined the line-up and was not counted as a wrongdoer. The twenty-seven who remained were charged with mutiny, a charge so seldom made in the Army—there are less than half a dozen cases on record—that it is correctly described as

"quaint." The maximum punishment is death. In this case, however, the Army decided to limit the possible maximum to life in
prison.

Perhaps half a dozen of the demonstrators, before their imprisonment, had taken part in peace parades or had met with peace
groups at one time or another in the Haight-Ashbury district, yet
no actual effort had been made to present the demonstration as
antiwar. It was for this reason, in fact, that several prisoners who
were intensely committed to the antiwar movement had refused to
take part in the protest. They had been sent to the stockade for
chaining themselves inside a San Francisco church to protest the
war. If the Presidio demonstration had been antiwar, they might
have joined it, but since it wasn't, they hadn't thought it worth the
trouble.

In the Sunday night meeting at which the prisoners had worked
out the details of the demonstration, there was virtually no discussion of U.S. policy in Vietnam. The list of grievances was aimed
entirely at stockade inhumanities—bad food, stinking toilets,
rough guards. It was like a Quaker meeting at which the body
rather than the spirit predominated, as one after another of the
soldiers stood and recited examples of bruises and biliousness as
reasons for the revolt. But among the complaints, Dean Rusk was
never mentioned. The stockade captain was cursed, but Lyndon
Johnson was not.

It is important to keep this in mind. The general public and,
most significantly, the Army quite clearly believed that the demonstration was an antiwar, anti-Administration, antimilitarist protest.
Those who sympathized with it thought it involved the constitutional guarantee of free speech. The Army, too, though it did not
sympathize, thought it was suppressing a mini-Continental Congress. Actually, the Army was simply putting down a plain old
prison rumble and didn't know it, or didn't want to acknowledge it,
finding it more convenient to pretend it was something else. None

of the attorneys for these men ever claimed that the Army had violated their clients' freedom of speech. They simply argued either that the defendants had been virtually out of their minds from fear or that they had been framed on a much, much more serious charge than was merited. They argued that the only part of the Bill of Rights violated by the Army was in the denial of a fair trial.

It is an illusion, then, to see the twenty-seven as pure in spirit, devoted to the cause of freedom and justice, sacrificing themselves so that this might be a brighter, better land in which to live. A few of them may have qualified for that star-spangled description, but not many. They were a very mixed bag. Expert observers are of the opinion that if there was anything approximating a common quality among them, it was their psychological insecurity. More than half the mutineers, tested by Army psychiatrists later, were found to be unfit for service. At one of the mutiny trials, Dr. Price Cobbs, the San Francisco psychiatrist who is co-author of the book *Black Rage* (his testimony was so impressive that of fourteen psychiatric experts used by the defense, he was the only one not cross-examined), testified that at the time of the demonstration the twenty-seven GIs were "psychologically denuded and vulnerable." To be exact, said Cobbs, "all of them, if given proper psychiatric testing by military authorities, would have been declared unfit for service."

When the first edition of this book appeared, the Army reacted in a frantically defensive way and, typically, managed only to get itself in deeper. For example, after I had appeared on a CBS radio program with Mike Wallace to discuss the book, Colonel H. H. Arnold Jr., Information Officer for the Sixth Army, wrote Wallace to protest: "The picture Mr. Sherrill paints of the mutineers as innocent youths is in actuality a far cry from the facts. . . . Among them, they had six charges of desertion and 72 separate occurrences of AWOL, which represented 4226 days of unauthorized leave. Fourteen other charges had been filed against them including assault, possession of narcotics, and others. In all, they had 34 convictions by courts-martial. In addition to these military offenses, information from civilian law enforcement agencies reveals 58 civilian arrests prior to entering military service. These arrests include grand theft, narcotics violations, assault, burglary, contributing to the delinquency of a minor and a host of misdemeanors ranging from joyriding to public drunkenness." Which, of course, helps to round out our picture of the men very nicely and underscores a major point made by the Special Civilian Committee appointed by the Secretary of the Army in 1969 to study conditions in the stockades.

Although the committee (which turned in its final report on May 15, 1970) made a point of *not* investigating prison brutalities, it could not fail to note one of the most invidious brutalities—the mere keeping of the unfit man in uniform, much less in prison. On this point it observed:

The Committee constantly encountered prisoners who were clearly unfit for military duty. Many of them were in the stockades' disciplinary segregation cells. They were in trouble because of emotional instability that made it difficult for them to stand the tensions of military life in general, and confinement in particular. This, coupled with a lack of self-control, precipitated outbursts of violent temper, fights with other prisoners, and insubordinate behavior. Others were so susceptible to suggestions that they were easily led into trouble by other prisoners. If one could read their life histories, he would probably find the frequently recurring picture of youths who suffered deprivation, rejection and harsh treatment from early childhood, or overpermissive treatment, and who turned in their mid-teens or earlier against the authority of parents, teachers and police, and were now resisting the authority of the Army and all personnel exercising it. . . .

It did not seem to the Committee that, even after a medical and psychiatric examination, placing a prisoner who had cut his wrist or arm in an administrative segregation cell to avoid a repetition of the act was an adequate approach to the problem. Such an act usually has pathological connotations, and calls for observation under psychiatric auspices, if not treatment.

Other prisoners who were seen in stockades' administrative segregation cells included a great variety of physical, mental and emotional misfits, sex deviates, drug addicts and others who were clearly unfitted for military service. In one cell Committee members saw a prisoner on a recurring LSD "trip" although he had not had access to the drug for several weeks. Others in various stockades included men in their early twenties who had been addicted to "hard drugs" for several years before they were drafted; known and suspected homosexuals; a transvestite who said frankly that he was more comfortable in women's clothes; and prisoners who were segregated while it was decided whether or not they were psychotic or pre-psychotic.

Several questions were uppermost in the minds of the Committee members after seeing the same types of misfits in the administration segregation cells of stockade after stockade: Why could not the prisoners who needed to be under medical or psychiatric observation, and perhaps under treatment, be in a prisoner ward in the post hospital? The answer to that question was that very few post hospitals have prisoner wards. Why, then, could they not be in small hospital wards in the stockades? The answer was that there are no such wards in any of the stockades in Continental United States studied by the Committee.*

But of course the most sensible question would be: What are they doing in the armed services in the first place?

Private Larry Reidel, for instance—where was Reidel when the 7:30 muster began? He wasn't outside in the line-up, waiting to disobey orders to prove a moral point. He was inside the mess hall, standing at strict attention with his nose against the wall because he had just beaten up another GI who had irritated him by chewing with his mouth open. First, Reidel had poured a pitcher of hot coffee over the other GI, and then he had gotten up from the table and kicked him in the face. When the sergeant told him he had better go on outside and make the muster, he ran through the door, saw the big group standing at attention, saw the small group

---

* Lest anyone suppose that this Committee was made up of what the military would call "bleeding hearts," we hasten to add that its membership was comprised of such practical fellows as James V. Bennett, for many years director of the Federal Bureau of Prisons; Austin H. MacCormick, executive director, Osborne Association Inc.; E. Preston Sharp, general secretary, American Correctional Association; Sanger B. Powers, administrator, Wisconsin Division of Corrections; Lawrence W. Pierce, chairman, New York State Narcotic Addiction Control Commission; and Richard A. McGee, president, Institute for the Study of Crime and Delinquency, Sacramento, Calif.

of protesters already gathering for their sit-down, and immediately headed for the small group—as he would have done in ninety-nine cases out of a hundred because he was a compulsive troublemaker and was naturally drawn to the "out" group. Major T. J. Chamberlain, the Army psychiatrist who looked him over, wrote this description:

> Sociopathic personality, antisocial type, severe chronic, marked by a long history of antisocial behavior, including stealing, assault and a general pattern of juvenile delinquency. This twenty-one year old white male initially entered the service under duress from his parole board in the hope that the Army would rehabilitate this individual. He has a long history dating back to his early teenage days of running away from his family, of truancy from school, of disrupting school when there, burglary, stealing, lying, assaulting other people, and, in general, being unable to control or unwilling to control his behavior. He has been seen over a long period of time by myself in the stockade. During that period of time he has knocked down and broken the jaw of a prisoner, he has set fire to a mattress, he has had many homicidal thoughts, and has fashioned a knife out of a razor blade and a toothbrush, etc., etc. . . . He has no loyalty to any group or any ability to control any of his impulsive behavior, and particularly his violent reaction to frustration, or any sort of threat by another individual. It is my opinion that no therapeutic, punitive or correctional intervention is going to make this person into anything that approximates a good soldier. . . .

A more down-to-earth appraisal of Reidel was given by David Lowe, one of the attorneys for the "mutineers": "Reidel is basically crazy. He is a very tough guy and he prides himself on being very tough. I think when somebody asked Reidel confidentially— not in presence of the court—what he would really like to be if he got out of the Presidio mess, he answered, 'The best burglar in the block.' He testified in his trial, in the mitigation, that if he got out he wanted to be a cabinetmaker. The only reason he said this was that once he locked himself in a cabinet to smoke pot, and he liked the sensation. One of the other prisoners said afterwards, 'Larry, that was a moving piece of testimony. Did you really mean that?' And Reidel said, 'Shit, no, I can't even stand the smell of sawdust.' That's the kind of guy he was. He's antisocial and all that. But mutiny? Nonsense. Mutiny is where a group plots to do something together. He wouldn't join together with the rest of those guys to do anything. He didn't *like* any of them."

Like Reidel, Private Nesrey Sood, twenty-five, was imprisoned for reasons that had nothing to do with ideology. He was no pacifist. He lived from moment to moment, looking for excitement, hating the Army, drinking, quarreling and worrying about his family. Sood, who had an Army IQ of 103, was a high school dropout who had been drafted despite the fact that he had three children and a wife to support. He had spent almost all of his two years of service in Alaska, and all but one month of that time in the stockade. When he was sober, his officers said, he was a very good soldier. But he wasn't sober often enough. Sood himself had admitted that he sometimes took drugs, that he drank a great deal of Thunderbird wine, and that he was often drunk while on duty. In fact, he once was caught on duty with a bottle of Seagram's and three bottles of beer. He had served time for hitting a sergeant, after first roundly cussing him out. He told another sergeant, "You stupid jackass. If you didn't have that gun, I'd beat your head in." He told his second lieutenant, "I ought to punch you out," but let the officer off with only a push. He hated Alaska so much he put in a petition to go to Vietnam, but when his order to ship out was issued, Sood was, as usual, in an Alaska stockade. His platoon sergeant recalls, "I think he had some kind of mental problem. He used to sit on a lawn chair in his cube after duty, wearing shades, staring at a revolving light and listening to hippie music."

Inevitably, the Army decided that it and Sood were incompatible, and so he was ordered to return to Fort Lewis, Washington, and pick up his discharge. Other things were on Sood's mind, however. He was having trouble with his wife, and he was afraid that his three small children were being mistreated. When he reached Seattle and started hitchhiking to nearby Fort Lewis, the first car that picked him up happened to be going straight through to Oakland, California—Sood's home town—and on an impulse he decided to just let the discharge paper lie at Fort Lewis while he went home to take care of his domestic troubles.

In Oakland he was picked up for being AWOL, was put in the Presidio stockade and eventually received a fifteen-year sentence. Although Sood's disregarded discharge, signed by Major General K. B. Lemmon, Jr., Alaskan commander, seems clearly to have been meant to get rid of him under any conditions—it reads: "In the event individual is presently in confinement, the unexecuted portion of the sentence of confinement will be remitted and expeditious action taken to effect discharge"—officials at the Presidio chose not to interpret it that way. Lieutenant Colonel Ann Wansley, chief of the Military Justice Section of the Sixth Army staff judge advocate's office, said briskly: "Certainly it is regrettable that the man did not report to Fort Lewis and pick up his discharge, but that was his decision." And when one of Sood's defense lawyers asked her, "Don't you think if it had not been for the fact that mutiny was being lodged against him he would have been out of the Army back in October?" the judge interrupted: "That question is objectionable. The cold hard facts of life are that discharge was not effected and he was amenable to military justice and, as a result, he is here today."

It hardly seems extravagant to conclude that the Army was determined not merely to punish but to get revenge. It even stooped to such petty vengeances as failing to deliver a letter to Sood from the Alameda County Probation Department, written to him at the stockade on the fifteenth of January, 1969, notifying him of a scheduled hearing to determine where his three children would be placed for rearing; the department had found them "alone and unattended in the home," which was in "a mess and clutter." The letter asked him to let the court know "your feelings regarding the children and possible plans for their future." The Army withheld the letter for eight days, delivering it two days after the hearing.

But that is getting ahead of the story. The point here is merely that the motives that placed most of the twenty-seven boys in that huddle were both nonpolitical and desperate.

Among the others in the Presidio huddle was Private Danny Seals, twenty-three, who described his father as an alcoholic, always stealing, fighting with his wife. Seals was one of nine children. At the age of eight he was shifted to another family for upbringing, and thereafter the transfers occurred regularly and often. He quit school in the tenth grade, and was often in trouble with the police. His Army IQ score was 64.* Dr. Earl Cohen, a psychiatrist who interviewed him before the trial, noted, "There is some evidence of impairment of intellectual functioning of a mild type. . . . There was some evidence of memory impairment for details involving recent events. . . . Judgment is questionable." Dr. Cohen described Seals as "an emotionally unstable personality of longstanding duration," which is quite understandable, considering the fact that he had been kicked in the head by a horse when he was a child and had indications of brain damage.

Private Richard Stevens, nineteen, was the son of a Church of God preacher who was constantly moving his family back and forth between Oklahoma and California. Stevens' Army IQ score was 66. The psychiatrist who interviewed him noted that when he attempted to do the simplest math problem, "He quickly became confused and his replies became so jumbled that one could not tell whether he was attempting to subtract, add, or was merely stating numbers at random." Stevens had tattooed himself on his hands and arms—with words such as "love" and "hate" and crude spiders. He had married his wife (seventeen at the time of the trial) when she was fifteen years old and four months pregnant; they had two children by trial time. During the past year he had gone AWOL about fifteen times, usually gaining his freedom, he said, by bribing guards with drugs. At another military base he had

* The Army IQ test measures the extent to which a man is trainable. The scoring range is from 40 to 160, with 100 showing an average susceptibility to training. A serviceman with a score of 60 would be marginally trainable; there wouldn't be many things he could do.

tried to escape from a shotgun-armed guard standing directly behind him, and he later thought that only the guard's inability to use the gun correctly saved his life. "There was a big explosion, and I didn't know whether I was hit or not," he said. "Then I looked around and saw the guard trying to fit the gun together." Stevens told a psychiatrist that he was a drug user himself and that before joining the Army he had supported himself mainly by selling items that he and his brother had stolen.

Private Ernest Trefethen, eighteen, had often been beaten by his father—an alcoholic who eventually had a "nervous break-down"—until his parents separated when Trefethen was ten. He ran away from home several times and was continually truant from school. He was made to see the school psychologist, but it did no good, and he gave up school in the ninth grade. He joined the Army on impulse, but as a San Francisco psychiatrist noted, "He almost immediately encountered even more problems than he had as a civilian. He found that he could not tolerate being confined in one area for very long. . . . Sometimes even if in the middle of a conversation, he would simply be obliged abruptly to leave the room." He was steadily AWOL, and he wound up in the Presidio. Trefethen's Army IQ was 94.

Private Francis Schiro was twenty-one. His mother was a beautician; his father had abandoned the family when Schiro was one year old. Later the father was reported to have been committed to a mental institution. His mother remarried. Schiro did not get along with his stepfather, frequently ran away from home, dropped out of school. He joined the Army on the promise that he would be trained to use heavy building equipment, but the Army went back on its promise and Schiro started going AWOL. Army IQ: 106.

Private Alan Rupert showed more courage than most soldiers are ever asked to show, merely by surviving his childhood with at least some stability and sanity. By the time he was fifteen his mother had lived with at least a dozen men. In a cruel exchange during the court-martial, the Army prosecutor forced a psychiatrist to say on the witness stand, in front of Rupert, what was quite apparent from the evidence and did not need to be said—that the boy's mother was a prostitute.* The men passed through the house rapidly, and Rupert never knew who his father was. His mother worked in bars, was an alcoholic, frequently beat Rupert; when he was thirteen, she and her current "husband" simply dropped Rupert off at a ranch, without a word of explanation, and left him to work there for a year. By the time he was fifteen he was made ward of a court. He had run away from home many times to avoid yielding to an impulse to kill his stepfathers. In the first eighteen years of his life he had lived in twenty-four states, and had gone to more schools than he could count. He joined the Army with great expectations, and immediately ran into the kind of brutal sergeants with which the services abound. It was, unfortunately, too much like home. He went AWOL four times, was thrown into the stockade every time, but twice escaped. It was idiotic for the Army to expect normal responses from Rupert; in the words of his court-martial psychiatrist, "To punish him for this seems to me to be equivalent to punishing a cripple for not being able to run a hundred yards in ten seconds flat." A month before the Presidio demonstration, an Army psychiatrist had advised authorities to discharge the boy; had they acted with reasonable speed on this advice, Rupert wouldn't have been in the stockade at the time of the demonstration.

Private Richard Gentile, twenty, came from a broken home,

* This exchange perfectly illustrates how the Army uses its court-martial procedures to dehumanize defendants. Dr. Kurt Schlesinger, assistant chief psychiatrist at Mt. Zion Hospital in San Francisco, was on the stand. He described Rupert as a rootless nomad and described Rupert's mother as neurotic-psychotic. But the Army's assistant prosecutor, Captain Carlotti, wasn't satisfied with that. He kept pressing for a more concrete description of the woman. Dr. Schlesinger said he didn't like to go into that with the son present, but Carlotti insisted. "Well, for want of a better word," said Dr. Schlesinger, "I'll use a euphemism—her conduct denotes randomness." Carlotti kept insisting that the doctor use a more common description, and finally Schlesinger gave in and said, "All right, Captain. He may take a swing at me for this, but his mother, in my opinion, is a prostitute." Private Rupert began crying. The defense asked for and got a recess despite Carlotti's objection, "I see no reason for a recess."

became involved in a drinking, fighting, joyriding bunch of young-sters, ran away from home several times, dropping out of school, and at the age of seventeen joined the Army on the promise that he would be sent to diesel and turbine engineering school. He was sent to cook and baker school instead, then shifted to the infantry. He served twelve months in Vietnam on reconnaissance and sniper duty, and was recommended for the Bronze Star for heroism in an ambush.

Gentile was one of the unusual ones among the twenty-seven; he actually was interested in the peace movement. He was, in fact, in the Presidio stockade at the time of the demonstration because of that interest. On October 12, two days before the sit-down, the entire Presidio post had been restricted so that none of the soldiers would be able to participate in a downtown peace march on that date; but Gentile had left the base anyway and taken part in it.

His Army IQ was 89; he was, in the words of the court-martial psychiatrist, "essentially a lonely, frightened boy." His shaky mental state did not reveal itself until after the stockade demon-stration. Several weeks later, becoming increasingly depressed from being locked up, he had a dream one night in which Bunch, the murdered GI, talked to him and told him to "Get out, get out." Gentile interpreted this to mean that he should kill himself, so he swallowed a can of chrome polish. He was sent to the hospital, then returned to the stockade. He escaped and went AWOL and was caught, and this time he cut his arm with a razor blade. He slit it from the bend at the elbow to his wrist, and it took eight MPs to hold him while it was sewed up. He spent three weeks in the psychiatric ward at the hospital and then, learning that they were about to return him to the stockade, ran away again and was not captured until he had reached Florida. Back in the stockade, he again had fights with the guards.

Although he was enthusiastic about the peace movement, it should not be presumed that he joined the sit-down demonstration to agitate for peace. He was there, as his psychiatrist said, simply because he felt a desperate need for identification—"to feel 'a part of' some group, whether it be a pot-party, a fight, a mutiny, a march, etc."

Private Patrick Wright, twenty, was another soldier with a chaotic childhood. He said he never knew his real father and that his step-father was "drunk all the time" and beat Wright's mother as well as Wright and his two brothers. Sometimes the stepfather threatened the family with a gun. The longest period Wright lived in one place was one and a half years, with an aunt and uncle to whom the court had awarded him because his mother and step-father had by that time abandoned him. Later he lived around with older brothers. He quit school in the ninth grade. The years he recalled most fondly were those between the ages of fifteen and eighteen, when he left home and roamed the country, working here as a bus boy, somewhere else as a farm hand, on down the road in a factory—"I was free, and no one was telling me what to do or yowling at me all the time." Then he joined the Army, and every-body began yowling at him again. He couldn't take it, couldn't take the senseless punishment, the senseless restrictions. Four times he fled the Army, four times he was captured and brought back. Wright's Army IQ was 90, but he was bright enough to recognize the Presidio stockade for what it was—"a crazy house." By joining the demonstration, he hoped to do again what he had been doing all his life—run away, run away from authority. As his psychiatrist summarized it: "The most striking characteristic about Patrick's personality is his fear of and bitterness about the ways of authority—particularly where he cannot see the sense of the authoritative demand. This fear is marked and life-long. For example, as a small child, he cut his finger tip off in a lawnmower. He was so afraid he would be punished and yelled at that he couldn't go into the house. A neighbor finally saw him bleeding and found help. He has consistently been unable to handle the demands of authority in all areas of his life—at home, at school, on jobs, in the Army. In each situation, he runs away."

Private Richard Duncan, twenty, was another whose Army IQ was low—62, to be exact. He was also another who came from a sordid home. His earliest memory was of his alcoholic father threatening his mother while Richard tried to keep his little brother quiet and out of the way so that his father wouldn't turn on them, too. Duncan was six years old at the time. He was often beaten. When he was about thirteen, his parents broke up. About that same age he began to have severe migraine headaches. In all his life before joining the Army he had only one friend, a young man two years older, more sophisticated, better read. But then his friend married and apparently was somewhat ashamed to have Duncan hanging around. One day Duncan overheard his friend telling his bride how stupid Duncan was, how comical, how irritating, and that he hoped Duncan would stop coming around. Duncan did; he became more withdrawn, took to drugs. His only pastime was to take long solitary walks. Strange fears began to seize him now. He was afraid that he might become as insanely violent as his father sometimes was; once, when he was drunk, he hit his hand against a fence and broke several fingers, which he felt only confirmed his worst fears. At eighteen, mainly because he "wanted to get it over with," he joined the Army. But he couldn't take it. Five times he fled, five times he was captured and brought back. His psychiatrist hardly overstated the case when he wrote in his report: "The personality pattern disturbance of this young man is of such severity as to render him totally unsuited for military service and in my opinion, could have been diagnosed long before the five AWOLs confirmed his inability, his inadequacy."

Private Larry Lee Sales, twenty-two, was the most remarkable case of all. His record began with a burglary in the first grade; as he said later, "I've been pulling burglaries ever since." He dropped out of school when the school psychologist said there was no point in his trying to go beyond the ninth grade. He served eight months in jail for burglarizing a safe. The year before he joined the Army he got into a knife fight with his father and attacked a friend with a pair of scissors. At fifteen he was arrested for carrying a pistol and a machete. He had taken potshots at cows and children. At sixteen he had been arrested for shooting up a house with a 12-gauge shotgun. At eighteen he was picked up in Las Vegas for possessing drugs and carrying a loaded revolver. He often used narcotics— LSD, amphetamines, codeine, cocaine, morphine, opium, everything. At least once he posed nude for a homosexual photographer. Before joining the Army he attempted suicide by slashing his wrists.

But the Army took Sales in without a question. He didn't join out of patriotism. He joined because he had just been released from observation at Modesto State Hospital; he went into the Army as an alternative to becoming a permanent resident in the insane asylum. He persuaded the Army doctor that if he couldn't make it in the Army, at least the Army could care for him better than the state asylum.

Of course he couldn't make it. After one day of basic training, he later recounted, "my nerves were about to blow." And since nothing was done for him at sick call, he went AWOL. After that, his memory went blank.

"They tell me," he has said, "that I wrote $500 in false checks while I was AWOL. When I'd been gone two weeks, I took an overdose of codeine. The nurse told me I was pulseless and had been pronounced dead on arrival at Scenic Hospital at Modesto. They were about to send me to the state hospital after three days, but Dad told them I was in the Army." His dad used the old argument, "The Army can take better care of him," so they phoned Fort Lewis, Fort Lewis phoned the Presidio, and the Presidio sent an ambulance to fetch Larry Lee. The Presidio psychiatrist looked him over and said, "My God, you're insane— what are you doing in the Army?"

The Army in San Francisco told him they were going to send him back to Fort Lewis for his discharge because the Presidio just wasn't giving discharges. So they packed him off to the Presidio's

Special Processing Department to wait for his convoy to Fort Lewis the next day. When he got to SPD, it was late in the afternoon and the specialist, who didn't want to be bothered making out the papers, told Sales, "I'm going to stick you in the stockade overnight and you'll get picked up in the morning. Then I won't have to make out the papers. They can do it up there."

It was October 1 when Sales entered the Presidio stockade. He waited around. He kept telling everyone he was getting out the next day. The other prisoners told him, "Don't count on it, some of us have been here three or four months waiting to get out." A little over two weeks later Sales was facing mutiny charges.

Some of the twenty-seven young men were bright enough, but the general level of scheming was so primitive and disjointed that it could never seriously be considered a unified effort "to override military authority"—a mutiny. Asked how they had decided upon sitting down in a group and singing "We Shall Overcome," one of the protesters told a reporter that there really had been no formal decision on this point. "That's just the way you have a demonstration," he said. "We all had seen it on TV. No one had suggested it."

If the Army did not actually push these men into taking action that could be called mutiny, did it not at least permit them to drift that way when it could have stopped them? There seems to be little doubt, on the evidence uncovered in the several trials, that the Army was guilty of one or the other.

During the month prior to the sit-down, Captain Lamont and his superior, Lieutenant Colonel Ford, had had "several conversations." "We had discussed mutiny," Lamont admitted on the witness stand. "Various prisoner actions in the stockade, such as in Cell Block Three, had led up to these conversations," he said. "We looked in the UCMJ [Uniform Code of Military Justice] and discussed the subject. Contingency planning is a normal function."

So Lamont was ready. All he needed was the occasion. That occasion quickly ripened after Bunch's death, with the riot in Cell

Block Three on the day of the shooting; Lamont had another
discussion with Colonel Ford, who predicted that the reading of
the mutiny article to the prisoners at that evening's muster would
soothe them. It didn't. Major John Williams, the stockade chaplain, said he found them on the day of the shooting "in a very
emotional state—they used the word 'murder,' " and the next day
he found them still to be "really, really uptight."

Army Field Manual FM 22–100, *Military Leadership,* page 40,
says that officers should act in situations where rumors and tension
are building up by "finding out and attempting to eliminate the
basic conditions creating uncertainty before they accumulate."
Lamont conceded that twenty-four hours after the shooting "the
mood of the prisoners was still tense. Other than officially announcing the death, announcing the memorial service and my staff
individually counseling prisoners, no other action was taken to
calm the prisoners."

Sometime between 5:30 and 6 o'clock Monday morning, October 14, Specialist E-4 Terry Michael Raines, an employee of the
stockade, showed up for work and at once learned from the
prisoners that there was going to be a sit-down. At first Raines
claimed he didn't tell Captain Lamont about this, but then he
changed his story and said, yes, he did in fact telephone Captain
Lamont and inform him that trouble was about to spill over.

Lamont then confirmed that Raines had phoned him to report
"rumors that prisoners would leave formation and that the press
and TV cameras would be there." The warning, however, seemed
to have little impact on Lamont. He did not get up and dress and
go to the stockade and attempt to calm the prisoners. In fact, he
did not even show up for work before his normal check-in time of
7:30. And he ordered his stockade personnel to take no excep-
tional steps to prevent trouble.

LAMONT: My words to him [Raines] were, "continue with your
   regularly scheduled formation as scheduled, and report to me if
   there is any further rumors or disturbances."
Q: You didn't tell him to contact the prisoners whom the rumors

suggested might be involved, and to attempt to reason with them about this matter?

LAMONT: No.

Q: Didn't you give it [the threatened demonstration] some thought?

LAMONT: No.

Q: And you, yourself, went back to sleep, did you?

LAMONT: Yes.

Q: Is that your standard procedure when you get a call in the middle of the night that some group of prisoners might be about to commit a crime?

LAMONT: It depends on the circumstances. . . .

Further testimony showed that the authorities had been alerted to the upcoming trouble as early as 3 A.M. Lieutenant John Joseph Tierney, who was operations officer at the post provost office, testified that when he heard of the sit-down at 7:30, it came as no surprise.

Q: At that time did you have any pre-information which caused you to be alerted or ready for the information you received?

TIERNEY: Yes, I did.

Q: And from whom did you receive that pre-information or knowledge that there might well be a disturbance?

TIERNEY: From the Duty Officer the night before.

Q: And what is that Duty Officer's name?

TIERNEY: Lieutenant Seine. I believe it was Lieutenant Seine that called. It might have been the Desk Sergeant, but it was about three o'clock and I wasn't taking notes.

While Captain Lamont lay sleeping, Sergeant Woodring was taking the threat of trouble no less placidly.

Q: On the morning in question, October 14, what time did you arrive at work?

WOODRING: As previously stated, sir, about 0630 hours.

Q: And when you arrived at work did you have any indication that there would be a demonstration on that morning?

WOODRING: I was informed—or, I received information that there would be some sort of disturbance, or something.

Q: What time did you receive that information?

WOODRING: At about 0630 hours, sir.

Q: And what action did you take between 0630 hours and 0730 hours on that morning?

WOODRING: I carried out my normal duties.

Q: You made no extra efforts to determine the nature of the possible incident?

WOODRING: Well, I inquired as to what sort of disturbance was going to take place. Other than that, I took no action.

Q: What did you find out in your inquiry?

WOODRING: Nothing, sir.

Q: Nothing?

WOODRING: (*No audible response.*)

Q: You weren't concerned, then, with the incidents which might take place?

WOODRING: No, sir, I was not concerned.

Q: Are you usually unconcerned with possible disturbances or incidents which might take place in the stockade?

WOODRING: It's not that I'm not concerned, sir. I've built up an immunity to them.

Q: Such that you are no longer concerned about them?

WOODRING: That I don't become excited at the first indication that there might be some trouble.

Q: When did you become excited in respect to the incident that did take place?

WOODRING: I don't recall that I did get excited, sir.

Q: Have you ever been involved, or observed a mutiny taking place before?

WOODRING: It was my first one, sir.

Q: And you weren't excited?

WOODRING: Just routine, sir.

Q: Routine mutiny?

WOODRING: Yes, sir.

Whether or not Captain Lamont had intended for his personnel to interpret his order in that fashion, without exception the stockade guards did nothing to attempt to prevent the demonstration, even as it began actually to develop.

When Reidel, having finished beating up another inmate in the

mess hall, came out and started toward the mutineers sitting on the
grass, Sergeant Morales saw him heading the wrong way but did
not try to stop him. Defense Attorney Lowe asked him, "Why
didn't you tell Reidel to go back into formation?"

A: I was under orders not to offer any hassle with the people, just
to proceed as normal.
Q: Were you under orders to let people join the group if they
wanted to join the group?
A: No, I never heard that.
Q: What did you hear?
A: As I stated, "to proceed as normal."
Q: From whom did you receive those orders?
A: I received those orders from Captain Lamont.

It was this kind of "alert indifference" on the part of the jail
personnel that has led some observers to suspect that the twenty-
seven soldiers were tacitly encouraged to trap themselves in a
situation which the Army could use as a punitive example.

Defense Attorney Terence Hallinan is one who holds the entrapment theory—"I feel that they were driven and enticed by
military authority into a cleverly devised trap." But of course for a
hot-blooded defense attorney to yell "trap" is not nearly as persuasive as for other, calmer gentlemen to hold the same opinion.
Congressman Robert Louis Leggett of California, for example, a
respected attorney, a former state legislator and a four-term
member of the U.S. House of Representatives, appraised all the
evidence and concluded:

"The confinement officer admitted that he was aware of the
pending demonstration the night before but did nothing to prevent
it. He admitted that his plan of action was that they should be
charged with mutiny. He probably, and with prior consideration,
refused to follow the standard operating procedure so as to inflame
the situation. He probably guided the situation so as to create an
incident and to permit it to get out of control. I would call this
entrapment. This is an example of the most dangerous and most

deplorable conduct on the part of the U.S. Army that I have ever had the misfortune to observe."

Those who harbor such suspicions point out that the Sixth Army's highest officers were unwilling to think of the disturbance in any terms except mutiny, even when they were advised to do so by their own investigators.

The first Article 32 investigation (preliminary investigation) was conducted by Captain Richard M. Millard, who recommended that the charges be reduced to willful disobedience and that the men be tried by a special court-martial.* Captain Millard insisted on the lesser charge despite intense pressure from his commanding officer, who all but ordered him to bring in a recommendation for mutiny charges. Millard nevertheless concluded:

> The charge of mutiny under Article 94 does not apply to the facts of 14 October 1968. There are three elements to the offense of mutiny, one of which is the intent to override lawful military authority. The element is absent in the present case. To charge [these men] with mutiny, an offense which has its roots in the harsh admiralty laws of the previous centuries, for demonstrating against the conditions which existed in the stockade, is, in my opinion, an overreaction by the Army and a misapplication of a statute which could lead to a further miscarriage of justice.

The six-month maximum sentences that a special court-martial could give, he wrote, should be punishment enough. "If it is not adequate, then the focus of the command should be on those conditions which lead to such demonstrations, for in my opinion, one does not give up six months' freedom to participate in a short demonstration unless the conditions leading to the demonstration are compelling."

Taking note of the findings of Army psychiatrists, Millard also recommended that several of the defendants be released from military service.

---

* For a description of the several types of courts-martial, see page 86n.

The Army commanders were highly offended by that report, and they were not pleased by the recommendations of Captain James Bradner, Jr., who conducted the second Article 32 hearing. He, too, saw the offense as something other than mutiny. He suggested the prisoners be tried by a general court-martial for willful disobedience, an offense that could bring maximum sentences of five years.

Not until still another captain held a third Article 32 investigation (normally only one investigation is held) did the commanders get the recommendation they sought: mutiny charges.

These charges appear to have been inevitable. Officers and noncommissioned officers who were privy to discussions of stockade discontent had been using the word "mutiny" even before the event, and once it occurred they were remarkably swift to brand the protest as this worst of military crimes.

Lieutenant Tierney, who had commanded some of the Military Police at the disturbance, testified: "When he [Captain Lamont] came outside of the compound, I asked him if he wanted to repeat the reading of the mutiny article. Earlier when he told me he was reading the article, I asked him why, because it was mutiny whether he was reading the article or not." Strange that Tierney should already have been so convinced, since at the moment he was calling it mutiny, Lamont *had not yet given the twenty-seven protesters the order to disperse,* the crucial order that the Army later made the basis for its official mutiny charge.

Sergeant Woodring, for another example, though he had no legal training and on the witness stand could not begin to paraphrase the mutiny article, no sooner saw the men break ranks than he knew they were mutinying.* Before they had regrouped in their circle on the grass, while they were still on their feet, walking past

* To be sure, Woodring had a very fanciful notion of what constitutes a crime, especially a crime as sophisticated as mutiny. Some time after the sit-down, a group of prisoners walked up the stockade stairs whistling in unison and Woodring yelled at them to "shut up or I'll charge you with another mutinous act."

him, he knew it was mutiny. They were guilty of disobedience and of breach of peace and perhaps of some other, lesser crimes, but the only charge that came to Woodring's mind, for some reason, was mutiny.

Q: When the prisoners walked out of formation, what did you do?

WOODRING: I immediately started to walk from the steps in the direction that the prisoners were traveling. I ordered them to halt, and they ignored me, and I then explained to them that what they were doing constituted mutiny. They continued to walk in the southeast direction.

Q: Where were you in relation to the prisoners when you ordered them to halt?

WOODRING: I had moved from the steps onto the paved area, and was walking in the same direction the prisoners were. Some of the prisoners were in front of me, some about even, and some were behind me.

Q: And briefly, specifically what did you say; what words did you use?

WOODRING: I stated: "I'm giving you an order to return to the formation." When they ignored that, I said, "What you're doing constitutes mutiny. I'm ordering you to return to the formation."

Q: Did you tell them they were guilty of disobeying the orders of an NCO?

WOODRING: No, sir.

Q: Did you tell them they were guilty of any violation of the code?

WOODRING: I didn't tell them they were guilty of anything. I said that what they were doing constituted mutiny.

Q: Did what they were doing constitute any other crime in the code according to your opinion?

WOODRING: Yes, sir.

Q: Did you inform them of that?

WOODRING: No, sir.

Q: Why did you pick mutiny?

WOODRING: Because I believed at that time that the act of a large group of prisoners, acting to override or overthrow authority, did constitute mutiny.

Q: Well, without knowing what the prisoners were eventually charged with, without knowing what they had in mind, you were

prepared to say they possessed the required intent for the commission of mutiny?
WOODRING: I have said it, sir. I must have had some foresight there,
somehow.

Sergeant Woodring's lighthearted explanation, however, was not
enough to dissuade some observers from a feeling of fishiness. As
attorney Lowe asked the Fort Lewis jury panel of high-ranking
officers: "Are any of you gentlemen so versed in the Code, so
versed in law that you can in a matter of moments reflect upon a
complicated, fast-moving, highly diffused factual situation and
decide that it is mutiny? You could only if you had been so
predisposed to believe it is a mutiny. Sergeant Woodring, like
Sergeant Morales, like Captain Lamont, like everyone else in a
position of command responsibility in that stockade, knew something was going to happen that morning. They knew it beyond
question, beyond doubt, but the minute that thing happened,
Woodring could say 'mutiny.' "

Why would the powerful, cocksure Army go out of its way to
destroy these pathetic waifs? The victory seems so slight and the
overkill so enormous. The answer is a fairly human one, not a
bureaucratic one. The Soods and Saleses of the Army are the
direct victims not of inflexible regulations handed down by Big
Army, by the Pentagon Army, but of the arbitrary emotions of the
Outpost Army—the uncocksure, aging human beings who run
things in the field and whose insecurities in a civilian-dominated
world are hidden beneath the uniforms of colonels and generals.

The chaos and the often ridiculous inconsistencies of military
justice are largely the fault of a tradition by which a commandant
is allowed to run his own outfit with all the autonomy of a medi-
eval fiefdom. Face and pride, so precious to the military, would
otherwise be lost. High Pentagon officials have admitted on the
record that they will go to almost any lengths to avoid interfering
with the generals who run the bases and will reverse their injustices
only when adverse public opinion mounts to threatening levels. As

a result, one finds trivial jealousies, grudges and a general's own political biases often dictating the conduct of courts under his command, as well as dictating, of course, who appears before them as defendants.

Examples are not hard to find. Captain Howard Levy was a New York Jew who offended the citizenry of Columbia, South Carolina, by helping Negroes in a voter-registration drive and who offended the other officers on the nearby Army post by refusing to join the Officers' Club. Given his indiscreet tongue, it was almost inevitable that he would wind up defending himself against serious charges—and he did. It was just as inevitable that Lance Corporal William Harvey and Private George Daniels would be sent to prison for six and ten years (later reduced to three and four years) for the crime of asking to talk with their commanding officer about the justice of black men being sent to Vietnam. They had made the mistake of irritating the Marine commanders at a time when their base, Pendleton, was considered an "extraordinarily dangerous" place, as one Pentagon official put it, because of the unrest of the troops. Also, the commandant was fed up with Black Muslims, and Harvey and Daniels happened to be of that religion. And one need not be surprised that Private First Class Bruce Petersen was given eight years in prison for possessing marijuana (enough, the police said, to mildly taint the lint in his pocket), when the ordinary sentence for possession is six months. Petersen was the editor of the underground newspaper at Fort Hood, Texas, that had embarrassed and enraged the commandant for months, printing news of disturbances on the base that the commandant wanted to keep quiet and that the local civilian newspaper did, indeed, suppress.

The same inevitable injustice descended on the Presidio because of persons who irritated the local commanders—the most irritating being the peace people and the hippie community of San Francisco, which, the Army believed, was ruining many of its soldiers; the San Francisco press; and Terence Kayo Hallinan, the fiery attorney who championed dissident soldiers.

The Presidio officers hated the peace people and the hippies so much, in fact, that they were secretly talking of moving the confinement facilities away from San Francisco. The suggestion was put to the Sixth Army commanding general, by Colonel Robert McMahon, infantry commander, in a memo in 1968:

The primary reason for this request is to prevent further unfavorable criticism of the Army caused by indifferent, irresponsible, ineffective soldiers awaiting disposition at Presidio of San Francisco. This problem is acute because the Presidio is located in the San Francisco area where the press is particularly inclined to give headline attention to sensational stories involving the Army. . . . The easy access from the city of San Francisco . . . not only permits, but encourages the two-way contact of troublemaker elements in the service with the press and other organizations that thrive on sensationalism. . . . The Haight-Ashbury district acts as a magnet for fugitives and contributes to the general problem. . . . A contributing cause to the recent adverse publicity has been the group of attorneys to whom many SPD personnel have turned for representation. These lawyers have employed techniques bordering on the unethical in order to achieve discharges for their clients. Soldiers have been advised to go AWOL or remain out of military control until they are dropped from the rolls of their organizations, and then surrender at the Presidio so they will be processed here in the atmosphere hostile to the Army.

Four days before the sit-down, Navy Nurse Lieutenant (j.g.) Susan Schnall had gone on her celebrated "Peace Bomb" mission, flying over the aircraft carrier USS *Ranger,* Oakland Naval Hospital, Treasure Island Naval Base, the Presidio and Yerba Buena Island. She dropped twenty thousand leaflets telling of the GI protest march for peace to be staged in San Francisco two days later, October 12. On the day of the parade, many West Coast bases held maneuvers to keep their men too busy to participate. The Presidio isn't laid out properly for maneuvers, so the commanders held mandatory company formations every two hours throughout that Saturday to prevent servicemen from joining the protest. Nevertheless many GIs were in the march and the Outpost Army was furious. In the forty-eight hours before the sit-down, it was rumored around the base that the prisoners were about to pull something "to attract the press," which also infuriated the officers. And when, at the sit-down itself, the prisoners interspersed choruses of "America the Beautiful" and "We Shall Overcome" with chants of "We want Hallinan! We want Hallinan! We want the press! We want the press!" the sit-downers became secondary antagonists. The colonels and generals were out to get these other forces which, by beguiling their GIs, had jeopardized discipline.

Intellectually they seemed perfectly aware that the demonstration did not fit the description of a mutiny. One may fairly assume this from testimony given by Sergeant Craig Black, the specialist who took video film of the demonstration for the Army, just as he had taken video films of the GI and Veterans March two days earlier. According to Black, when he showed both films to a group of eight top officers from the base, "someone at the meeting said that the reason for the demonstration was to support the GI and Vets March and someone else said that it was to protest the killing of a prisoner. *I didn't hear anyone say that one reason for the demonstration was to avoid doing something they were going to be ordered to do."* (Emphasis added.)

When the top officers discussed the demonstration privately, they did not talk about anyone's "intent to override military authority"—or mutiny. And if they did not honestly view it in that light, why should they charge mutiny if it was not to strike back, through these prisoners, at that greater grudge target which included "peacenik" civilians, the press—and civil rights attorneys, as embodied in Terence Kayo Hallinan?

Could the commanding cadre really have reacted so violently to one attorney? The reaction may have been illogical and extravagant, but it was not unreal. Some of the local Army leaders were convinced that Hallinan, who had visited the stockade on October 13, had instigated the demonstration that occurred the next day. And their theory was perhaps not totally absurd. According to one prisoner, Hallinan had told the GIs in the stockade that there were

a number of lawyers in the Bay area standing ready to help them.*
At the trials of the "mutineers," one GI defended himself on the
grounds that he had no criminal intent and that Hallinan had
misled him, sneaking into the stockade disguised as a priest
several days before the demonstration to advise him that it
wouldn't be mutiny if they sat down. A guard also testified that
he had seen Hallinan sneaking in. When Hallinan was asked if he
had done this, his reply was not entirely direct. "Well . . . there's
no need for me to sneak in," he said. "I can go in in my regular
disguise as an attorney."

There is no doubt that Hallinan is a tricky, smart, tough
attorney. "I did smuggle out Richard Bunch's suicide notes," he
conceded, "the day before the mutiny."

One of seven sons of Vincent Hallinan, Terence inherited all his
father's nonconformity. Vincent Hallinan was the presidential
candidate of the Progressive Party in 1952, a year when the party
was widely considered to be dominated by Communists and fellow
travelers. Vincent Hallinan didn't mind the company at all. He was
also legendary on the West Coast for his brilliant legal services to
Harry Bridges, the longshoremen's boss. None of his sons can yet
match Vincent's radical record, although one of them is making a
game effort as an official of the Communist Party in New York.
And Terence—something of a street-fighting delinquent in his
younger days and an amateur boxing terror in his later youth—is
now well on his way to building a legal reputation no less feisty
than his father's.

It took Terence Hallinan two years to win his law license. The
committee of bar examiners said he had been arrested too many
times for pro–civil right and pro-peace militancy, and Hallinan
got around that block with the help of the State Supreme Court.
But he immediately proved he had no intention of settling down

* This, actually, was no news at all. Several months earlier the commanding officer of the Presidio had written a letter—later disclosed to the
public—in which he had alluded to the unpatriotic character of about one
hundred lawyers in the area who were helping soldiers.

when he took the case of a reluctant soldier who was en route to Vietnam. Hallinan boarded the Air Force bus taking the soldier to the Vietnam-bound plane and pulled his client off—while Army guards seized other portions of the soldier's body and tried to hang on. Though Hallinan won the tug-of-war, he lost the subsequent court-martial; but he made the trial colorful enough to win the lasting enmity of the military authorities. "That," he recalled with satisfaction, "was when they began to really get down on me."

On the day after the demonstration, he went to the stockade to see if any of the men needed counsel. The Army had changed the rules overnight, and he was forbidden to talk to anyone who had not written a letter to him asking his help. Hallinan had one client there, however, and they couldn't keep him from seeing this boy. "As I came out of the room," Hallinan said, "they were having rec period and the yard was full of prisoners. So I got up at the top of the stairs and yelled, 'Are any of you from the twenty-seven?' A bunch of kids came over and started talking to me. The guards came running out, grabbed me and hustled me out of the gate. As I was going, I yelled over my shoulder, 'Write me! Write me! Terence Hallinan, 345 Franklin Street.' The next day I had some nineteen letters. I ended up with seventeen clients, but three have escaped. Two just grabbed some paint buckets and brushes and told the guards they were on work detail and kept on walking. The third one sawed through the bars in the infirmary." Hallinan grinned as he told about it.

Nonconformity being the identified enemy, the Presidio and Sixth Army authorities apparently were determined to let nothing deter them from delivering a crushing punishment against every man involved, even those who joined the sit-down out of a misunderstanding or halfheartedly or by misadventure. And to achieve this punishment the Army was apparently ready to use every slip and dodge that is permissible under the Uniform Code of Military Justice.

The extent of the Army's hostility is best illustrated by the case of Private Edward A. Yost. Yost was not one of those defendants who, because of their psychological problems and bizarre, anti-social behavior, could have been expected to receive unsympathetic treatment from the Army. Yost was a perfectly ordinary GI, a good soldier, and his fate in the Presidio trials accurately portrays the implacability of military justice.

Private Yost, of Vacaville, California, was a holder of the Combat Infantryman's Badge (not lightly given, as every GI knows), the Purple Heart and other medals won for combat service with the 9th Infantry Division in Vietnam. He was a light-weapons infantryman. One day, while he was working with a mop-up team on patrol in the Mekong Delta, a booby trap went off and gave him extensive injuries over his face, chest, shoulders and abdomen. While he was being removed from the scene, a sniper shot him in the shoulder. He spent two weeks in a hospital in Vietnam, then he was shipped to a hospital in Japan, and finally he was returned to Letterman Hospital in San Francisco.

Meanwhile, he was having other problems. The Army had failed, for reasons unknown to Yost, to start his allotment to his former wife and he had fallen behind in child-support payments— no trivial matter in the State of California. Deciding that his financial situation was getting desperate and that he couldn't solve it by lying around Letterman, Yost went over the hill and returned to Vacaville, where he got a job working with a furniture company.

But Yost liked the Army, and being AWOL bothered his conscience. In September, 1968, he got a lawyer to ask the Army what would happen to him if he surrendered to the military authorities. The reply was: probably nothing. Confinement in the stockade, the Army said, would not be likely "because having surrendered, confinement would not seem necessary to insure his presence at the trial."

So Yost surrendered on September 20, 1968, and was thrown into the stockade.

Still, Yost had no grudge against the Army, or if he had a grudge, it was such a slight one that his overseers at the stockade could not detect it. Every officer and noncommissioned officer attached to the stockade and called to testify at Yost's trial—with the exception of Lamont, Woodring and Morales—described Yost as a model prisoner, dependable, willing and correct; they testified that they would be happy to serve beside him in battle. He himself testified that he had been proud to serve in Vietnam, despite the consequences, and that he would willingly serve there again. He was no pacifist, and he disliked those who were. Furthermore, he had no patience with soldiers who denounced the service.

Then why was he among the twenty-seven protesters? The answer is an intertwining of reasons, the principle one being that Yost's hearing was very poor. Not only had the Vietcong booby trap ripped through his flesh at countless places, it had also blown out his right ear drum and damaged his left ear as well. Consequently he often did not have an immediate grasp of what was going on around him. And when another of the "mutineers," a boy he had gone to high school with, broke ranks and walked past him at the morning line-up on October 14 and said, "Come on, let's go," Yost went. He wasn't quite sure why he was going, but he went.

In one sense, Yost was not happy about the stockade. He thought it was sloppily run; he thought it was a bad specimen of Army routine. Thus he may not have been altogether opposed to being part of a protest. But that would have been a fleeting emotion. Basically, he was uneasy among the other twenty-six, and he stayed because getting into a stupid position is much easier than getting out of one. He stayed. But photos taken by the Army of the protest group show Yost on the perimeter, often ducking his head in what clearly seems to be embarrassment.

With Yost, then, the demonstrators sat down in the prison yard. According to testimony, Captain Lamont then approached the demonstrators, and Private Walter Palowski stood and said, "Captain Lamont, I have a list of grievances that I want to read to you." He began at once on the list. The demonstrators wanted the shotgun details eliminated at the stockade, they wanted psychological evaluation of all custodial staff, they wanted improved sanitation facilities. . . .

After Palowski had read these three demands, Lamont interrupted and began reading from the mutiny article in the Military Code. Outraged and frightened now that their plan was being frustrated by Lamont's unwillingness to listen, the group began to yell and chant their protest expressions and songs even louder.

A question arises: Why didn't Lamont listen to the entire list of grievances and respond to it? Army Regulation 633–5, Section VI, 45-b, gives this advice on the use of force at Army confinement facilities:

In the event of an attempted group or mass breakout from a confinement facility, a riot, or some other general disorder, it will be made evident to the prisoners concerned that authority prevails, that order will be restored, and that means are available to restore it by the vigorous application of force, if necessary. *If the situation permits, an attempt will be made to reason with the prisoners engaged in any disorder* prior to the application of any force. This is not to be interpreted as requiring bargaining with or making concessions to prisoners while in a state of revolt. [Emphasis added.]

The situation at the Presidio was nothing so disorderly as a mass breakout; everyone was squatting in one place. It was not a riot; the men had quieted to let one of their members read from a list. If a commander is required by Army regulations to attempt to reason even with men who are breaking out or rioting, how much more stringently is he required to reason with men who are simply sitting and singing?

Lamont acknowledged under questioning that the atmosphere at the sit-down was relatively tranquil.

Q: During the course of incidents of things that were taking place did you feel the stockade was threatened?

LAMONT: No.

Q: Did you feel a threat of physical violence?

LAMONT: No.

Q: Did you witness anyone being threatened?

LAMONT: No.

Q: Were there any attempts to destroy any articles around the grounds?

LAMONT: No.

Q: Would it be fair to say the incident was peaceful?

LAMONT: Yes.

But Lamont did not attempt to reason with the men. He was not even willing to hear out their grievances. Why not? Lamont said his first response was to be "dumfounded" that they would read such a list to him. Then he said he was already aware of the grievances, but "I don't think any of them were well-founded. Some of them had merit for discussion."*

But Captain Lamont was in no mood for discussion.

Q: Did you attempt in any way to reason with them by responding to their questions or their requests?

LAMONT: No.

Q: Did you feel that any response directly to their questions would constitute a concession?

LAMONT: At that time we were at a disadvantage, guard force-wise, and I felt, in the manner in which the grievances were being stated . . .

Q: Did you feel personally apprehensive as you stood before the group?

LAMONT: You mean, was I afraid for myself?

Q: Yes.

LAMONT: No.

* At one of the preliminary hearings, however, Captain Lamont conceded under questioning that the prisoners' petition for a psychiatric examination of the guards was perfectly in line with good custodial work. "I think," he said, "that when you are dealing with prisoners it is not an unreasonable request." So of the grievances he heard before he interrupted the reading, Lamont agreed that at least one-third were reasonable.

Q: Then when you said the conditions, to wit, the lack of suitable guard forces at the moment, were not conducive to answering their questions, you weren't afraid that they were all going to jump on you and attack you, were you?

LAMONT: No. I felt that the way they were expressing themselves, and the form in which they were holding it, could only have led to making concessions, to have got any kind of cooperation from them.

Q: You felt that it would be making a concession to have taken the piece of paper from Private Palowski's hand and saying— say, "I'll look into it. Now, please get back in."

LAMONT: I was not offered that piece of paper.

Q: Do you feel it would have been a concession had you merely replied to his grievances and said, "Appropriate action will be taken"?

LAMONT: At the time, Palowski was not very interested in hearing what I had to say, but more in what he had to say.

Q: Well, of course, what you had to say, from your own testimony, wasn't responsive to what he had asked, or what he had said.

LAMONT: I don't think they knew that at the time, because up until that point, all I had said was, "Give me your attention."

Q: The group was quiet at that point, was it not?

LAMONT: While Palowski read, yes.

Q: Considering the tension that you had previously testified to, then, it was your opinion that it would have been a concession to have responded in some way to their grievances which they voiced?

LAMONT: I would have been perfectly willing to accept any grievances if they had been expressed by formally coming to me and stating them, or that they had problems that they wanted to have looked into. But in the manner in which they expressed them . . .

Q: Well, of course . . .

LAMONT: The method they chose, I felt it was inappropriate at that time to reason with them.

Q: Do you not agree [with] the very provisions, or the very form of AHR633–5, which recommends reasoning to be applied in those situations where there are disorders, and, generally speaking, improper things being done?

LAMONT: I feel I complied with those guidelines, as well as could be, under the circumstances and conditions we had at that time.

Or, as he put it in later testimony: "I chose not to reason any further than I did." When one is on the winning side, one can ignore the regulations with impunity. Captain Lamont was determined to finish his reading of the mutiny article, which he had broken off when the group began shouting again. He retreated to an MP's sedan parked outside the stockade fence. The sedan was equipped with a loudspeaker, and Lamont used it to read the mutiny article and to order the mutineers to disperse and return to their prison barracks.

The most important question raised in any of the trials was raised in the Yost trial at this point by his defense counsel: "Did the group know it was receiving an order?" The significance of this matter was laid out plainly by the military judge in his instructions to the jury panel. Not only must Yost and the other defendants have been aware of the order to be guilty of mutiny; they would have to be aware of it even to be guilty of the lesser offense of disobedience. "I would like to advise you again," said the judge, "of *the requirement that these accused had knowledge of the command is an essential element of the offense of mutiny,* the lesser included offenses of willful disobedience of an order of a commissioned officer and the failure to obey a lawful order." (Emphasis added.)

When Captain Lamont first approached the group, he gave them no order to disperse. At the trials he was determinedly candid about that.

Q: Did you give the prisoners an order at that time?
LAMONT: No.
Q: It's a fact, isn't it, that at no time inside the stockade did you give the prisoners a direct order?
LAMONT: That's correct.
Q: Are you absolutely sure about that?
LAMONT: Yes.
Q: When was the first time that you gave an order?
LAMONT: The first order I gave was over the public-address system on the sedan outside the compound.

Q: At the point you left the group to go outside the compound in order to get on the PA system, did you, in any way, indicate to the group by a signal, or by directing your NCO's to indicate that you were leaving the immediate area to go out of the stockade?

LAMONT: No.

Q: I understand, then, you did not direct any of your people to indicate—

LAMONT: No, I did not.

Q: —that you were leaving, going outside the stockade? Did you make any specific effort to attract the attention of the group, other than speaking on the PA system?

LAMONT: No.

Q: Did you have a police siren readily available?

LAMONT: I am sure there was one on the vehicle.

Q: Were there other possible signalling devices that could have been used to avoid the possibility that someone may not have known that you had left the group?

LAMONT: What was the question—were there others?

Q: That's correct. Were there other signalling devices, such as a red light on the car, or headlights, or automobile horns?

LAMONT: I believe there was.

Q: And you did not use any of these?

LAMONT: No, I did not.

Q: The group was in a circle, was it not?

LAMONT: Yes.

Q: So that some members in the group, while you were speaking on the PA system, had their backs toward you, is that correct?

LAMONT: That's correct.

Q: So unless they turned their heads a hundred and eighty degrees they would not have seen you, is that correct?

LAMONT: Correct.

When Lamont began using the loudspeaker, his was a mystery voice, not only to the men who were sitting with their backs to him but to some of the others as well. For he had somehow slipped out of the stockade yard and to the sedan without being noticed even by some observers on the spot who were standing nearby and watching everything that took place. Sergeant Woodring, for example, admitted at the trial that he had *not* seen Lamont leaving the grounds.

Q: Are you indicating to this court, then, while standing six to eight feet from Captain Lamont, you don't know where he went? You don't know how he got there?

WOODRING: I'm not indicating anything, sir. I'm stating a fact. I don't recall how he got over there.

Q: Did you hear any special signals, or did you see other officers or non-commissioned officers indicate to the men of that group that Captain Lamont had now left the area and had gone some 50 feet to that new location?

WOODRING: No, sir.

Q: It is possible, then, that some of the members of that group never saw him leave or arrive at that new location, is it not?

WOODRING: It's possible, sir.

Furthermore, as other witnesses testified, Lamont was not in complete view of the group while he was using the loudspeaker. The front left door of the sedan was open in front of him.

Q: At the time you were at the public address system in the sedan, did the group appear to be quite engrossed in its singing and chanting?

LAMONT: Yes.

Q: Did you observe any of the individuals whose backs were to you, turn around and look at you?

LAMONT: I don't recall.

At one of the preliminary hearings it was revealed that Captain Lamont, before giving his order and before again reading the mutiny article over the loudspeaker system, had failed to identify himself. To be guilty of even willful disobedience, a soldier must know the order comes from his commanding officer. There was no certainty, however, that *any* of the demonstrators knew who was addressing them, although of course it is reasonable to assume that at least half of them—those facing the sedan—did know. (But certainly not Private Sood, who had just been imprisoned and had never seen Lamont in his life.)

Still, the more important question remains: Could they hear him? Everyone admitted that the twenty-seven young men were making a great deal of noise. Even when Lamont first approached them and stood only eight or ten feet from the group and began reading the mutiny article, they were chanting and yelling at a very high volume. Lamont stopped reading the article because "I felt that the prisoners, after they started singing and chanting again, *could not hear me.*" (Emphasis added.)

When he resorted to the use of the loudspeaker, did they stop and listen? Not at all. They increased their volume. Lamont admitted that the sound of their voices when he was reading over the loudspeaker system, as compared with when he was inside reading to them, was "much louder . . . screaming. They got very, very loud."

And later he gave this testimony:

Q: And what was the group doing, if anything, while you gave this order?

LAMONT: They were continuing to sing and chant.

Q: And what volume, tone or pitch, as compared to when you were reading from the portions of the Manual for Courts-Martial over the loudspeaker system?

LAMONT: The ones I observed were screaming just as loud as they could holler.

Q: Did the volume or pitch change at all during the period of time you were giving the order?

LAMONT: Yes, they were—they were—I don't know how to describe it. They were screaming as loud as I believe they could.

The loudspeaker system wasn't operating perfectly, and this was the first time in his life Lamont had ever used such a device. Some witnesses said they heard static, some said they heard feedback, some said they heard both (and these were prosecution, not defense, witnesses). At one point Lamont had to stop while a

military policeman regulated the speaker so it would stop making
what one witness described as "a keening noise." Lamont conceded under questioning that it was "quite possible" that his voice
might have been distorted enough that it was unrecognizable by
the men who had their backs to him.

One of the most authoritative witnesses recruited by the defense
was Dr. Vincent Salmon, a Ph.D. in theoretical physics who for ten
years had worked for Jensen Manufacturing Company, a maker of
highly regarded loudspeakers; he was Jensen's top physicist in
charge of designing and testing. In 1949 he had joined the staff of
the Stanford University Research Institute, where at the time of
the trial he was senior research scientist and manager of the sonics
program, dealing with all phases of acoustics. In other words, for
the past thirty years he had performed the most highly advanced
research into noise control, hearing loss, underwater sounds, audio
engineering and electroacoustics.

In his testimony before one of the courts-martial, Dr. Salmon
used the man in the circle of twenty-seven who was *nearest* the
public-address system as his guinea pig and presumed he was
*facing* the loudspeaker (though, in fact, the nearest men had their
backs to Captain Lamont). This hypothetical soldier would have
been in the best position of anyone in the circle to hear Lamont.
Dr. Salmon furthermore assumed for his calculation that the men
"were not singing at double forte nor double piano but were in
between" (though Lamont said they actually were screaming at
the top of their lungs). Even assuming those ideal conditions, said
Dr. Salmon, he figured the public-address system was operating at
91 decibels and the men were chanting at something like 98
decibels, moderately figured, and therefore the chant overwhelmed
the loudspeaker by 7 decibels. "The man nearest the public-
address system may have heard a few words," Dr. Salmon said,
"but certainly, in my mind I'd have no doubt that he would have
great difficulty in understanding *what* was being said over the
public-address system. For men more distant than the nearest man,

this situation would be more reinforced. . . . My conclusion is, under these conditions it would have been—I have very strong doubts in mind—it is my opinion the men could not have understood the message."

This was under ideal conditions, Salmon emphasized. But if the men were grouped in an uneven cluster (as they were) instead of an even circle, the noise they were making would have had an even greater masking effect. And if the men were screaming (as Lamont testified they were) rather than merely singing loudly, the masking factor "would be increased at least 5 decibels." It would be more reasonable to assume, then, that the men were drowning out Lamont by at least 12 decibels or more.

If this were true for the average demonstrator, with good hearing, what was poor Yost's share of Dostoevskian justice—Yost, the soldier who had left most of his hearing in Vietnam? He was not sitting in the best position. In fact, he was sitting in the worst. Sergeant Woodring testified that Yost had his "right side and back" to Lamont, and it was Yost's right ear that had received the most severe damage from the land-mine explosion.

Captain Ronald S. Reiter, chief of the Audiology, Otolaryngology Service at Madigan General Hospital, had tested Yost. Because of the "unusual hearing loss" in his right ear and also the milder loss in his left, Yost (the captain testified) would need a 20-decibel increase in a sound over that which an ordinary person would need to receive it clearly. Put in more practical terms, said Captain Reiter, Yost's hearing was so bad that if he were discharged honorably he should apply for a pension from the Veterans Administration.

It was the possibility of a sentence that would prevent Yost from receiving a pension that seemed to worry his defense counsels most. As one of them pleaded in his closing remarks to the jury:

There are many punishments, as was expressed by some of my fellow counsel. There is some awesome punishment, and it is awesome indeed, the potential that you carry over this man's head. You can . . . among other things adjudge a dishonorable or bad-conduct discharge and strip this man of his medals, his buttons, and get him right out of the Army. You can do it here today. That is your prerogative. But is this necessary for the Army? Is this the best way for society? Is this the best for this man? I think not, and I beg you to think not, because not only has this man earned the right to have this piece of paper hanging on his wall someday that he served his country honorably, but he also has the right to come in some years from now, perhaps when these wounds start acting up, when he is 30 or 35 years old, he has the right to have the Government take care of him like they have so ably taken care of all of our veterans and to be treated for those wounds, if they act up, or he has earned the right to be compensated, as one of our expert witnesses testified, for his ear. His ear drum was blown out serving his country, and I believe that he has earned his right for that sixty or seventy small dollars a month that he has earned in that service, but he cannot do this, gentlemen, if you impose a punitive discharge.

But the plea was not sufficient. The Army was so determined to show no mercy to the "mutineers" that none could escape. Yost—whose attitude in the stockade had never been even surly, much less mutinous, and could not conceivably be thought to harbor the necessary "intent to override military authority" that constitutes mutiny; whose record in the Army was not only honorable but valorous; who was sitting with his back to Lamont during the disputed period and was least able, for this and physical reasons, to hear the captain's command—Yost was given a sentence of nine months in prison and a bad-conduct discharge, which, in terms of depriving him of veteran's benefits, was as crippling as a dishonorable discharge.

According to his civilian attorney, Lowe, one of Yost's Army lawyers asked the members of the panel later if they hadn't believed the sound expert and the audiologist. Yes, they said—but Yost was guilty anyway.

In that trial, the jury of three lieutenant colonels, a major and a captain needed only twenty minutes per defendant to bring in their verdicts. The other three defendants received sentences of six, three and two years.

It is painful to think that fits of temper, plus pressure from commanders, plus public opinion, somehow are supposed to equal justice, but that is just exactly what the equation came to at the Presidio. Not that the local commanders wanted it that way. They would have much preferred to leave out the public-opinion factor.

The subjective involvement of key Presidio officers was illustrated when Colonel James Garnett, chief legal adviser to the Sixth Army Commander, General Stanley Larsen, was being cross-examined by attorney Hallinan. The official record of their exchange reads only: "Mr. Hallinan and the witness argued briefly." What actually happened was that Hallinan baited him a bit and Garnett lost control and screamed at Hallinan, "Why, you're nothing but a smart-aleck who's trying to get press!" Hallinan began screaming back at him, and in a moment the captain conducting the hearing was yelling for the bailiff, apparently with the intention of having Hallinan put out of the courtroom, although it didn't get that far.

To understand just what it meant to have Garnett call Hallinan names, one must realize that the captain running the hearing was *under* Garnett. No one, then, was surprised when the captain came in with recommendations that the men be charged with mutiny.

When the first court-martial panel brought in a verdict of guilty with a penalty of fifteen years at hard labor against Private Sood, the public was outraged. On the same day that General Larsen "reviewed" the case and cut the sentence to what he considered a humane seven years, public opinion boiled over through Congress. Representative Robert Leggett put a special call on the floor of the House, and for the next few hours he and a group of seven other California Congressmen denounced everything about Army justice. Their words fill thirty pages of the *Congressional Record*.

Secretary of the Army Stanley Resor had known the storm was

coming, and he had been working hard to bring matters under control. In the early days of the trials he had been on the phone to the Presidio frequently. Now he sought to cut the Sood sentence still more, and as swiftly as possible. Ordinarily when a trial record is completed, it is reviewed by the local commanding general and then in due course mailed back to Washington for further action by the board of review. In this case there was no such dilly-dallying. A lieutentant colonel was used as a messenger boy, and he flew the Sood trial record back to Washington and delivered it by hand that same day to Secretary Resor's office, so that Resor's legal counsel could take it right over to the Judge Advocate General, Major General Kenneth Hodson, to act on immediately. The general had no more than half an hour to review the voluminous trial record, which suggests he knew very well what was expected of him before he ever got his hands on it. He performed as expected, reducing Sood's sentence to two years.

It not only was unusual for a judge advocate general to make a clemency ruling before the board of review had handled the case; it may have been the first time in history for such speedy action. That it was done to satisfy the public cannot be doubted. In the hours before Congressman Leggett led the long denunciation of the military courts and the military prison systems on the House floor, his office was overrun by officers from the Pentagon, seeking copies of his speech or news releases or some clue to what he was going to say. They went away empty-handed. Finally, shortly before the Leggett broadside began, the Pentagon announced the reduction. The Army was *scrambling*.

This immediate slashing of the sentence was a heavy reproof to General Larsen and Colonel Garnett, but they would not heed it. In less than a month Larsen had approved two other convictions, reducing the sentences only from sixteen to five years in one case and from fourteen to five years in the other. Once again the Pentagon dropped the sentences to two years.

And *still* Larsen and Garnett pressed the Outpost Army's

vendetta.* Along came the trial of Private Yost, the courageous veteran of Vietnam who had lost his hearing—a perfect opportunity for the Presidio to pull back without loss of face. Yost's attorney, David Lowe, put it up to the prosecution. "Look, we've got a disabled hero," Lowe remembered saying. "You can see the Pentagon would prefer these sentences were lighter. Maybe we can work a deal. We can't plead the mutiny because there wasn't a mutiny, but we will plead guilty to disobedience of an order if you want it, if you'll agree to recommend a year and a bad-conduct discharge." The prosecutors said they would check with the Presidio. They checked and came back with the word from Garnett to go for broke.

As we have seen, in Yost's case the court nevertheless did give a light sentence (nine months), lighter even than the defense had offered to take. By the time the trial of the fourteen defendants opened at Fort Ord, California, the weight of public opinion had made itself fully felt. The sentences that came out of Ord ranged from three months to fifteen months, and two of the fourteen men even got off with convictions of disobedience.

Hurrah for pity at last. Well, in a way. The later sentences in the Presidio case may have been more merciful than the first, but as a measure of justice the three-month sentences were no more reliable than the fourteen-, fifteen- and sixteen-year sentences of the first three trials. Where men motivated by the same impulses perform the same act, perform it at the same time and in the same place, and come away with unreviewed sentences as disparate as

* Larsen may have been feeling more Pentagon pressure than he let on. Early in March, two of the excellent Army defense attorneys, Captains Emmitt Yeary and Brendan Sullivan, told the press that they had been telephoned at home by a mysterious "Major Jenkins," who said he was an old friend of General Larsen's, having served with him years ago in the 82nd Airborne Division. "Jenkins" said he was acting as the general's intermediary in an effort to "get off the hook"—which, said "Jenkins," was the general's deepest desire. General Larsen denied knowing a Major Jenkins, and the Army refused to permit civilian defense attorneys to call Larsen into court and question him on the matter.

three months and sixteen years, it is quite plain that the system which passed judgment on them is racked by the most arbitrary gusts of emotion and self-interest. The very success of public opinion in shaping some of the Presidio judgments only underscores the fact that many thousands of courts-martial send young men unjustly to prison without a voice being raised on their behalf.

*Epilogue:* A year after the last of the trials had ended, the Military Court of Review, still feeling intense public pressure, threw out the mutiny charges with the explanation that there was "insufficient evidence that they intended in concert to overthrow military authority"; but the court upheld lesser convictions for "willful disobedience," except in the case of Private Larry Lee Sales, whose charges were dismissed because the review court said it was not convinced that he was mentally responsible for the offense—in other words, it was not convinced he could distinguish right from wrong. But because the men had been deprived of the right to bail while making their appeals, they had all finished serving their time in prison before the court acted; in any event, their less-than-honorable discharges remain. If anyone benefitted by the Court of Military Review's action, it was only the Army, which hereafter can exclaim, to any who care to listen, "See how merciful we ultimately were."

# 3. At All Costs, Discipline

T HE MOST DISCOURAGING THING about the "Presidio 27" trials was that they were not unusual. If the certainty of conviction seemed to hang over them from the beginning, this was quite in keeping with the Army's record of getting convictions in 95 percent of all courts-martial. And if the great, melancholy heap of evidence produced by these trials showed injustice by civilian-court standards, it must be mourned not for the blighted lives of the individual defendants so much as for the national threat that all military justice poses.

Chief Justice Warren, usually a defender of the military, warned in 1962:

Events . . . have required a modification in the traditional theory of the autonomy of military authority. These events can be expressed very simply in numerical terms. A few months after Washington's first inauguration, our army numbered a mere 672 of the 840 authorized by Congress. Today, in dramatic contrast, the situation is this: Our armed forces number two and a half million; every resident male is a potential member of the peacetime armed forces; such service may occupy a minimum of four percent of the adult life of the average American male reaching draft age; reserve obligations extend over ten percent of such a person's life; and veterans are numbered in excess of

22,500,000. When the authority of the military has such a sweeping capacity for affecting the lives of our citizenry, the wisdom of treating the military establishment as an enclave beyond the reach of the civilian courts almost inevitably is drawn into question.

In the intervening eight years since Warren gave that warning, the numbers that so frightened him have grown. There are now 28 million veterans and another 3 million men are currently in uniform. If they, by their experiences, have developed a tolerance for unconstitutional trial procedures and for unconstitutional and inhumane punishment, it means that the minds of nearly one-half of our male population above the age of eighteen have already to some extent been polluted by militarism, a militarism that is much more dangerous than the economic brainwashing that the military-industrial complex has found so successful.

The Army is quite frank about, and in fact proud of, its mission to condition not only the bodies but the minds of those under its control. In the pamphlet, *The Fort Knox Experiment,* for example, in which the Army praises its methods for "developing the 'whole' man . . . in contrast to just exposing them to information," it says: "The Army today is the only organization in America equipped to conduct this kind of efficient training of our citizenry. The Armed Services have an extraordinary opportunity since they control the time and attention of the trainees 24 hours a day, seven days a week."

One favored military method of conditioning a man into docility is to make trial and punishment not only arbitrary but unpredictable. Refusing to wear a uniform has resulted in sentences ranging from simple discharge to three years in prison. Refusing to obey an order has resulted in sentences ranging from a few weeks to sixteen years. Holding an antiwar bull session while in uniform on base has resulted in everything from an administrative discharge without punishment to ten years in prison and a dishonorable discharge. So long as a serviceman can assure himself, "I have the right to act, within constitutional limits," he is a potential troublemaker. The less assurance a serviceman has of possessing any practical rights, the more likely will he be to shrink from action beyond that authorized by command.

This is the theory that inspired the Army in the case of Private Joe Miles. A handsome, popular black, Miles had received an award for being an outstanding platoon leader during basic training. But Miles was a political militant, and when he was moved to Fort Jackson, South Carolina, he became a founder of GIs United Against the War in Vietnam. When authorities observed Miles' influence over the other men, they shipped him to Fort Bragg, North Carolina. Hardly breaking stride, he immediately began organizing a new chapter of GIs United at Fort Bragg. There he received, on his written request, permission to distribute copies of the Bill of Rights at a specified time and place. But when he started handing them out, he was arrested for "distribution of unauthorized material." The next day the charges were dropped without explanation; at the same time he was informed that the Army had revoked its permission to distribute leaflets, the revocation being retroactive. A week later he was transferred to a post in northern Alaska.

During 1969 at least half a dozen young men who were members of such organizations as the Progressive Labor Party and the Young Socialist Alliance were drafted into the Army. Before induction they told their draft boards of their membership, but they were taken anyway. Then they were dismissed from the service with less-than-honorable discharges on the grounds that they belonged to subversive organizations.

Recent action in civilian court indicates there may be a way to salvage some the men who have suffered in this way in the past. On May 14, 1970, Federal Judge Charles A. Tenney of New York ordered the Army to change the "undesirable" discharge it had given to Andrew D. Stapp in 1968 to an "honorable" discharge.

Stapp, the irrepressible organizer of the American Servicemen's Union, had been kicked out of the Army on the grounds that he had "close, continuing and sympathetic association with the Communist Party" and with other forbidden organizations on the Attorney General's list. Ruled Tenney: "Since Stapp is charged with associations and beliefs, and not with any military misconduct or matters affecting his military record, the allegations failed to state a basis for a less-than-honorable discharge."

Of course, this ruling will not block future Army action against men who offend it politically; the ruling will only make the Army more circumspect in the reasons it publicly gives for the discharges.

Are these gross inconsistencies accidental, or are they part of the Army's strategy to keep its personnel off balance, insecure, rattled—and therefore more malleable? The latter. The Army admits it. Lieutenant Colonel Theodore E. Hervey, a high officer in the Pentagon's military personnel office, was asked about the arbitrary variations in the way the Army applies the rules and in the sentences that result from courts-martial. "The varied responses our commanders make to the dissidents," Hervey replied, "is going to keep them off balance. Whereas if our commanders always attacked at dawn [always applied the same laws the same way] they would know what to expect."

Before he had stopped talking, Colonel Hervey had given a perfect illustration of razzle-dazzle justice. First he said, "We do not control a soldier when he is off duty, off the post and out of uniform—so long as he does not commit a civil offense." When he was reminded that Second Lieutenant Henry Howe, Jr., in the first of the great freedom-of-speech cases arising from the Vietnam conflict, had been sentenced to prison for picketing against the war when he was off duty, off the post and out of uniform, but had committed no civil offense, Colonel Hervey—in the kind of reversal of the field for which the Army is notorious—waved this aside with: "Oh, well, it depends on what activities the soldier is engaged in. Again, we get back to the necessity of taking each individual case on its merits."

Ordinarily, this kind of "conditioning" is applied only to enlisted men and junior officers. But occasionally it happens at the top. After disagreeing wholeheartedly and publicly with the Administration's pursuit of the Vietnam war, and after participating in a peace vigil, Arnold True, a retired admiral who has a high reputation within the Navy as a destroyer tactician, was officially summoned in December, 1966, to the office of Rear Admiral John E. Clark, commandant of the Twelfth Naval District in San Francisco. As he entered the Federal Building, True noticed in the lobby a poster which read: "Let it be clear that this Administration recognizes the value of daring and dissent—that we greet healthy controversy as the hallmark of healthy change." Apparently it was an old poster, for the quote was signed by John F. Kennedy. True remarked upon this poster when he met Admiral Clark and asked if the philosophy had been superseded by another. "No," said Clark, "but it doesn't apply to members of the naval service," and he informed True that, even though he was retired, if he continued to criticize the Administration's Vietnam policies "the next interview might not be pleasant." True took that to mean that he might be court-martialed. Only the intercession of then Deputy Secretary of Defense Cyrus R. Vance prevented the unpleasantness from occurring, for True refused to shut up.

On the other hand, "taking each individual case on its merits," the military decided there was nothing wrong with Major General Francis S. Greenleaf's public intrusion into Administration policy matters on the Vietnam war. Perhaps that was because Greenleaf, deputy chief of the National Guard Bureau, is *for* the war. In November, 1969, he sent out an official memorandum to all National Guard outfits urging members to "drive their automobiles with the headlights turned on and turn their porch lights on at home" to counteract the November 15 Vietnam Moratorium demonstration, which he called a "betrayal." His memorandum urged Guardsmen not to violently assault the demonstrators even though "to act with restraint in the face of what many of the Guardsmen, I know, believe to be a dishonor to our country requires a patience and understanding that are above and beyond what most Americans are ever asked to perform." The Pentagon decided to ignore that inflammatory note.

The greater the number of men under arms, the narrower the tolerance for policy disagreement and unorthodox behavior and the greater the need for the mental-conditioning effect of courts-martial—or so the military believes. During one year at the peak of World War II, when 12.5 million men and women were in uniform, there were 750,000 courts-martial. (At the end of the war some 45,000 persons who had gone through the military courts were still in prison.) Not long ago one of the judges of the Court of Military Appeals predicted that in the next war possibly 20 million people will be under military law. If the ratio holds, this means that about 1.25 million courts-martial will be held in a boom year of the next international conflict, or quite enough military justice to submerge the Bill of Rights for a time.

It has also been suggested that, in addition to threats and courts-martial, the military uses its stockades and brigs to remold the minds of recalcitrant servicemen. This point was made by Dr. Samuel Nelken, a member of the University of California Medical Center faculty, in his testimony at the Fort Ord portion of the Presidio trials. Referring to the treatment of GI prisoners at the "thought-reform universities" directed by the Chinese Communists during the Korean War, Nelken said: "We believed at that time, and properly, that the brainwashing methods used by the Chinese were cruel and unusual punishment. But we found in the [Presidio] stockade the same methods being used to break prisoners: isolation, confusion, threats of death and taunts about death of fellow prisoners." Of these techniques, he said, none was more important than the element of uncertainy and confusion. "The rules were changed sometimes from week to week, sometimes from day to day; the prisoners were shifted almost daily, so they almost never slept twice in the same place."

One must understand the purpose of military justice. It is not even remotely related to protecting the innocent. The comforting old saw, "Better a hundred guilty escape than one innocent man be punished unjustly," has no place in the military even as a myth. Only in recent years, in fact, has the military establishment even bothered to pretend from time to time that courts-martial result in justice.

Blackstone, England's eminent legal authority of the eighteenth century, charged that the military system of justice was "built upon no settled principles, but is entirely arbitrary in its decisions and is something indulged rather than allowed as law." Colonel W. Winthrop, the most respected nineteenth-century commentator on military affairs in this country, wrote that "Courts-martial are not courts, but are, in fact, simply instrumentalities of the executive power to aid him in properly commanding the army and enforcing discipline therein." This was precisely the opinion also of General William T. Sherman, who was a lawyer as well as an arsonist. Sherman once put it this way: "The object of the civil law is to create the greatest benefit of all in a peaceful community. The object of military law is to govern armies composed of strong men. An army is an organization of armed men obligated to obey one man." A similarity of spirit is evident in the present-day appraisal given by Senator Sam Ervin, chairman of the Senate's Constitutional Rights Subcommittee. "The primary purpose of the administration of justice in the military services," Ervin said, "is to enforce discipline plus getting rid of people who think they are not capable of contributing to the defense of the country as they should." Subservience or disreputable ouster, no other choice.

From ancient times the mode of military justice has been much the same. Whether one refers to the operation of the Roman *magistri militum,* to Emperor Charles V's penal code of 1532, to the Articles of War of Maximilian II of 1570, to the Articles of War of Free Netherlands twenty years later, to the more sophisticated articles of Gustavus Adolphus of Sweden in 1621, to the British Articles of War and the British Mutiny Articles, or to our own military codes—everything hinges on the whims of military author-

ity. The civilian ideal has always been maximum freedom, restricted by law only so far as is necessary to permit others equal
maximum freedom; the military ideal has been just the opposite—
maximum restriction by law, with only so much freedom as is
necessary to encourage re-enlistment and prevent a harmful slump
in morale.

The job of drafting the original military code for this country in
1776 was so distasteful that most members of the Continental
Congress committee assigned the task shirked it, and the job was
left to John Adams. Adams had such a strange notion of what the
new nation stood for that he copied the handiest tyrannical code
available—namely, that of the British military, which in turn had
been shaped in imitation of some of the sterner European codes. It
was Adams' timorous notion that "nothing short of the Roman
and British discipline could possibly save us."

Adams also put together the first Articles for the Government of
the Navy, which were essentially the same as Oliver Cromwell's
Navy Articles of a hundred years earlier.

Adams himself was surprised that he got by with these harsh
and archaic regulations, which were intended, as he says, to produce not justice but discipline. Later he wrote, explaining his
goals:

There was extant, I observed, one system of Articles of War which
had carried two empires to the head of mankind, the Roman and the
British; for the British Articles of War are only a literal translation of
the Roman. It would be vain for us to seek in our own invention or the
records of warlike nations of a more complete system of military discipline. I was, therefore, for reporting the British Articles of War
*totidem verbis*. . . . So undigested were the notions of liberty preva-
lent among the majority of the members most zealously attached to the
public cause that to this day I scarcely know how it was possible that
these articles should have been carried. They were adopted, however,
and they have governed our armies with little variation to this day.

He wrote that about a century and a half ago, but it could have been written on the eve of the First World War, for by 1916, when the military code was allegedly revised, not one change had been made in the Roman-English system adopted by the Continental Congress. The 1916 revision simply reshuffled old articles, put them in more modern language and left the fundamentals. Much the same appraisal could be made of the "revisions" of 1806, 1874, 1920 and 1948. In every practical aspect, the American soldier lived under the same code of justice from the beginning of this country until 1950.

Likewise, although the Navy Articles were slightly revised in 1800, no other noteworthy changes in Navy law were made until 1950, and the sailor who fought in World War II was governed in all judicial matters very much in the same way, and to some extent with the same language, as the British sailor of three centuries earlier.

Adams' Army and Navy Articles were so garishly out of harmony with the Bill of Rights that Secretary of War Henry Knox wrote President Washington in 1789 that governmental propriety "will require that the articles of war be revised and adapted to the Constitution." They never were. The philosophy of discipline at all costs, of the primacy of order and rank, of the need to crush and intimidate men into a narrow mold—this philosophy continued to prevail.

As for physical punishment, the record is just as grim. Adams, disturbed by the extreme barbarity of the flogging in the British military services of that day, deliberately wrote his Continental Articles to be more "humane"—the maximum number of lashes that could be dealt an American serviceman under those articles was a mere one hundred. Yet the articles were barbarous enough. In the 1790s American soldiers were sometimes punished by any one or a combination or all of the following: being whipped, having head and eyebrows shaved, being tarred and feathered, being branded on the forehead. Flogging on board a Navy ship was legal until 1850. Flogging in the Army was permitted off and on until 1861. Branding was not outlawed by statute until 1872, although it had been outlawed by regulation in 1861.

But if legal punishment today is somewhat more civilized, the rules by which military trials in this country are conducted are, despite some refinements, hardly closer to the U.S. Constitution than they were at the beginning. Bill-of-Rights guarantees—bail, indictment by grand jury, trial by impartial judge and jury of peers —are nullified. As for that most elusive but most central theme of constitutional justice, "due process," the U.S. Supreme Court—which has done virtually nothing over the years to extend constitutional protections to the serviceman—issued one of its most cynical rulings in 1911, to the effect that, "To those in the military or naval service of the United States the miliary law is due process." What the military wants to do, it does; and that is the law. This is the tradition.

The shaky efforts to construct an indigenously American code of justice, with at least a passing relationship to the Constitution, have all failed. No really serious demand for reform was made by the public or by Congress until after World War I. Four million Americans went into uniform during that war, and many of them resented the stern and sometimes brutal justice of their new life. Nor were they reticent about expressing their anguish and disgust in letters to their Congressmen. One Congressman, Dan V. Stephens, told the House of Representatives on March 3, 1919, "It is conceded on all sides that courts-martial procedure during the present war has been atrociously harsh, brutal, and unjust. There is hardly a Member of Congress who has not directly received convincing evidence of that fact through innumerable justified complaints from his constituency, establishing beyond all doubt that courts-martial are not worthy of the name of courts."

World War I produced such cases as these: A recruit refused to surrender his cigarettes to an officer and was sentenced to twenty years at hard labor. For being "disrespectful" to an officer, a soldier received five years in prison. A young soldier, for being AWOL twenty-seven days, was sentenced to forty years in prison. Another AWOL soldier was sentenced to life in prison. Two young soldiers, having had no sleep for five days, dozed on guard duty and were sentenced to be shot. Petty-larceny cases sometimes ended in sentences of ten years and more. Thirteen Negro soldiers were convicted of murder and executed two days later—four months before their "appeals" were processed in Washington.

These may have been exceptionally harsh sentences, but there were so many thousands of other sentences almost as harsh that the returning doughboys, thoroughly disenchanted, demanded that Congress reform the military code of justice. However, the 1920 Articles of War that resulted from this demand were in fact no reform at all and actually perpetuated the old system. The best description of military justice during World War I was written in the *Cornell Law Review* of November, 1919, by the courageous and persistent S. A. Ansell. Ansell was Acting Judge Advocate General of the Army during the war, and, because he was outspokenly in favor of reform, he was demoted from brigadier general to lieutenant colonel after it. "The existing system of military justice," wrote Ansell,

is un-American, having come to us by inheritance and rather witless adoption out of a system of government which we regard as fundamentally intolerable; it is archaic, belonging as it does to an age when armies were but bodies of armed retainers and bands of mercenaries; it is a system arising out of and regulated by the mere power of Military Command rather than Law; it has ever resulted, as it must ever result, in such injustice as to crush the spirit of the individual subjected to it, shock the public conscience and alienate public esteem and affection from the Army that insists upon maintaining it. . . . The system may well be said to be a lawless system. It is not a code of law; it is not buttressed in law, nor are correct legal conclusions its objective. The agencies applying it are not courts, their proceedings are not regulated by law. The system sets up and recognizes no legal standard, and has no place for lawyers and judges. Whatever is done with the final approval of the convening commander is done finally beyond all earthly power of correction.

An even more piquant, but no less accurate, description of military justice in that era was given in the *Minnesota Law Review* in 1918:

A court-martial is merely an agency "appointed" by the commanding officer for the training of the soldiers in discipline, and though one is sentenced by such a tribunal to death or to a long term of imprisonment, he is not deprived of life or liberty or in fact punished at all, but merely trained and educated and disciplined. A criminal sentence in the Army, in short, serves the same purpose as the manual of arms or the setting up exercises.

This same "lawless" quality was observed through World War II. A 1943 text used by the Judge Advocate General's School at the University of Michigan conceded the point: "Strictly speaking, a court-martial is not a court at all in the full sense of the term but is simply an instrumentality of the executive power of the President for the enforcement of discipline in the armed forces." And in 1946 an article in the *Wisconsin Law Review* summed up the system of justice that had destroyed the lives of thousands of GIs in World War II: "The system is so flexible that it is almost entirely up to the commander to determine not only who shall be tried, for what offense, and by what court but also what the result shall be in each case."

To make sure that the commanding officer could work his will upon justice, it was commonplace in World War II for courts-martial panels to administer stupefyingly heavy sentences and then leave it up to "the Old Man" to cut them down to whatever dimensions and shape he envisioned justice to be. Thus the general courts-martial at Norfolk automatically administered fifteen-year sentences in each of thirty-seven cases, which gave the admiral who was the courts-martial convening authority plenty of margin; and he, in turn, in each case reduced the sentence to three years.

These were no acts of mercy; they were, in fact, the first real sentences given to the victims, the fifteen-year sentences being only proxies which the admiral—without hearing. testimony or reading the trial record—could treat as he chose.

After World War II, so unhappy were the GIs who had experienced military justice that the American Bar Association, at the reluctant request of the War Department, set up a study committee headed by Arthur T. Vanderbilt, dean of the New York University School of Law. The committee in due time reported what was already quite obvious: that military commanders were rigging their juries, rigging sentences and disregarding all pretense of formal procedure. Other study groups were similarly critical. And, since Defense Secretary Forrestal wanted to unify the services anyway, this was used as a good excuse to write a reformed uniform code of justice under which all the services would operate.

By previous standards, the 1950 Uniform Code of Military Justice was indeed a major step forward. For the first time in our history a military court of appeals was set up; for the first time in our history a qualified lawyer was required for the defendant in all general courts-martial; for the first time a certified law officer (judge) was required for all general courts-martial. And, most important, the new code included an article (No. 37) which prohibited the commanding officer from exerting his influence on the conduct or outcome of the trial.

Regrettably, the paper reforms of 1950 have not resulted in much reform in practice. Fearful that anarchy would result from the slightest easing of disciplinary justice (just as military authorities once feared anarchy would result from the abolition of the lash), the commanders have quietly transferred the evils of the old Articles of War to the adminstration of the UCMJ. The grossest of the surviving defects are these:

*Vagueness of Law.* It is here, in the wording of the UCMJ, that the overriding element of arbitrariness begins. One of the honored boasts of our politicians is that "This is a government of laws, not of men"—meaning that there must be a set of rules (the Constitution and the statutes derived from it) by which the governors as well as the governed agree to abide, and that the people in power can't just make up new rules as they go along. It means, too, that the law must be clear enough to the governed that they can be reasonably sure that they are obeying it and reasonably aware of their violations. But the military system of justice undercuts this proud old conception, being in fact set up consciously to give the local commanders the widest possible application of imperiousness. For example, Article 89—"Disrespect Towards a Superior Officer"—is defined in the *Manual for Courts-Martial* as including "marked disdain, indifference, insolence, impertinence, undue familiarity, and other rudeness"—which could mean any number of things, depending on the depth of spleen of the accusing officer. So could Article 133—"Conduct Unbecoming an Officer and a Gentleman." As for Article 134—"The General Article" (which, it is said, includes *fifty different offenses,* ranging from abusing animals in public to wearing unauthorized insignia)—it is a singular twist of justice.*

Edward F. Sherman, a professor at Indiana University Law School and an expert in military law, and Melvin Wulf, legal director of the ACLU, are trying to free two black Marines who were put in prison (with three- and four-year sentences) for making "disloyal" statements—supposedly a violation of Article 134. "Disloyalty" is a typically vague charge characteristic of military justice. The *Manual for Courts-Martial* defines disloyalty as "praising the enemy, attacking the war aims of the United States, or denouncing our form of government."

Sherman and Wulf reasonably ask in their brief:

Who is the enemy? . . . What constitutes praise? Can one applaud

---

* Articles 133 and 134 will be discussed and amply illustrated in the chapters dealing with the case of Howard Levy (page 126) and the case of Henry Howe (page 183).

the peace efforts of the Soviet Union in the India-Pakistan dispute? Can he praise the educational programs of Premier Castro? Can he comment favorably on the tenacity of Ho Chi Minh? As for "attacking the war aims of the United States," is it an attack on the war aims of the U.S. to call for escalation of the war? To urge that we pull out of Vietnam? Can a serviceman be sure what the war aims of the United States are? "Denouncing our form of government" is similarly unhelpful. What does it mean? Can a soldier advocate abolition of the electoral college system established in the Constitution? Can a serviceman urge taking away constitutional powers of the Supreme Court or denounce the school desegregation decision? What elements are so basic to our "form of government" that they cannot be denounced—federalism, capitalism, democracy, welfare state programs, the draft?

*Command Influence.* The corruption of the military system of justice runs through every layer, but it starts at the top, where the whims of the commandants flutter like pigeons over a courtyard. General courts-martial are not convened unless the commanding officer believes the defendant is guilty; and since the officers who make up the trial panel know that the commandant is of this persuasion—and because they must often look to the commandant for promotion—they will most often come through with the verdict he wants. It is, in fact, that simple.

The commanding officer is not supposed to interfere with the process of military justice, but it is virtually impossible for him to refrain from doing so even if he wanted to. Most commanding officers certainly do not want to refrain from controlling the court, for they believe it is their best way to exert control over their troops.

The commander decides when and whom to prosecute. He controls the investigation of the charges and can (as was seen in the Presidio case) overrule the officer who conducted the preliminary investigation. The commander can personally select the jury members from among officers who are beholden to him for favors, promotions and other career opportunities; he also picks the prosecuting officers and the military defense attorneys. Although the staff judge advocate is supposed to be a neutral administrator of portions of the trial procedure, he is in fact the commanding officer's attorney and, as such, represents the commander's wishes in all that he does. The staff judge advocate is supposed to review the pretrial evidence impartially, and he is also supposed to review the trial record and the sentence to see if all was conducted in a legal manner and on the basis of his study make recommendations to the commander. In theory the SJA is a referee who has the advantage of being at some distance from the court play and there-fore better able to observe it objectively. But in practice the SJA—who deliberates daily with the commander upon the needs of discipline—acts with the same subservience as any attorney on the payroll of a powerful, hard-driving executive.

Not until 1969 was the *Manual for Courts-Martial* amended to actually outlaw a military commander's giving the court members "pretrial orientation"—which is a euphemism for letting the court members know which way he wants their verdicts to go. Whether or not the practice will be really outlawed is yet to be seen. A commander who violates this can only be court-martialed, and where is the higher officer who will hold him officially accountable for doing what virtually all officers believe a necessity—ruling their ranks with complete control?

Senator Charles Goodell of New York, who once served as an attorney in the Judge Advocate General's office, knows about these command pressures. He once defended a soldier charged with desertion and won an acquittal for his client. "Well, this created a major controversy," he recalled, because the verdict went against the base commandant's wishes. "Several of the panel were trans-ferred, the judge advocate was called on the carpet—and I was reassigned to prosecution."

Another military lawyer involved in that same case was Irving Peskoe, now an attorney in Homestead, Florida, and a colonel in the Air Force Reserve. Peskoe once again was caught in the squeeze of command pressure in the spring of 1969, when Senior

Master Sergeant John H. Smith, who had returned from a tour of duty in Vietnam only a month earlier and was stationed at Homestead Air Force Base, was ordered back to Vietnam to stand trial on charges that he had paid only $17 for $60 worth of goods obtained at a base PX. The charges against him were pressed by a native Vietnamese girl who was later fired by the PX. It was a matter of Sergeant Smith's word against hers. Smith was a veteran of twenty-one years with the Air Force; he was married and the father of two boys. He had a clean record.

Before Sergeant Smith left Vietnam he had asked his superior officers whether, considering the fact that this charge was hanging over him, perhaps he shouldn't stay on until it was cleared up. No, no, no, go on home, they said. And then, a month later in America, he was being hailed back to a Vietnam court-martial. It was at this point that attorney Peskoe entered the case. He attempted to obtain an injunction delaying the trial, arguing (among other things) that the witnesses Smith needed for his defense had since been transferred back to the States. Peskoe did not get the injunction, but he got plenty of front-page publicity. As one newspaper pointed out, "The civil action Sgt. Smith instituted to stop the order, the court-martial, loss in job performance [Smith was a supervisor of aircraft maintenance with the 4331st Tactical Fighter Wing], attorney's fees, transportation for the 12,000 mile round-trip and other costs may make the total bill as high as $20,000."

Smith was found innocent, came back to Homestead and went to work again, and the only thing that hung on was the bad odor of it all—that and the irritation of Colonel Wiltz P. Segura, top-ranking Air Force officer at Homestead. The day after Peskoe tried to get an injunction on Sergeant Smith's behalf, a letter came from Washington authorizing a reserve position for Peskoe on the judge advocate's staff at Homestead. Segura objected. He wanted no lawyers on his base who bucked his wishes. He wrote the Pentagon demanding that Peskoe be kept away from Homestead. So he was.

Peskoe now has to travel two hundred miles to do his reserve officer duty, at Patrick Air Force Base, whereas if he had not offended the base commander by his independence, he could do his reserve duty five miles from home.

In the summer of 1969, Lieutenant Thomas McGuire, twenty-five, of Niles, Michigan, a lawyer, charged that the highest officers of the 6th Cavalry at Fort Meade, Maryland, were demanding that courts-martial turn in more convictions and stiffer sentences, and that these officers were plaguing defense attorneys with veiled threats and unveiled hindrances. The next quarterly evaluation of Lieutenant McGuire's performance—a routine report made on every officer by his superiors; usually the evaluations are full of praise—noted that McGuire was immature, irresponsible and possibly even disloyal. The next thing McGuire knew, he was in the Panama Canal Zone training for jungle warfare, a stopover on his way to Vietnam. McGuire claimed that his performance evaluation was simply his superiors' way of getting revenge for his criticism of their meddling in the military trial procedures. An Army review board agreed with him and ordered the evaluation removed from his record. McGuire also asked why, if the Army considered him immature, irresponsible and possibly disloyal, it would want to trust him to lead troops at the front. The question was never answered.

As a rule, the commanders try to show at least a touch of reticence when they are communicating their wishes. Not many are as outspoken as Rear Admiral T. Ruddock, Jr., U.S. Navy Retired, who once served as president and permanent member of the Twelfth Naval District's court. He let the other officers of the court understand that he thought it "would be very foolish" of them not to render such verdicts as would enable them to obtain good reports from him, although he "certainly" did not want them to think he was trying to influence their decisions. As the Court of Military Appeals later described the old sea dog's routine: "Every time a new court convened, Admiral Ruddock conducted a short period of indoctrination. He 'usually' informed new members that the Table of Maximum Punishments provides 'tentative guidance.' He stated that he was familiar with the presumption of innocence but did not recognize it as a constitutional right because he believed that persons in the military service had no constitutional rights. [One officer] who had served intermittently as law officer for the court had heard Admiral Ruddock say at various times that 'anyone sent up here for trial must be guilty of something.' "

In the most notorious recent case of command influence, Major General Thomas Lipscomb, commanding general at Fort Leonard Wood, Missouri, in the mid-1960s, laid such a heavy hand on the courts-martial under his authority that the military board of review in Washington eventually reversed the verdicts or modified the sentences (where there were guilty pleas) in ninety-three cases. So flagrantly did General Lipscomb enjoy his authority that he became the only commander on record even to be investigated for command influence. He was accused of appointing as jurors only senior officers whose careers depended on his favor; of ordering the fort's legal officer to lecture court-martial juries on the need for discipline; of threatening a defense lawyer who challenged one of Lipscomb's hand-picked jurors; and of reprimanding court-martial officers for handing down sentences that were too light for his taste. The Army looked over the evidence and decided General Lipscomb had done nothing out of line. And indeed, according to military tradition, he had not.

One of the civilian defense counsels in the Presidio trials, Joseph Manzella (a former Navy officer), did not endear himself to the military judge when he addressed himself to this truism: "As your honor is well aware, one of the greatest evils of the military tribunals is command influence, which is the most serious threat to justice in the military court-martial. As of this date, only one commanding officer has been investigated for it, and after a lengthy hearing nothing was done about it. Now, your honor is quite aware that there is no direct influence from the command or convening authority directly to the court [Manzella's one distorted effort at either politeness or sarcasm], but in the *sub rosa* method, through his aides who carry this word via the Officers' Club and their other social gatherings, it is quite apparent that the word permeates down as to this desire, where subconsciously all the members of the court really want to do what they feel the 'Old Man' would like done in this situation."

And then Manzella, having somehow up to that moment escaped a sword thrust, plunged on to the next most obvious feature of that trial and all military trials: "For one thing, I think that this is nothing more than a stacked jury. . . ."

Which brings us to that natural auxiliary to command influence.

*The Stacked Jury.* In a civilian court the defense attorney seeks to obtain a varied jury—a plumber, a banker, a schoolteacher, a bus driver, etc.—a cross-section of society that will see a question from different viewpoints and thus may very likely disagree. That is how hung juries are made. But in military court, as ACLU attorney Paul Halvonik learned so very well in the Presidio proceedings, "you are not only stuck with a jury that's homogeneous, but one that is homogeneously agreed on the one basic issue in the trial—whether the most important thing in this world is obedience and whether you can shaft somebody completely if you feel they disobeyed or didn't act properly. So you've got the worst possible jury that you could possibly have."

If that is the whimper of a losing attorney, it must be counted a general one, for virtually every defense counsel who goes up against a military court has the same complaint. The same lack of variety, the same overwhelming homogeneous quality, was noted in the first trial of Private Zaino by his attorney, Manzella, the opening of whose blunt summation has already been given, and which continued: "Every member of this court is currently in the infantry or has been in the infantry. Mostly all have the Combat Infantryman's Badge, and with the star indicating that they were in combat in two wars. And how this group, primarily of all infantry officers, was selected—now, I realize that Fort Lewis is an infantry based camp, but I think this is not a proper, random selection, but nothing more than the convening authority's attempt to stack this jury. I would like to know why the general saw fit to select a group of officers from the Infantry Training Command rather than from a true representation of all the officers within the Sixth Army." (To which the trial judge responded: "We are not going into that any further.")

The U.S. Constitution guarantees unbiased jurors. The Military Code does not. Bearing in mind that a central question of the Presidio trials was to be the propriety of holding protest demonstrations, consider these responses by a member of the panel from which one of the early Presidio jurors was being selected:

DEFENSE ATTORNEY: Colonel, do you believe in the right to demonstrate?
COLONEL: No.
ATTORNEY: Maybe you didn't understand my question. Let's forget about the Army for a moment. Do you believe that civilians have the right to express their views in peaceful demonstrations in support or in opposition to an official policy?
COLONEL: No.
MILITARY JUDGE (*interrupting*): Colonel, you know the Constitution provides that right.
COLONEL: I don't care.
ATTORNEY: OK, we'll challenge him for bias.

In a civilian court a juror will be knocked off the panel by the judge if the defense attorney can show that he is biased against his client. But not until late 1969 did the military judge have anything to say about it; the question of a prospective juror's bias was left up to *a vote of the other members of the jury*.* When the above colonel was challenged for bias, the officers on the jury voted to

---

* Judge Homer Ferguson of the Court of Military Appeals, commenting on this unique practice, admitted, "I think we have had cases where even the man himself [the challenged juror] voted on whether he should be excused."

accept their brother as unbiased and fit to serve.

From the selecting process of another Presidio jury there came these other responses: One lieutenant colonel said that parades and demonstrations against the war in Vietnam "annoyed" him, but he wouldn't let that keep him from giving a fair decision to somebody charged with antiwar demonstrating. Another lieutenant colonel said he felt the reports in the press that called the sit-down a mutiny were accurate—but he hadn't formed any opinion about the case. A colonel on the panel who was in the ROTC Division of the Sixth Army complained that there were "incidents that occur on campuses throughout this Army area almost on a daily basis" which had "an adverse effect" on his ROTC, but he said he wouldn't allow that to prejudice him against sit-downers and protesters. And he said he didn't have anything against the ACLU, although he had found in his experience with them that ACLU attorneys were "misinformed, in a frequency of the cases I got involved in."

Although the mutiny arrests brought about the most explosive publicity in the Presidio's history, a colonel said he had read only the headlines mentioning the affair and that these had not interested him enough to make him read further. Also—or so he claimed—nobody who worked in his office at the Presidio was much interested either.

Q: You say you heard it [discussed] perhaps in office talk. Can you recall what you heard in the office talk, if you recall?
COLONEL: Yes. "Have you seen the morning paper?" "Yes, I seen [sic] the morning paper." And some person would mention, "Well, I seen [sic] they had trouble up in the stockade"—but not anything in detail.

This colonel also had a low opinion of demonstrations, although he stopped short of calling them criminal.

Q: How do you feel about demonstration and protest?

COLONEL: I'm wondering who's paying these people who can afford this time to go out and do it. . . .

Q: Do you feel that a protest is ever a legal means of expressing a
grievance?

COLONEL: I can only presume it is. I would have to say that I feel
that a protest is *not necessarily an illegal* means of expressing a
grievance. That would be the best answer I could give you on
that one. [Emphasis added.]

Much of the defense's argument would, as has been seen, rest on
the fact that the stockade was run in an oppressive, sloppy, perverse way and that therefore the group of protesters had reasonable complaints to make, even if they chose the wrong way to
make them. But the defense could hope for little attention from
this colonel, who had been an inspector general from 1964 to
1966, visiting prisoners in stockades and listening to thousands of
similar complaints.

Q: During this two-year period, did you have the opportunity to
check on the complaints or grievances of people who were resid-
ing in the stockades as prisoners?

COLONEL: Yes.

Q: Did you find that any of those complaints were justified?

COLONEL: Yes, I'm sure there must have been some. In fact, I
know—I recall one.

Why didn't attorney Halvonik challenge these colonels and try
to have them tossed off the jury? "I didn't make any challenges for
cause," he explained, "because it's insane to do it. I never challenge for cause in a military trial. All it does is set the rest of the
panel against you because they think you have insulted a brother
officer."

*The Defense's Obstacle Course.* Of all the Army's petty mean-
nesses in the Presidio trials, none matched its refusal to take verbatim transcripts of the preliminary hearings and to supply the
defense in the later trials with transcripts of the earlier trial records.
Thus the defense was deprived of a way of determining if prosecu-

tion witnesses were lying or were changing their testimony. The denial of verbatim transcripts was done in an especially shabby way, for the defense attorneys had been assured that such transcripts were being taken and then they discovered—too late to set up tape recorders of their own or to hire court reporters—that the Army had secretly rescinded the order for verbatim reporting and was taking the record only in paraphrase. To defense protests, the Army replied that it could not afford to hire the necessary secretaries and that the base had no tape recorders available.

Records needed by defense attorneys are sometimes destroyed or "lost" by government agents (as will be seen in the Levy trial, Chapter 4). Witnesses for the defense are sometimes threatened with court-martial if they testify (as happened at the preliminary hearing for the "Fort Jackson Eight"). There is hardly anything that military investigators who gather evidence for the prosecution will not do, or have not done—including the planting of fingerprints. In one case, a suspect's family was locked in a room for thirteen hours while Air Force investigators searched for smuggling clues. About 40 percent of the cases reversed by the Court of Military Appeals are for improper, or illegal, investigations; but just as commanders are never prosecuted for jury-tampering, military investigators are never punished for illegal procedures.

Typical of the highhandedness employed quite successfully by the military was the case of Captain Joseph P. Kauffman. He may or may not have been guilty of conspiring to sell information to the East Germans (a court-martial in 1962 said he was guilty), but the method used to convict him hardly spoke well for the democracy he was accused of betraying. He was put on temporary duty at Travis Air Force Base, California, to get him away from his home in Atwater, California, so that the Air Force investigators could ransack his home—without a search warrant—on three occasions. Then his room was wired so that Army officials could record his conversations with his attorney. He was packed off to Wiesbaden, Germany, for trial, too far away for his civilian attorney to help him and where the jury panel that judged his fate would be composed of career officers who lived under daily bombardment of propaganda about the horrors of the Communist East. To top everything else, he was not permitted to face his chief accuser, a defector from East Germany, who was allowed to wear a disguise while in court.

To obtain confessions that would implicate some of the prisoners in the Fort Dix rioting of June 5, 1969, the Army's Criminal Intelligence Division reportedly used bribe offers and threats. Determined to convict Private Terry Klug of inciting the riot (he was acquitted at his trial), the CID selected several prisoners and put the screws to them. One was Private Miguel Morralles, who had been in the stockade a long time and had expected to be released in three weeks. One of the agents said to Morralles: "So you think you're getting out. We don't think so. We think you were the one who started the riot. Think about it." Three days later Morralles signed a statement implicating Klug. But at Klug's trial Morralles braced up and told how the statement was obtained from him. He said the CID had warned him it was the only way he could get out of jail on time. "Klug, Klug, Klug, they kept asking questions about Klug," Morralles testified. "They put his name in my mouth." Another who was forced to name Klug in a statement was Private James Eastman, nineteen, who has such claustrophobia ("I can't stand small areas, I lose control") that a year earlier he had had to be taken from jail and put in the more spacious confines of Marlboro State Mental Hospital. He was a prime candidate for CID treatment, and with the threat of solitary confinement hanging over him, he too signed.

The military attorneys appointed to help defendants in general courts-martial* sometimes are of great integrity and courage. But

* There are three types of courts: summary, special and general. Theoretically the defendant can be represented by an attorney at any level of court, but actually no serviceman ever gets a counsel for a summary court-martial, where the court consists of one officer who acts simultaneously as

whether military or civilian, the defense attorneys in these proceedings are under critical handicaps. They have no subpoena powers of their own, little freedom of cross-examination, no power to call military witnesses. They must make their requests for witnesses *through the prosecution,* and if the prosecution doesn't think the witnesses should be called, they aren't.

---

judge, jury, prosecuting and defense attorney, and where one month is the longest jail sentence that can be imposed. It sounds mild, but one must remember that a summary court-martial still goes on the serviceman's record as a federal trial, and the idea that a man's record can be smeared permanently at the whim of one officer is something that even most members of the Judge Advocate General's office will admit is a shame and an abomination. Only enlisted men can be tried by summary courts, of which about 25,000 are held each year.

And only enlisted men get to experience a special court-martial, where sentences of up to six months in prison and a bad-conduct discharge can be imposed (about 75,000 a year, lately). Punishment is swift and sure. For example, a soldier who worked in the special processing detachment at Fort Hood, Texas, disclosed that it is commonplace there for trial records to be typed up in advance, complete with guilty verdicts and six-month sentences. Heretofore only about 5 percent of the accused in special courts-martial were appointed military counsel, and as often as not these "defense attorneys" were not competent. A U.S. District Court in Utah threw out the special court-martial conviction of a private in 1965 when it discovered that one of the man's defense attorneys, who ordinarily worked as a veterinarian, had learned everything he knew about military law in a two-day crash course and that his other "counsel" had learned his military law in a college ROTC course. The District Court discovered that "Their advice to the accused on various legal matters was based upon *consultation with the officer who had drawn up the charges."* (Emphasis added.) The private had requested qualified attorneys to represent him, but the authorities said there was none available; furthermore, the District Court disclosed, the private was warned "not to raise any question with regard to his legal representation with the convening authority or before the court-martial."

Reform, however, may have arrived. A statute that went into effect in 1969 provides that "the accused must be afforded the right to be defended by qualified lawyer counsel at special courts-martial unless the commander certifies one cannot be obtained."

The general court-martial, which is the kind virtually all of the cases discussed in this book were assigned to, handles the most serious breaches of military law. It is the only court-martial that can sentence a man to death, and it is the only court-martial that can hand down a dishonorable discharge. Justice is dispensed by a military judge and a jury of at least five military personnel, usually officers. The defendant is guaranteed trained legal counsel.

In one set of the Presidio trials, the defense attorneys wanted to call General Larsen, commanding general of the Sixth Army, to wring from him testimony that would show that the jury panel set up by him guaranteed that no officer below a certain rank, and no noncommissioned officer with less than eighteen years' service (it is said the old noncoms are the harshest jurors), would sit on the jury. When the request for Larsen was made, the military judge threw the press out of the courtroom and upbraided the defense lawyers for trying to "embarrass, harass and intimidate the Army."

In that same trial (it was the trial in which Yost was a defendant) the defense wanted to call Dr. Joseph Katz of Stanford University, one of the foremost behavioral psychologists in the country, who was prepared to testify that the men were not mutineers but were in fact supplicants, like children who do something nasty to attract the attention of their parents and thereby tacitly beg their parents for protection from themselves as well as from others. Defense attorney David Lowe explained, "We had Dr. Katz examine the transcripts of other trial proceedings, documents, statements by the Army about physical conditions, the psychological records and tests of all the twenty-seven who were tested. These are voluminous documents. We told the Army that Dr. Katz would testify. And they refused to let us call him. The Army said he hadn't actually interviewed the accused and therefore the Army wouldn't pay his way. So I volunteered to pay the transportation and fees of all such experts (I would have had to raise the money). The Army denied our request. The Army's prosecutor and the military judge have the power to say who we bring and who we don't bring."

Illustrating the extent to which the military will sometimes go to frustrate the defense is the case of Captain John J. McCarthy of the Green Berets. McCarthy was convicted of murder in a court-martial in South Vietnam after Major Sully H. Fontaine, who had vital information for his defense, was ordered to stay away from the trial because his testimony might have revealed the extent of secret

American operations in Cambodia. Or so the army claimed. In any event, the weird aftermath of the trial would suggest that the Army felt somewhat ill at ease about its conduct of the case. The *New York Times* reported that the army refrained from discharging or stripping rank from McCarthy even after he was convicted. And instead of holding him in prison during his appeal—as would doubtless be done even in civilian procedure after a murder conviction—it permitted him to go on serving in a fairly normal fashion at an Army post near his home in Arizona.

In another Green Beret case, this one at Fort Bragg, North Carolina, where Captain Jeffrey R. MacDonald was charged with the murder of his wife and daughter in 1970, MacDonald's defense attorneys were physically assaulted by military police. Army investigators had found pieces of hair in Mrs. MacDonald's hand and the prosecution wanted to take hair from Captain MacDonald to see if it would match up. His attorneys contended that this would, in effect, force him to testify against himself, contrary to Constitutional protections, and they refused to let the Army have samples. Not to be dissuaded, the MPs followed MacDonald and his attorneys away from the hearing and forced their car off the street. Then the MPs pulled one of the attorneys out of the car, threw him to the ground, where he landed face down, breaking his glasses. The MPs pushed the other attorney around when he went to rescue his colleague. Both attorneys were hospitalized. The hair samples were obtained.

Civilian and military defense attorneys who are aggressive on behalf of their clients are often threatened. Lowe was warned that if he didn't stop his unorthodox tactics—such as asking to question General Larsen—military authorities were prepared to have him reprimanded by his state bar. ("I encouraged them to go right ahead," Lowe recalled. "I said, swell, because then we'd have some hearings the Army would *really* be interested in.") Attorney Terence Hallinan says he was told that the Army was gathering evidence in an effort to have him charged with fomenting the mutiny. But the military defense attorneys have had to withstand the most intense pressure. Captain Emmitt Yeary was twice threatened with court-martial, once because he spoke to the press (his remarks were taped by an Army investigator) and once because he stayed up so late one night preparing his defense case that he was a few minutes late the next morning reporting to his Presidio office. Captain Brendan Sullivan, another outstanding defense attorney, told Lowe that before the trials began he was warned by a superior officer that he would be under surveillance constantly. The officer reportedly warned Sullivan, "I've got men who can look through a keyhole with both eyes." On another occasion the Army let Sullivan know its suspicions of him by requiring the defendants to strip and be searched after Sullivan and another lawyer had left them.

Such dealings inhibit justice in the services more than civilians might think. It is a rare military lawyer who has the courage to question the system, knowing that transfers to bleak outposts, loss of promotion and mysterious difficulties can come his way if he does. Not many will continue to speak out as Captain Sullivan did. Almost immediately after his part in the trials had ended, he was ordered to Vietnam without the ninety-day notice or thirty-day leave that officers usually get before going. He received his orders one day short of the deadline after which he would have been ineligible for Vietnam service. (The order was later rescinded because of public and Congressional protests; the Army tried to pretend it was an ordinary transfer, but they could not explain how it was that of Sullivan's graduating class of one hundred officers he was the only one to receive orders to Vietnam.)

Far from intimidated by it all, Sullivan went right on talking frankly to the press, scoffing at the military-court system as little more than a travesty of the civilian system of justice. "We have in the courts in this country the principle that we have the adversary system, with one lawyer fighting against another, using every tool within his possession, bounded only by ethical considerations to help his client," Sullivan said at one of his press conferences. "Do we have that in the military? I say we do not because the defense attorneys do not have the power, or the will, or the freedom, to go ahead and use every legitimate tool on behalf of their client. You're a captain, you're not a lawyer in there [in the military courtroom]. Sometimes you get the impression you are fighting the whole Army."

To discuss military justice only in terms of courts-martial, however, is to ignore perhaps the most questionable procedure of them all—the administrative board. It is the smoothest way to achieve the ouster of unwanted men from the service. In fact, it is such a handy maneuver (making absolutely no demands on the military's marginal sense of fair play) that administrative discharges have become very popular with commanders in the past twenty years. In 1968* alone nearly eleven thousand men were removed from the services with "undesirable" administrative discharges based on what military authorities conceived to be misconduct or unfitness.

The categories of misconduct range from AWOL to "other good and sufficient reasons," but by far the most common reason for giving a man an undesirable discharge for misconduct is that he has been convicted in a civil court. This means that he is punished twice for the same offense: once, perhaps lightly, by the civil court and a second time, with extreme weight, by the military, since the undesirable discharge will stick with him for life and will often come between him and the job he wants. Judges of the Court of Military Appeals, including even the most conservative member, Judge Robert Quinn, have often stated their suspicions that the administrative discharge is used to get around the difficulties of proving a serviceman's guilt in a fair trial. But they have been expressing their suspicions for more than a decade, with no resulting reform that can be measured.

* Although this material was updated in the summer of 1970, no later figures could be obtained from the Pentagon, which guards its information closely, especially if it believes the information will be used in a critical way.

The criterion in the military services for judging the fairness of dismissing a man from the service without a trial and with a less-than-honorable discharge can be summed in one word: convenience. The reputation of the individual is held to be secondary to the convenience of the services. If this means convicting a man on hearsay evidence or on unsworn testimony or on a fabric of rumor, nevertheless it is done. The late Judge Paul J. Kilday of the Court of Military Appeals expressed this point of view quite candidly:

> Here you have men who are convicted administratively by being given discharges. . . . But then you have the practical situation. If you have a fellow aboard ship who pretty nearly everybody on the ship figures is a homosexual and you have everybody upset, or you have a barracks thief who is such a good barracks thief that you have not been able to catch him with the goods, but you have got it reasoned down that he is the only one who could be doing it, what are you going to do, keep the homo aboard ship or send him to another one? Are you going to keep the barracks thief there?

The military's answer to those questions has been: No, even though we haven't enough evidence to support a court-martial, we will get rid of the man for the good of the service. It may ruin him, but it will help us.

The administrative-discharge process includes no rules of evidence, no due-process guarantees, no statute of limitations on the evidence that can be used. The defendant has no subpoena powers, no right to confront his accusers. A defendant can find himself facing rumors and indiscretions that are fifteen or twenty years old and that he can scarcely remember the origins of, much less construct a defense against.

A Navy man of fourteen years' service was discharged on the basis of a homosexual charge that was ten years old and which the Navy had known about all along and despite which it had twice re-enlisted him. A major was dismissed from the Army with an administrative discharge (he asked for a court-martial but was refused) because some unidentified foreign nationals accused him of homosexual conduct; when he asked the field board to present him with the evidence, he was shown only an unsigned, unsworn, Thermo-Faxed copy of the charges. A Navy veteran one year short of twenty-year retirement was dismissed administratively because he wasn't able to pay for his wife's fur coats as fast as she bought them. A Marine was given an undesirable discharge, under less-than-honorable conditions, for no reason except that he had been involved in a serious automobile accident in Haiti.

The defects of the administrative board are much the same as those that afflict general courts-martial. As a representative of the Fleet Reserve Association once told a Senate subcommittee: "The proceedings looking toward the issuance of the discharge are initiated in the first instance by the commanding officer; the commanding officer appoints all of the personnel connected with the field board hearings, and ordinarily such personnel will be junior to him. Under the circumstances, the average board member probably is more inclined to follow or accept the recommendation of his commanding officer than to take steps to see that the individual appearing before the board is accorded any great degree of protection insofar as basic rights are concerned."

Going back a few years to find a superb example of the uses to which the military puts administrative discharges, we come upon the ruined life of Marine Technical Sergeant Boniface (which is not his name, though everything else is factual), a veteran of seventeen years of unimpeachable service, including twenty-two months overseas in World War II, participation in the Iwo Jima campaign, and three months as a combat cameraman in Korea, where he took part in the Inchon landing and the Naktong River operations. He was no hero, but he had served well and honorably and had received four good-conduct medals.

In 1958 he was stationed at the Pentagon. As frequently happens around large conglomerate institutions of that type, homosexuals made use of the toilets as hunting grounds. They appeared to be especially thick around Pentagon Toilet No.

2D617, so policemen hired by the General Services Administration teamed up with Army Criminal Investigation Division agents to rout them out. Half a dozen agents stationed themselves conveniently to peek through the cracks around the stall doors and to peer under the doors and over the top of the stalls; other government detectives hid out in the ceiling crawl area, taking photographs of what went on in the stalls; still other agents hung around outside the toilet room to follow suspects and find out their identity.

On July 11, 1958, Walter Bruce, a special agent for the Office of Naval Intelligence, was handed a dossier on Sergeant Boniface. Bruce looked through the material and saw that it was (in his own words) "very shoddy investigative work," saw also that the material made no mention of witnesses and that the material had been collected by an anonymous investigator; Bruce wanted no part of it, and when his superior insisted that he take over, Bruce asked hotly: "What the hell do you want me to do with this piece of junk? I don't have an official contributor, and I don't know who did this, and I would prefer to do some investigative work to find out more."

No, no, said his superior, no more investigations were necessary, for Boniface had been identified and observed taking part in perverse acts, and Bruce's only job was to interview the suspect and, hopefully, make him confess.

As it turned out, that wasn't difficult. But exactly what Boniface confessed to isn't clear. Threatened with a court-martial and public notoriety and shame if he didn't confess, Boniface panicked and did as he was told. His panic was caused by being shown an indistinct photo of a Marine and being assured that the Marine was none other than himself, being perverse. Under the direction of military agents, he wrote out and signed a six-page confession to the effect that on two occasions while he was sitting in a toilet stall "an unknown man in an adjoining stall had reached under the partition separating the stalls and felt my leg and, proceeding further, had performed an indecent act" on him with Boniface's passive cooperation. That's what the written confession said, but Boniface later insisted that what he had told Bruce was that an unidentified man in the next stall had borrowed a book of matches from him and, on returning them, had suggested that they go for a ride and that he, Boniface, had told the man to "get lost."

Because he had confessed, Boniface was advised to escape trial by asking for an undesirable discharge. The advice was given by a Navy officer, supplied as his counsel, who was not an attorney.

Sergeant Boniface was the victim of bluff. He had been told that there were corroborating witnesses, but there were none; he had been told that the evidence against him was sufficient to merit a court-martial, but it was not—for one reason because Section 25, Chapter VI, of the *Manual for Courts-Martial* states: "Ordinarily, charges for an offense should not be preferred against an individual if, after investigation, the only available evidence that the offense was committed is his statement that he committed it."

On September 5, 1958, Boniface was expelled from the Marine Corps with an undesirable discharge. Four years later, in 1962, Boniface's civilian attorney finally forced the Navy to name the two witnesses who allegedly had seen Boniface commit the homosexual act. But at a subsequent trial in the U.S. District Court, neither of the witnesses could identify Boniface and one of the witnesses admitted that "I never personally saw any homosexual acts because I was stationed outside the toilet." After four years, the Navy had finally made clear that it had no case against a seventeen-year veteran except the confession it had frightened out of him.

The Pentagon files are full of cases not only of mature servicemen like Boniface but of seventeen- and eighteen-year-olds who were strong-armed into accepting an undesirable discharge after committing indiscretions that, at worst, can be condemned as human. A. F. Zerbee, counsel to the Catholic War Veterans, wrote the Senate Constitutional Rights Subcommittee in 1966:

> Very frequently these young men—with no juvenile or adult police records—will commit a minor civilian offense such as joy riding, public drinking, fighting or other minor disturbances. If the soldier is arrested by the civilian police and convicted for the misdemeanor, he is returned to his post and ordered before an Administrative Discharge Board and awarded an undesirable discharge. His offense did not deserve a trial by court-martial, yet the mandatory issuing of the undesirable discharge for the light civilian conviction sends the young man back to civil life as an outcast, and the condemning castigation on the face of his discharge certificate renders him undesirable for employment.

Along with his letter Zerbee sent excerpts from letters which had been received from "undesirables." Samples:

> I have written you before about trying to get my discharge reviewed but, however, it did me no good. I was 17 years of age when I entered the service and 19 when I received my bad conduct discharge. I have been going to night school for 3 years but it does me no good for I cannot get a decent job because of my discharge.

> I understand there are exceptions in some cases and it may sound selfish, but I am asking that my case be made one of those exceptions, because since my discharge, which has been over 3 years, I have gotten married and have a family and another one due, and I have been unable to find employment of any kind due to my discharge. If my discharge can't be reinstated, and I can't re-enlist, could you please give me a letter of recommendation so that I might get a job to support my family?*

Against the thousands of individual hardships of this type, the military weighs its own convenience, and invariably chooses the latter. The administrative-discharge routine, for example, helped get the Army out of an embarrassing situation in 1969 involving the famous case of the "Fort Jackson Eight"—the dissident soldiers who were arrested for holding a boisterous bull session outside

---

* These, and the Boniface case, are from the Senate subcommittee's hearings on military justice.

their barracks to denounce the Vietnam war and white racists. Fort Jackson officials claimed the men were arrested for refusing to obey an order (though it was admitted that no direct order had been given) and for creating a riotous situation (though the MPs were not called, and one noncom at the scene had been so unimpressed by the danger that he left to get a sandwich).

Some of the dissenters were held incommunicado in the stockade for two months; others were held under barracks arrest. All were threatened with court-martial. If the Army had gone ahead with its threat, the result would have been such a classic freedom-of-speech trial that the Uniform Code of Military Justice might have been seriously shaken. As public support of the imprisoned men increased, the Army dropped all charges against two of them and neatly got rid of the other six either by mutual-consent undesirable discharges or by undesirable administrative discharges.

As a result of military courts-martial, which is poor enough justice, or their poorer substitute, the administrative discharge, more than half a million veterans are now on the labor market bearing the burden of a less-than-honorable discharge which, for the rest of their lives, will make them unwelcome to most employers.

Nor should it be supposed that the military would like to extricate itself from its own harsh discharge system and modify the penalties that it now feels compelled to administer. Several times in the recent past, proposals have been made that would have given the military just such an opportunity, and in each case the proposals were rejected (except by the Air Force, which has by far the fairest record in dealing with its problem servicemen). The late Clyde Doyle, Congressman from California, introduced legislation in the early 1960s that would have enabled men receiving less-than-honorable discharges to remove themselves from that perpetual blacklist by living exemplary lives for, say, three years thereafter. The bill passed the House but, as a result of intense opposition by the Army and Navy, died in the Senate.

# 4. The Levy Affair

Aɴᴅ ᴘʟᴇʙɪᴀɴs, ғʀᴇᴇ-ᴛʜɪɴᴋᴇʀs, and Israelites not only entered and contaminated the Army, but even succeeded in placing themselves [in responsible positions]. What did they plan to do, these republicans whose beliefs contradicted the principle of passive obedience and were incompatible with Caesarian militarism? Above all, what did those Jews plan to do, who, having renounced the commercial and financial dealings found appropriate by their co-religionists, proposed to follow a military career? What evil thoughts of gain attracted them here? Or what treason did they think of carrying out? The time had come to chase them away.

So reads a portion of Alexandre Zévaès' *L'Affaire Dreyfus*. But one must be cautious in likening the affair Levy to the Dreyfus case. There are points of similarity, though not always exact ones. Alfred Dreyfus, a career artillery captain, was convicted of treason in 1894, which was only the beginning of a court fight that was to drag on for a dozen years and become one of the most important political controversies of France at the turn of the century. Howard Levy, very reluctantly a medical captain, was convicted of acts of disloyalty in 1967 after a trial that briefly caught the imagination of the nation and of Western Europe, but almost immediately was forgotten. There was a question of national anti-

Semitism involved in the Dreyfus affair; anti-Semitism also probably added to the enthusiasm with which Levy was pursued, but it
was the kind of anti-Semitism which in the South, where the affair
took place, cannot be separated from its xenophobic reaction to
the cities of the North, especially New York. Decisive evidence
against Dreyfus was contained in a letter he was alleged to have
written offering the sale of secrets; an important, but not dominat-
ing, piece of evidence against Levy was a letter in which he counseled against fighting in Vietnam. Perhaps the most fascinating
similarity between the two cases was the fact that Dreyfus would
surely have been exonerated if a secret dossier had not been
produced against him; against Levy, too, a secret dossier was
produced, this one making the difference between whether or not
he was to be court-martialed.

But the real likeness between the two cases, the striking repetition of history, was in the role that society's view of militarism
played in the two trials. As Roger Soltau said of the Dreyfus case,
"Complex as it was, it can be reduced ultimately to a simple
choice between two conceptions of society which had, ever since
the Revolution, been struggling for mastery in the French mind
. . . the basing of society and civilization on certain elementary
individual rights, the other based on authority as external and
prior to individual citizens."

If one substitutes "American mind" for "French mind" in that
passage, he has a perfect summary of the choice that also was
distilled from the Levy trial.

Howard Brett Levy of Brooklyn, New York, shared the feeling
common to most doctors: he was not ecstatic about serving his
hitch in the Army. He had received a good medical education, at
New York State University's Downstate Medical Center, but as a
doctor he was not yet earning high fees. For credit references on
his Army data sheet he listed only his Mobil Gas credit card, the
New York Telephone Company and Field Brothers Clothing in

Coney Island. But he did not know how to get out of going into the Army, so he went.

His 1963 Ford broke down three times en route to Columbia, South Carolina, and he reported to Fort Jackson late, eight days after he started the trip. Already he was out of step with the Army. And things never changed.

On July 17, 1965, four days after he arrived at his new home, he learned that the blacks in nearby Newberry County were carrying on a voter-registration drive as part of a regional effort led by Dr. Martin Luther King. Levy didn't like the South, he didn't like the Army, and he was bored stiff; so he drove twenty miles over to Newberry to see if he could get involved in something that would revive his spirits.

What he got involved in eventually led to a three-year sentence in a federal penitentiary. Possibly Levy was misled by the lethargic air of Newberry County, although surely the viciousness he shortly ran into should have cleared his thinking on that point. Many a Northerner has miscalculated the depth of the spleen in these backwash Southern areas. Newberry County is that kind of place.

Thirty-five percent of Newberry County's 28,000 citizens are black. They live like most blacks in the South—badly. But the whites aren't much better off. The Newberry County Development Board boasts that "present unemployment in our county is at the lowest level in past history," but it also admits—or rather it also boasts, since this would be very attractive to employers looking for cheap labor—that about 17 percent of the population is jobless, which is about the same rate as at the bottom of the 1930s depression. Virtually all of Newberry County is rural, a handsome rusticity with piney-wood thickets, heavy vines, lush fields and Black Angus cattle. A commercial farmer with enough land and enough money can do well. But like many rural areas of the South, Newberry is losing population. Those who remain are having an increasingly hard time "just hanging on." They do not like change, because change means letting go. Thus the white residents of Newberry did not like the voter-registration drive.

Newberry County's official slogan is "The County of Friendly Folk," but Dr. Levy did not find it so. Even before the registration drive, there was racial tension in Newberry. Three months before the drive opened, half a dozen hooded men took an eighteen-year-old black from the jailhouse in Prosperity and treated him roughly. Later one of Prosperity's two policemen and one of its two night watchmen were arrested as suspects in the second-degree lynching. In short, when Levy, unhappy soldier, drove to work with the blacks, the atmosphere in the town of Prosperity and the county of Newberry was crackling with hostility.

The work took nerve, and on more than one occasion Levy showed that he had nerve. One of the other workers in the voter-registration campaign later recalled the time a white volunteer was beaten in Whitmire (population 2,663) and held for questioning by police. The worker and Levy decided they had better go rescue the volunteer before there was more trouble. They ran into a "mob of thirty-five or forty white men who threatened us with physical violence and swore at us and insulted our racial backgrounds. Dr. Levy refused to be intimidated. He was pretty courageous because he certainly didn't have to be there or anything." Levy not only kept up his door-to-door recruiting of new black voters; he also set up a printing press to turn out leaflets and newsletters to encourage the movement.

One of Prosperity's best-known residents was James B. West, special agent of the Army's Counter Intelligence Corps. West had been living in the town for four years when Levy appeared on the scene. He was a close friend of both the chief of police and the sheriff. One white resident described him as "one of the worst bigots" he had ever known. In a county where so few people live, the lives of men with feelings as intense and as contradictory as those of James West and Howard Levy are destined to cross. And so they did.

West was born in central Florida, a section where a number of brutal attacks have been made on Negroes in recent years and where black men are no more welcome than in Mississippi. He grew up in South Carolina, and joined the Army in 1940. Beginning in 1950 the Counter Intelligence Corps had used him for spotting evidence of "treason, sabotage, disloyalty, and disaffection." He retired from the service as a chief warrant officer in 1961 and became a civilian employee of the intelligence group in 1965. He claimed that he could not recall when he first became aware of the name Howard Brett Levy, but "offhand I would say December of 1966." Even for an offhand remark, this was rather inaccurate. Evidence shows that West was putting together a case against Levy as early as February of 1966. And there is further evidence, strong evidence, that West must have known about Levy's voter-registration work with Negroes in West's home town in the summer of 1965. At Levy's trial, West refused to answer questions as to whether he had ever investigated Levy's activities in South Carolina. "Well, I will have to decline to answer that. . . . This possibly could be a security matter."

Exactly when did West take the trail of Howard Brett Levy? It is important. At one point in his testimony West claimed that he did not join the civilian intelligence group until the first of November, 1965. But later defense counsel Charles Morgan again asked, "When did you say you started into this?" and West, seeming a bit uncertain this time, replied: "I didn't start into this until—well, it would have been the summer of 1965. You see, I was not assigned to this until November of 1965, and then I didn't have—I could only do very limited work after being assigned here until I got a badge and credentials, and it takes some time, and prior to that there were other men that had worked on the thing. I did not myself."

"So in the summer of 1965 . . ."

"Somewhere. I don't know."

What a strange intelligence agent, unable to recall when he started a case, unable to recall when exactly he went to work. There were so many things that slipped his mind. He could not even remember the tumultuous voter-registration drive in his home town in the summer of 1965, much less whether or not Levy's name had come up at that time.

This bit of forgetfulness may be a good criterion of West's general credibility. Is it really possible that he could not remember hearing of the voter drive in Prosperity? At last count, 750 people lived in Prosperity, but more leave every day. If you travel at thirty miles an hour, you can drive from the town limits to the center of Prosperity in one minute, thirty seconds. There isn't a place to eat in Prosperity. The city jail, the police station, the city clerk, the city treasurer and the superintendent of utilities are all housed in a building about the size of a two-car garage. The biggest building in town is the Lutheran church. Business in Prosperity consists of: a florist, a bank, a hardware store, a barbershop, a five-and-ten-cent store, a farm and garden center, two grocery stores, three filling stations, a finance company and a very small pants-manufacturing plant.

Special agent West claims he was unaware, amidst all that bustle, of the most critical social upheaval to hit Prosperity since the Civil War. For some reason, Levy's attorney was unconvinced by this forgetfulness and argued stubbornly that West had begun pursuing Levy because of his pro-Negro activities long before he began to chase Levy as a "security risk."

As early as February, 1966, according to records, West was interviewing disgruntled servicemen about Levy. One of these was William Cain, who had worked under Levy in the Dermatology Clinic from July, 1965, until January, 1966, and become thoroughly fed up with the captain because "Levy spoke favorably about those persons who burned their draft cards, feeling that this was their right, and they should not be prosecuted for this. I would not consider Levy a loyal American because of his statements condemning U.S. policies. On one occasion, I told him that I did not consider him very loyal to the U.S., and he became quite angry. Levy was quite pro-Negro, took the side of the Negroes when discussing civil rights matters and appeared to think more of the Negroid race than the white race." Cain's statement ends: "He often visited a young Negro private who was confined in the post stockade for failing to obey two direct orders from an officer, although *I am unaware just what their association together was.*" (Emphasis added.) A very deft touch, that last—just the right brushing of perversion to be effective. However, it was not true; the prisoner visited Levy in his offices to be treated for a skin ailment. "Their association together" was medical.

Sergeant First Class Debevion Landing was another Levy aide who worked against Levy. Landing had written Captain Walter C. Rose, who had been an adjutant in the Medical Corps at Fort Jackson before his transfer to Hawaii, telling Rose that Levy wasn't measuring up to his idea of an officer. (These were, one eventually concludes, rather presumptuous enlisted men, who felt no hesitation in rating a captain for attire, conduct, bedside manner and loyalty.) Rose told Landing, as Landing put it, "to keep quiet and that he would be contacted by counterintelligence personnel." And, in due course, Landing heard from agent West.

Of all the partnerships in this anti-Levy movement, none was so smooth and congenial as that between agent West and Sergeant Landing. Landing is middle-aged and a native of Millen, a Georgia town of slightly over three thousand population. At the trial he slipped into the patois of his native region, using the comfortable word "nigger" ("I have heard Dr. Levy make the statement that if he was a nigger he would not go to Vietnam and fight")—and then denying that he said it that way. Sergeant Landing declared he was unaware of any racial discrimination in this country. In his testimony, Landing joined a long list of prosecution witnesses who had selective memories. Although several of Levy's remarks burned holes in his brain, he claimed he could not remember talking to even one person about these remarks. (Another soldier disputed that claim under oath.) Landing also admitted disobeying a direct order given by Levy, who thereupon threatened him with administrative punishment. Yes, he could remember that. And he remembered very well indeed overhearing Levy say that he would like to date one of the attractive female Negroes he had treated. He could remember very distinctly hearing Levy declare on one occasion that he was an atheist. With engraved clarity he could recall Levy had said he wouldn't go to Vietnam even if ordered. Equally well remembered was Levy's damnation of the Special Forces as thieves and murderers.

This last recollection is curious. From the emphasis that the prosecution placed upon the statement, one would have supposed that Levy had gone around damning the Special Forces constantly. Sergeant Landing, however, whose ears were well tuned to incriminating remarks, could recall hearing Levy condemn the Special Forces only once. Specialist Ronald E. Novak, also an aide to Levy, said he had heard the doctor criticize the Special Forces only "two or three times," and only when he was explaining to them why he wouldn't train them.

Under oath Landing admitted that he had been near enough to overhear remarks made by Levy perhaps a dozen times a day, every workday, for more than a year. But the above are the *only* remarks in all that time—and Levy was a talkative fellow—that Landing could recall.

Perhaps it was because he got some steering from agent West.

Q: Now, what question did Mr. West ask you that you responded to with the statement that Capt. Levy had expressed the desire to date Negroes?

LANDING: I guess he was talking along the line of how—about the Special Forces.

Q: Do you mean if he asked you a question as to how Dr. Levy felt about Special Forces, you answered that he would like to date Negroes?

LANDING: I said along the line. I didn't say that was the question. I said along the line, sir.

Q: Fine. Since you have specific quotes in your statement here that relate back pretty far that you state now that you remember Dr. Levy making, I am going back much less far in time and asking what Mr. West said.

LANDING: *I believe Mr. West wanted to know if there had been any remarks made like this.*
Q: About dating Negroes?
LANDING: Or to this effect, I believe, sir.
Q: He was generally interested in Dr. Levy's thoughts about Negroes in general?
LANDING: *He asked a lot of questions about them, yes, sir.* [Emphasis added.]

As for the reason Sergeant Landing had told West about Levy's atheism, well, yes, the secret agent from churchgoing Newberry County had asked specifically about that.

So bitterly did Fort Jackson's commanders later react against Levy, it is difficult to believe that at first there was no outward show of antagonism toward his presence on the base. But this was the fact. From the time Levy arrived at Fort Jackson until late June, 1966, his commander at the base hospital was Colonel Harry J. Grossman. Members of the Army's Special Forces—the Green Berets—were receiving training at the hospital, and Colonel Grossman had heard that some of the aidmen were complaining about antiwar statements Levy was making. He called the captain in and orally reprimanded him for it. "I told him to desist from injecting his personal political comments into his training," Grossman recalled. "I did not give him a written reprimand or levy any disciplinary action against him. It was never brought to my attention that Levy refused to train the Special Forces medical personnel." Grossman said he was aware that Levy had been denied a security clearance because of his relationship with some "radical" organization in New York prior to his enlistment, but this didn't impress Grossman nearly so much as the fact that Levy, in Grossman's description, "performed his professional duties in the Dermatology Section in a very good manner."

In recollecting Levy's trespasses, Grossman did not seem much interested in Levy's handling of his Special Forces role. Further evidence that this leisurely attitude prevailed even up to early October of 1966 was a statement given at that time by Lieutenant Colonel Jackie Jacob, chief of professional services at Fort Jackson hospital and thereby Levy's superior. "I know of no orders or directives from this hospital or the Surgeon General's Office requiring Captain Levy to instruct and train Special Forces medical personnel, although Special Forces personnel are receiving training at the hospital." This statement was made on October 4—seven days before Colonel Grossman's successor as head of the hospital, Colonel Henry F. Fancy, called Levy in and upbraided him and gave him both oral and written orders to train the troops. Obviously, what had become of almost hysterical importance to Colonel Fancy was not, in fact, important enough even to be known by Jacob or other top officials of the hospital. So far as Jacob was concerned, "Captain Levy has performed his duties in a very satisfactory manner, and I know of no instance when Captain Levy refused to instruct Special Forces medical personnel or allow them to observe treatment of patients in his section." The only thing Jacob could think of to criticize Levy for was that sometimes he didn't wear his cap to work and sometimes he wore his white smock outside the clinic, which was against regulations.*

Another of Levy's superiors, Major Nelson R. Jensen, Jr., who came to the hospital on July 15, 1966, as chief of the Department of Medicine at the hospital, was just as relaxed about Levy. On October 26 he told agent West that, so far as he was concerned, Levy carried out all his assigned duties "without conflict." He said he had heard that Levy didn't like the Special Forces men to hang around his office because they annoyed his other patients, espe-

---

* Although Levy would never in a lifetime have been able to adjust to the Army's nitty way of wanting a doctor to wear a cap to work, he was further handicapped in his adjustment by skimpy indoctrination. Most incoming Army doctors go through a six-week indoctrination training period at Fort Sam Houston, Texas, but the class was overcrowded at the time Levy joined the Army, so he went straight to Fort Jackson, where he received only six hours of indoctrination training. It wasn't enough.

cially his women patients. But, in general, Levy's record was clean so far as he knew.

At first Colonel Fancy, the hospital's new commander, was no different in his acceptance of Levy. He first met Captain Levy near the end of July, 1966. It was a routine get-acquainted meeting. Fancy had just taken over as commander of the hospital and he wanted to meet the fifty-two doctors on his staff; Levy was No. 14 to have that pleasure. Although Levy's dossier was already flagged —and although the officer who was to become Fancy's executive assistant, Colonel Chester Davis, whose most distinguishing feature was his caterpillar mustache, had privately pointed out Levy's flagging because "he's a pinko, or something"—Fancy claimed he did not mention the subject in this meeting with Levy, "although I recognized it as a potentially serious matter."

For the next two months Colonel Fancy apparently took no special interest in Levy. In fact, even by the time of the trial he had not learned how properly to pronounce his name (he was saying it as if it rhymed with "bevy"). However, in addition to being told by Davis that Levy was a "pinko," Fancy had learned shortly after he arrived that some others on the base were offended by Levy. Colonel William A. Rawlins, then Fancy's personnel officer, came to him with the vague information that the "previous commander had had some problems with Captain Levy but that he felt there were no particular problems with the other medical officers as far as he knew." This was quite correct. Some of the other medical officers liked Levy and some didn't, but they all admired him professionally. Some agreed with his position on Vietnam, some didn't, and with the latter he often argued, but there were no hard feelings. One thing all agreed on: Levy did not try to hide his feelings or proselytize in secret. He came right out and said what he wanted to say. He argued with doctors, he argued with nurses, he argued with some enlisted men, he even argued with some patients. As for his scuffed shoes and longish hair— two matters Fancy was to make something of later on—the truth is that doctors get by with more in the Army than do ordinary officers. Traditionally, they are not compelled to maintain polish for the sake of polish.

What, beside these trivial matters, did Colonel Rawlins say the previous commander had had trouble with Levy about? Well, it seems that Levy hadn't joined the Officers' Club. He didn't want to join because he didn't like Officers' Clubs, and so he didn't join. Even by Army standards, this was no great crime.

That was the sum of it in July.

In August and September, Colonel Fancy received complaints from a Sergeant George B. Curry, who was the noncommissioned officer in charge of Plans and Training for the Special Forces aidmen. Curry said that Levy wasn't giving the aidmen any training. Curry, in fact, with those other subordinates of Levy's, had been hard at work for months undercutting Levy.

At first most of the juicier information collected by Curry and Landing was passed on to West, not to Colonel Fancy, and whatever Fancy received he treated as of less than earth-shaking importance. But then West embraced Fancy and let him in on their program. It began slowly at their first meeting, on October 2. By trial time Fancy and West claimed that they had "forgotten" most of that first conversation. The colonel remembered vaguely that "I told him that I had no definite problems with Captain Levy, but that I had observed his practice of dermatology in his clinic, I had observed that he was somewhat brusque with patients and rather argumentative, but, in general, I told him that I had no outstanding problems with Captain Levy."

Up to this point Fancy did not exactly dislike Levy, but neither did he like him. Fancy was not yet ready to participate in the attack on the captain, but he was already picking at him in small ways. For example, though Fancy as a rule filed in his doctors' personnel records all letters received which commended them for their good patient treatment, he withheld filing a letter of this type about Levy. He wasn't trying to "get" Levy, but neither was he trying to help him. Mainly, he simply wanted to ignore the dermatologist, whose office he visited only twice in the first three months.

Although Colonel Fancy said later that Sergeant Curry had been complaining for two months about Levy's failure to train Special Forces aidmen, Fancy also claimed that he did not tell West about this at their first meeting because "I wasn't sure of my information. I had not checked into it." From this one would judge that Colonel Fancy had himself not placed a very high priority on the training of Special Forces aidmen, since he had let the rumors go by for two months without bothering to make one phone call of inquiry to Levy.

From his side of the desk, agent West listened politely to the colonel and then in his smiling, easy way began to lace their conversation about Levy with new meaning—faintly dangerous, smelling of something that was not quite treasonous but certainly not patriotic. As West was to tell the court, describing his tactics with considerable pride: "I ask questions and anyone intelligent, such as Col. Fancy, can deduct from the questions I ask what I am getting at."

Fancy deduced so well that he later was able to tell the court that West had told him "there was some possible evidence emerging and suggested that Capt. Levy was attempting to influence the performance of duty in foreign affairs by Negro enlisted men. . . . In other words, what Mr. West told me was to the effect that Capt. Levy had been having some dealings with Negro personnel, which dealings and discussions were of an unpatriotic nature." West later denied under oath that he told Fancy any such thing, and although it might be convenient to suppose simply that one of the two men was lying, the answer probably lies in West's boasted technique of asking questions in such a way as to impart information. In any case, the important point is that, from the outset, West was obsessed with the subject of Negroes.

West's visit shook Fancy, and for the next week the colonel made inquiries at the hospital about Levy's activities. He was told

once again that the Brooklyn doctor was something less than
enthusiastic about training Special Forces. Now Fancy was becoming nervous. On October 7, for the first time, he went to G-2
headquarters (the base intelligence office) and leafed through
Levy's dossier, stopping here and there to read closely. One of the
things he read was the statement, given by Levy to an Army
security agent more than a year earlier, that under certain circumstances he would feel it his duty to his country to disobey an
order.

So Levy was like that. Pushed far enough on a point of conscience, he could be counted on to balk. Three days later, October
10, West and Fancy talked again. This time Fancy could talk more
concretely, more robustly. He talked with West about his deter-
mination to give Levy both an oral and a written order to train the
aidmen, and if Levy refused to obey (something that was to be
determined, he said, by talking with Levy's Special Forces students), Fancy would take appropriate action.

Some of the above account of what Fancy said to West comes
from statements in West's official agent's reports. But during
Levy's court-martial, thanks to some slip-of-the-tongue testimony
by West, a great deal more was suddenly discovered. Fancy, West
said, had not just vaguely speculated about the possibility of
Levy's refusing to obey the order; he had said that Levy had
already *absolutely* refused to give Special Forces training.

This was a major revelation. Levy could not be convicted of
disobeying an order if Fancy knew he would disobey it, and if the
order were given primarily to get Levy in deeper trouble. In the
*Manual for Courts-Martial,* under Article 90, "Assaulting or
Willfully Disobeying an Officer," the Army warns those who would
prosecute: "Disobedience of an order which has for its sole object
the attainment of some private end, or which is given for the sole
purpose of increasing the penalty for an offense which it is expected the accused may commit, is not punishable under this
article."

It cannot fairly be said that West and Landing, those good and loyal Southerners, had a "private end" in bringing about the downfall of Levy, a pro-Negro Jewish Yankee. But if Fancy told West on October 10 that he positively knew that Levy would not obey the order that he planned to give on October 11, and if the giving of the order seemed aimed at accomplishing nothing more than an increase in punishment (or, as Colonel Fancy said in his schoolmarmish fashion, "I regarded this as a strong corrective measure, a strong educational measure"), then the order was illegal and Levy could not be found guilty of disobeying it.*

* During the trial, evidence was given on the critical issue of whether or not Levy was lured into an entrapment. Twice Captain Richard M. Shusterman, the government's prosecuting attorney, asked West if Fancy had told him on October 10 that Levy had already "absolutely refused" to train Green Berets. Twice Shusterman carefully chose those words and twice—as Shusterman saw a key part of his charges begin to fall apart—West said, yes, that's what Fancy had said, absolutely.

Then a break was called in the trial. West went to the toilet. Captain Shusterman hotfooted it right in behind him and had a sharp discussion with him about what had transpired in Fancy's office on the tenth. But still West didn't understand what Shusterman was getting at.

Defense counsel Morgan, who had seen them buzzing in the toilet, got West back on the witness stand and asked him what they had talked about. Oh, about the conversation on the tenth, he said vaguely. For a moment Morgan was afraid that the agent had caught on to the trouble he was raising for the prosecution, but he soon discovered that West had not. Morgan put the key question to him again: Did Fancy have knowledge on the tenth that Levy would *absolutely* disobey the training order if given?

WEST: On the 10th, yes, that is correct.

MORGAN: That is correct, right?

WEST: That is correct.

This made five times West corroborated the word "absolutely," and he soon did it twice more. Then Captain Shusterman took over again. Fixing West under a stare of such intensity that West at last began to pay attention to the signals, Shusterman said in a slow, firmly coaxing voice that put just the right emphasis on the key words:

"If, on the 10th of October, Col. Fancy had told you that Capt. Levy *ABSOLUTELY* refused to train Special Forces personnel, *why isn't that in your* [written] *statement?*" (Emphasis added.)

West's eyes opened wide. He thought he had caught the right signal at last, but he wanted verification from Shusterman.

WEST: I don't know whether—you are using the word absolutely.

Morgan jumped to his feet, ready to harpoon the floundering witness. "*You* used the word absolutely!"

Fancy did give the order, and Levy did refuse to obey it. Yet neither because of this disobedience nor on account of the information he had seen in the G-2 files on October 7 did Colonel Fancy feel compelled to bring prompt charges against him. He did not do so, in fact, until December, and even then he did not consider pressing such charges as would result in a court-martial. No, "I took the initial steps toward developing an Article 15 [a mild, nonjudicial-punishment type of action that does not even go on a man's record] and to do this I sent Colonel Rawlins to Fort Bragg to obtain sworn statements from the members of Class Number Nine specifically concerning the dermatology training [they had received or had not received from Levy]."

This was the first investigation Colonel Fancy had personally supervised—the first time he had filed charges against an officer— and he had no intention of punishing Levy severely. For an officer, the Article 15 procedure would normally result in nothing stiffer than a reprimand.

From what happened next, one may assume that the Judge Advocate General's office, when it heard about the upcoming Article 15, was unhappy about Fancy's mild approach. So, it may be assumed, was the G-2 office. G-2 was quick on the phone to Fancy and urged him again to look through the Levy dossier. "We have some new stuff," they told him. After he had read it, the JAG office phoned Fancy and asked for a chance to discuss the secret information with him, and asked him to hold off on the Article 15 hearing. Now the noose was tightening. The pressure was enough

---

But Shusterman and West had finally made contact, and in a moment West was tumbling out denial upon denial. No, no, he had not meant to say absolutely. Looking at Shusterman for understanding and forgiveness, he said, "I see what you mean now." Again, a moment later in his testimony, he said, "I was incorrect and I did not get that point there."

MORGAN: What did you refresh your memory with a moment ago?
WEST: In regards to this information?
MORGAN: Yes.
WEST: I didn't catch that absolutely. I see where that makes a great difference in there on that question. . . .

to make Fancy change his mind. "I felt as a result of this review that the dossier did contain sworn statements which added to the case, and I decided that the court-martial proceeding would be more appropriate than an Article 15 proceeding."

Fancy admitted that it was nothing he knew about Levy, nor even anything about the way he did his work—including his refusal to train the aidmen—that made him press court-martial charges, but something in the dossier prepared by West that made him do it. It was not until after "reviewing the dossier and talking with the Judge Advocate" that he felt "charges of a more serious nature were present." What did he see in the 180-page dossier? Levy doesn't know. His attorneys don't know. Nobody knows but a few senior Army officers and Mr. West of Newberry County.

In the Judith Coplon case, which went to a federal Appellate Court in 1950 seeking reversal on the grounds that wiretap information used against Miss Coplon was not furnished the defense, the court ruled: "Few weapons in the arsenal of freedom are more useful than the power to compel the government to disclose the evidence on which it seeks to forfeit the liberty of its citizens. . . . A society which has come to wince at such exposure of the methods by which it seeks to impose its will upon its members, has already lost the feel of freedom and is on the path towards absolutism."

At Levy's trial, his attorney dragged details from Fancy, bit by bit, with Fancy resisting all the way, until it was clear that the Levy case was getting special attention from the top, from Major General Gines Perez, commandant of Fort Jackson. "Subsequently," Fancy recalled at last, "there was a conference, a brief conference, with the commanding general, Colonel Meeting and the chief of staff, with familiarizing, but the commanding general did not tell me what action to take." By that time, the general didn't have to put it in words. In fact, from the moment the staff judge advocate's office recommended that Fancy reconsider the Article 15 hearing and to think, instead, along the lines of a general court-martial, he must have known he was listening to the voice of Major General Perez. The staff judge advocate is the commanding general's lawyer; he does what the general wants done—as, indeed, what officer on the base didn't (except Levy, perhaps)?

Perez, who has since been transferred from Fort Jackson, was not the sort of officer to overlook an opportunity to make an example for the sake of discipline. A native of Spain, Perez graduated from the University of Arizona with a master's degree in metallurgy in 1933 and also a reserve commission in the cavalry. Just before World War II swept this country into all-out mobilization, he was ordered to active duty with the 1st Cavalry Division and served with it in the Pacific, winning the Distinguished Service Cross, Silver Star with Oak Leaf Cluster, Bronze Star with four Oak Leaf Clusters, Legion of Merit with Oak Leaf Cluster, Purple Heart and other ribbons and decorations. Obviously a brave man, he was much admired by the militarists of South America, who had larded his chest with crosses and military orders and medals. Needless to say, General Perez didn't admire Levy's philosophy. Somehow the word got down to Fancy: think again. And obviously Fancy did.

But if the things Levy had done and said around the base were so insignificantly irregular that Colonel Fancy thought first of a reprimand only, couldn't one assume that the threat of an enormously greater penalty stemmed solely from Levy's preservice activities with a leftist organization in New York? It was logical to think so. And if that were true, wouldn't this (Levy's defense counsels later asked) clash with the recent ruling of a federal Appellate Court (*Lenske* v. *United States*) in overthrowing the conviction of a left-wing lawyer on the basis of information supplied by an Internal Revenue agent who disliked the lawyer? In throwing out that conviction, the court wrote angrily: "We reverse. This court will not place its stamp of approval upon a witch hunt, a crusade to rid society of unorthodox thinkers and actors by using

Federal income tax laws and Federal courts to put such people in the penitentiary. This court will not be so used."

This point was raised by Morgan simply out of instinct, out of the ritual that he had learned within the moderately constitutional framework of the average civilian court. However, he was not so simple as to think that it would have any bearing on the military court. As has already been pointed out, military courts do not have to pay the slightest attention to the precedents established in the lower federal courts, and there is considerable dispute over whether they have to pay attention even to the U.S. Supreme Court.

The Army will not say what is in Levy's G-2 dossier, although the information there is the sole basis for the serious charges raised against him, and although both the U.S. Constitution and the U.S. Uniform Code of Military Justice require that an accused man be given the right to confront his accusers. The Army simply violated these protective statutes and got away with it, as it usually does.

Fancy claimed under oath that he was most impressed by the "information that Dr. Levy had been to eight meetings of a political organization or an organization in New York where they had some lectures." But the Army had known about these meetings since early 1965; Levy himself had so informed it both in writing and in interviews. When Levy filled out his Armed Services Security Questionnaire on January 28, 1965, he had told in full of his brief association with the Militant Labor Forum, an organization which federal agents and security officers apparently look upon as ominous. Unfortunately for him, when he was again asked to fill out a security questionnaire six months later, he forgot to put in this rather trivial data about the MLF. And this gave the Army the excuse it needed to flag his file.

When the Army sent a counterintelligence agent to interview Levy on October 4, 1965, about this flagging, he was once again perfectly frank about the MLF episode, and why not? The Levy that emerges from this earlier period is hardly a sinister character but only a young man who, trying to feel his way into the social jousting of his time, subscribed to a number of leftish magazines—the *Militant,* the *Nation,* the *Monthly Review, Liberation,* the *National Guardian*—and sometimes braved the filth of the New York subways to attend meetings where social issues were debated. Or Levy may simply have been driven by a healthy curiosity. Later, when he was serving the Army in the South, he attended several Ku Klux Klan meetings just to see what they were all about.

"Although I am not positive of the dates," Levy told the counterintelligence agent who interviewed him, "as well as I can remember, I attended about eight meetings of the Militant Labor Forum during the period September or October, 1964, to not later than May, 1965. I attended most of the meetings during this earlier period. I learned of the MLF from their advertisements of meetings in the local New York newspapers, and attended these meetings purely out of interest in the various speakers that they had and to learn of their ideals and purpose. I attended most of the meetings of the MLF in a one-story 'walk-up' loft which was located somewhere, I believe, around University Place, near Twelfth or Thirteenth Street, in Manhattan. On one occasion I attended an MLF meeting in a place that may have been called the Palm Tree Ballroom, Manhattan. On this occasion Malcolm X was the guest speaker. I also attended one meeting in Newark, New Jersey. Normally there were about seventy-five to a hundred persons at the meetings, except at the meeting where Malcolm X was the speaker there were several hundred people present. . . . At one meeting there was a type of debate between a Mr. Watts from *Liberator Magazine* and a Mr. Van Dyke, a writer for *National Review* magazine."

Any meeting, no matter how remote the loft or how grubby the ballroom, that includes a member of the *National Review*'s stable of writers, is hardly a subversive gathering. In any event, Levy was a loner in all this. "During the time I attended meetings of the

MLF I made no friends from this group and engaged in no social intercourse with others who attended the meetings or were members of the MLF."

It would be naïve to suppose that the Army had sent around an agent to interview Levy at this late date out of any desire to clear his record of the flag. If that had been its objective, it could have taken care of the problem months earlier. It seems clear that the agent sitting across the table from Levy on October 4, 1965, was asking questions in order to make Levy utter the kind of rebellious statements that could entrap him. And Levy obliged, though not quite so clumsily as the Army might have liked. There is one significant alteration in Levy's statement. At first he is recorded as saying, "I do not know if I would or would not obey certain military orders given me by a commander, *and I cannot say that I would be completely loyal to the U.S. in certain situations where I questioned the United States' decisions or where I felt that the action or decision was morally or ethically wrong."* (Emphasis added.)

But Levy did not quite mean that. His quarrel was not with the United States. He felt no hostility toward the United States and did not think a situation could arise in which he would be disloyal. The United States, he felt, was being victimized by the same people who were victimizing him—the military—and if he were ever disloyal, it would be a disloyalty aimed specifically at the military. So, three days later, he scratched through the above italicized portion of his statement and substituted: "I am able to envision situations in which I could conceivably refuse to obey a military order given me by a commander. This would be in such a situation in which I felt that the order was ethically or morally incorrect. I would add that this cannot be a criteria of loyalty, inasmuch as in such an unusual situation it might be more loyal not to obey the order. There is ample historical evidence to suggest that this has sometimes turned out to be the case."

Section I of Army Regulations 600-31, Subsection 4, gives this advice to commanders:

Flagging actions have a serious effect on the morale and the military careers of the individuals concerned. Such actions should be taken only, if after careful consideration of all the factors involved, it is determined that flagging action is necessary to protect the interest of the government. Commanders therefore will take rigid controls to insure that . . . individual cases are processed expeditiously and with due regard to the interest of the service and the rights of the individual.

The rule says "expeditiously." Yet Levy's dossier had been flagged from the day he entered service, and no action was taken to remove the flag until he was under court-martial charges a year and a half later. At that time the "pinko" flag was removed (he had been cleared) and a *new* flag was put in its place because of the court-martial. In other words, it was evident that the Army did not at any time intend to clear Levy until he could be squashed for something else.

The case was so stacked against Levy that when he went to trial he had absolutely nothing going for him but a stable of very militant, witty, sharp, unfrightened attorneys, of whom the most flamboyantly adept was Charles Morgan, Jr. Morgan had first gained national attention four years earlier as the young attorney in Birmingham who denounced the "good people" of his home town for allowing ruffians to burn Negro churches and kill innocent blacks. For that sacrilege he was all but stoned. Since then he has been the American Civil Liberty Union's top troubleshooter working out of Atlanta. He is a massive man physically; his briefs are about equally divided between the law and passages from literature, especially irreverent literature. It was, and still is, Morgan's contention that the court-martial of Howard Levy for breach of Army regulations was a complete farce, contrived to disguise the *real* reasons for putting him in the penitentiary: that he had befriended Negroes in South Carolina and had attended debates of a radical organization in New York.

Reading the formal charges against Levy, however, one could detect no hint of these motives. Levy was asked to defend himself against these accusations: that he had refused to obey the lawful command of Colonel Fancy to establish and operate a training program for Special Forces aidmen in dermatology; that, with the design of promoting disloyalty and disaffection among the troops, he had said the United States was wrong in being involved in the Vietnam war, that he would refuse to go if ordered, that blacks should refuse to go to Vietnam because they were discriminated against in this country, and that Special Forces personnel are liars and thieves and killers of peasants and murderers of women and children—"which statements," the charge ran, "were disloyal to the United States and prejudicial to good order and discipline in the armed forces"; and that he had been guilty of conduct unbecoming an officer and a gentleman by making the above remarks, which were "intemperate, defamatory, provoking, and disloyal."

After the trial had ended, Morgan looked back on these charges with a temperate eye: "The problem with Levy was, he was tried and convicted of crimes that don't exist. Like witchcraft and heresy. That's exactly what he was tried for. We went through a lot of years in this country with everybody thinking witchcraft and heresy were not things to be tried for, but that's what he was tried for, that's what he was convicted of, that's what he's serving a sentence for."

There had been two additional charges based on a letter Levy wrote to Sergeant First Class Geoffrey Hancock, Jr., a veteran of Vietnam. In this letter Levy had written such things as:

The only question that remains is essentially 1) were we merely naïve and therefore did we make unintentional mistakes or 2) does the U.S. foreign policy represent a diabolical evil? As you would guess, I opt for the second proposition. Is Communism worse than a U.S. oriented government? Are the North Vietnamese worse off than the South Vietnamese? I doubt it. . . . Geoffrey, who are you fighting for? Do you know? Have you thought about it? Your real battle is back here in the U.S. but why must I fight it for you . . . ? To destroy a child's life in Vietnam equals a destroyed life in Harlem. For what cause? Democ-

racy, Diem, Trujillo, Batista, Chiang Kai Shek, Franco, Tshombe—
Bullshit?

That letter was sent to Sergeant Hancock in September, 1965,
when Hancock was still in Vietnam. Far from persuading him the
war was unjust, it angered him. He didn't agree with Levy, and the
letter made him distressed that Levy was a captain in the Army.
Hancock did nothing with the letter until more than a year later
when he saw on a TV program that Levy had been arrested and
charged, at which time he hunted up the letter and passed it along
to Army authorities. They, in turn, forgot about it for a while, then
remembered it and dragged it out and slapped further charges on
Levy. The prosecution, however, made a technical error of some
sort in writing up the charges based on this letter, and so these
charges were dropped, cutting three years from the maximum
imprisonment hanging over Levy.

The ten men who decided Levy's fate were not a jury in the
constitutional sense; they were not unbiased (in the context of
their careers) and they were not his peers, though the Constitution
presumes to guarantee both. They were simply a panel of ten
dedicated Army officers. Each and every one promised under oath
to give Levy a fair trial, but promises cannot overcome such
obstacles. Thinking of these ten men, Levy's attorney Morgan said
later, "Any trial lawyer would trade every right in the Bill of
Rights for the right to choose the jury."

Dr. Levy was a civilian through and through, though he had
worn, piecemeal and in a sloppy fashion, the uniform of the Army
for nearly two years.

All the men on his panel were career Army officers; their
average length of service was slightly better than nineteen years.

Dr. Levy held the rank of captain; every man on the panel was
his superior in rank. The tone was set by the colonels.

For his verdict Dr. Levy, a Jew, looked to ten men who were
Catholic and Protestant.

If Dr. Levy had obtained notoriety around Fort Jackson and Columbia, it was not for his failure to train a few medics but for his enthusiastic support of the civil rights movement. Eight of the ten members of his panel were Southerners.

Next to his advocacy of the black man's cause, Dr. Levy's most inflammatory statements had been against U.S. participation in the Vietnam war. Four of the ten panel members were veterans of that war, a period of service to which they were grateful for helping them in their careers.

The ten impaneled majors and colonels had been selected from a panel approved by the base's commandant; they must have known that they would have not been sitting there and that the court-martial would not have been convened were not General Perez convinced of Levy's guilt. This conclusion was not peculiar to Levy's case; it is the conclusion correctly arrived at by every court-martial panel. The *Manual for Courts-Martial* specifically states that courts-martial should not be convened unless the evidence is heavily stacked on the side of guilt.

Looking up at that row of solemn-faced "jurymen," who stared coolly back through nineteen eyes (the twentieth eye had been lost in Vietnam), attorney Morgan, fortifying himself with the humor that he tapped throughout these weird proceedings, recalled one of his favorite passages from Kafka's *The Trial:*

"You know the Court much better than I do, I feel certain, I don't know much more about it than what I've heard from all sorts and conditions of people. But they all agree on one thing, that charges are never made frivolously, and that the Court, once it has brought a charge against someone, is firmly convinced of the guilt of the accused and can be dislodged from that conviction only with the greatest difficulty." "The greatest difficulty?" cried the painter, flinging one hand in the air. "The Court can never be dislodged from that conviction. If I were to paint all the Judges in a row on one canvas and you were to plead your case before it, you would have more hope of success than before the actual Court."

The judge for this trial was Colonel Earl Brown, the top lawyer in the Judge Advocate General's office, sent down especially from Washington to steer the Levy court-martial successfully to its conclusion. Did he play his part sincerely? Certainly it cannot be denied that the Army's machinery ground Levy down much more smoothly because of Colonel Brown's part in the trial. But just how sincere was he? And if he was not sincere, what a pitiful example he is of what the Army does to a man's spirit. The reason these questions arise at all is that Colonel Brown is no longer in the Army; not long after the Levy trial he left the Army for a post on the law faculty at Columbia University, where he joined a group of other professors in signing an ad in the *New York Times,* on February 15, 1968, which read in part:

We believe that the United States cannot by *acceptable means* succeed in its attempt to secure and maintain the control of the Saigon government over the territory of South Vietnam by military force. . . .
We believe that the terrible violence that the war is inflicting on the People of Vietnam is destroying the society we seek to protect. [Emphasis added.]

If Brown did not believe the United States could by acceptable means succeed in keeping the corrupt South Vietnamese government in power, then it could only mean that he believed the United States was using unacceptable means. Did this mean illegal means? War crimes perhaps? In 1967 he helped send a young doctor to Leavenworth for saying that. Would he really have enough gall to sign his name to a Levy-like statement less than a year later, and, if so, what sort of man must we judge Earl Brown to be?

As for the second part of the ad, this was what Levy had in mind, too, except he saw it applying especially to this country rather than to Vietnam. The expenses of a war that was supposed to be protecting the American way of life, in some remote fashion, was in his view destroying all attempts to raise the life of the Negro to truly American standards. The same Earl Brown who presided over the trial of Howard Levy for saying such things in 1967 echoed Levy's complaint in 1968. What must he have felt like when he did this? And if he felt nothing, what kind of man is he?

At first, during the court-martial, it seemed that Brown was a complex man, but later it turned out that he was only confused. What appeared to be sophistication, in the early days of the trial, later was discovered to be merely a kind of desperate flippancy.

For example, the mushy garbage that floats throughout the Uniform Code of Military Justice—phrases of indecipherable vagueness such as "conduct unbecoming an officer and a gentleman"—were picked over by Judge Brown as though they still contained some food value. But the longer he picked at them, the easier it was to measure his talents.

"Conduct unbecoming an officer and a gentleman" is an offense totally alien to civilian concepts of justice except for the civilian laws against pornography, laws whose standing grows shakier every day. The Constitution has decreed that a man cannot be convicted of an offense that is so vague nobody knows what the law covering that offense means. You can be convicted of murder if you kill somebody in a planned assault. You can be convicted of jaywalking if you cross the street where there is no pedestrian right-of-way. You can be convicted of littering if you throw paper on the sidewalk. But what action can you describe specifically (an action not covered by some other statute) that is "conduct unbecoming an officer and a gentleman"? The *Manual for Courts-Martial* gives this counsel:

There are certain moral attributes common to the ideal officer and the perfect gentleman, a lack of which is indicated by acts of dishonesty [Levy was altogether too honest for his own good] or unfair dealing [Levy might have escaped punishment if he had cheated on his superior officer's orders, but he didn't], of indecency or indecorum [would one statement, in private, that he would like to sleep with a good-looking black woman be sufficient?], or of lawlessness, injustice [he spent his weekends helping the Negroes of Newberry County fight injustice], or cruelty [the very thing he wanted to escape, which is why he refused to teach the Green Berets].

The charge can hardly be considered seriously. It would be equally hard to take seriously Judge Brown's remarks to the court that "any officer who is convicted of conduct unbecoming an officer and a gentleman violates this article." It is a perfectly circular argument.

Among Judge Brown's other revealing rulings, none got closer to the heart of his approach to law than the one he made when Morgan asked a friendly witness, Captain Joseph H. Feinstein, chaplain, what he thought the words "disloyal" and "disaffectionate" meant. It was a reasonable query. After all, perhaps the most serious charge against Levy was that he had said things that tended to promote disloyalty and disaffection among the ranks. Morgan had asked if he thought Levy was loyal to the United States, and Feinstein said he thought so. To make this answer meaningful, of course, the court would have to understand what the witness meant by the words "loyal" and "disloyal"—or the witness would have to understand what the court meant—and that was the reason Morgan had asked the question. Immediately Judge Brown cut him down, ruling: "I'll permit this witness' testimony whether or not he thought that under the circumstances the accused was disloyal or not because that is in issue. *But I am not particularly interested in any witness' idea of what is or is not disloyal. I will define that term to the court myself.*" (Emphasis added.)

But he did not do so at the moment, and Morgan pressed on.

Q: With respect to his character, is he loyal?
FEINSTEIN: I believe he is.
Q: Now, what do you base that belief on?

Brown cut him off again, saying, "You are asking strictly for a conclusion of this witness under what circumstances a person may be disloyal or may not be disloyal to the United States. *I don't think you have any expert who can testify as to that."* (Emphasis added.)

What a strange admission for the judge to make, that the meaning of loyalty is so abstract and elusive that it would be beyond the ability of the defense to obtain "any expert who can testify as to that." Could Judge Brown, then, define the terms? Morgan asked, and Brown sidestepped an answer. He was equally evasive later when Morgan, pressing the same line with another witness, Captain Robert Petres, a physician, again ran up against Judge Brown's trouble with definitions.

MORGAN: Did Dr. Levy ever talk to you about Vietnam?
PETRES: No, sir. No, we didn't talk about Vietnam, not at length. No, we never talked about Vietnam at all.
MORGAN: He never made you disloyal, did he?
PETRES: No, sir.
MORGAN: He never made you disaffect, did he?
PETRES: What does disaffect mean?
MORGAN: I don't know.
JUDGE BROWN: Mr. Morgan, if you don't know the questions, don't ask them.
MORGAN: Could I have a meaning from the court what disaffection is?
JUDGE BROWN: Should have asked it before you asked the question.
MORGAN: I asked for a ruling on disloyalty the other day and you said you would supply it before the case went to the jury. I am trying to make out a case of proof on disloyalty and disaffection. I have difficulty understanding what the words mean. . . .
       I am trying to get from you now a ruling as to the legal definition of disaffection.
JUDGE BROWN: And I am going to tell you now that you don't need it at this time. *All you have to do is ask this witness what he means by the use of that word.* [Emphasis added.]

Once again the judge had gone full circle. If that wasn't confusing enough to Morgan, eventually Judge Brown *did* hold an out-of-court hearing and expounded on his preferred definitions of disloyalty and disaffection, proposing words—"unfaithful," "disgust," "discontent"—that were no more definite than the words defined. He hemmed and hawed a while and finally said that he wasn't sure that those were the definitions he would stick with to the end of the trial "because I am not satisfied with them myself." Nevertheless, he repeated them substantially at the end of the trial when he was giving instructions to the panel, equating disaffection, for example, with "disgust and discontentment, ill will, disloyalty and hostility."

Thus was Levy convicted for a crime that the judge himself could not define to his own satisfaction.

Morgan, as we have seen in earlier excerpts from the trial record, was also up against some of the most forgetful witnesses ever paraded through a court. Army witness after Army witness could not recall key details. Sergeant Landing, for example, on whose word the Army based much of its case, worked under Levy several hours a day for more than a year, and yet he could not recall one single thing that Levy talked about except the half-dozen statements on which the court-martial rested.

Morgan was also plagued with some of the tidiest people in the world. They burned things. Crucial notes that might have helped Levy's case—sorry, they were burned. To appreciate Morgan's ordeal, consider this cross-examination of Colonel Fancy, who had just testified that when he ordered Levy to train the Special Forces, Levy had answered that he wouldn't because they were killers and thieves:

MORGAN: You didn't remember on January 13, 1967, what he [Levy] said, did you?
FANCY: No, I did not.
MORGAN: But you now remember?
FANCY: Yes, sir.
MORGAN: You tend to remember things later better than earlier?

FANCY: No, I reviewed some notes that I had after the Article 32.
MORGAN: Do you have those notes?
FANCY: I don't.
MORGAN: Did you destroy them or have them in your possession
some other place?
FANCY: They are all destroyed.

Fancy wasn't the only man who was fast with a match. This is
an exchange with agent West:

MORGAN: What was that paper you were referring to there?
WEST: Just a card on the dates so I would remember when—
MORGAN: You don't keep any notes?
WEST: No, our notes are destroyed in our office. We have only a
field office. My office is in Atlanta and they are destroyed after
thirty days after the report goes in after they see them there.
MORGAN: Where did you get the information that is on here, on
these notes you are referring to?
WEST: I got the information from my agent's report. I have burned
copies of them now.

Against the charge of disobedience, the defense could have
raised the rebuttal that—contrary to Army myth—disobedience is
rather common and seldom punished, especially among Army
doctors. In a panel discussion sponsored by the Harvard Medical
School a couple of years ago, Colonel James B. Caskie, base
hospital commander at Fort Devens, Massachusetts, admitted,
"I've refused to obey orders many times in my twenty-year career
and haven't been court-martialed yet." If physicians in the Army
are doing their jobs conscientiously, they are normally given considerable leeway as to what outside orders they will permit to
break into their patterned professionalism. After the imprisonment
of Levy, another physician at Fort Jackson refused to train Green
Beret medics and nothing was done to him. The rules are flexible,
and if they were imposed on Levy, it was because the Army decided he was worth singling out.

The delicacies that must be observed by superior officers in
handling doctors in the service is recognized by most military

physicians with experience in this problem. No less an authority than Colonel Richard L. Coppedge, former chief surgeon of Special Forces and developer of the Special Forces aidman concept, testified on this point:

In their training, medical people—physicians—are certainly taught to differ from their instructors or their superiors on any point. If you feel a patient should be treated one way and the professor feels he ought to be treated another way, it is your patient, and really he [the superior] has got to justify to you in effect, with the treatment he thinks is better. Well, in other words, it's not so much an appeal to authority on this but an appeal to reason. This can't be entirely discarded like that just because you put on a uniform. Certainly the uniform adds to the authority—makes authority a little more acceptable perhaps. This makes handling physicians one of the most difficult jobs in medical service. In my own experience, in war times, it is required of a senior staff officer or hospital or medical commander—more time is required of such an individual in handling people, particularly his physicians, than any other single segment of his duties. You've got really talented people here, and in order to exploit them, in order to use them and employ them, it demands a little extra attention—quite a bit of extra attention.

Colonel Fancy gave Levy no extra attention, until he had decided to help purge him. Colonel Coppedge said if he had been in Fancy's shoes, he would have tried to show Levy the positive side of the Special Forces aidmen's work because he thought Levy was just the kind of man the Army needs. Why? "Because I think Captain Levy is interested in the society around him. He's interested not only in individual patients and cities, but he's interested in the people around, and that's the kind of person that we need."

Maybe there is, in fact, no positive side to the aidman's duties. But if there is, Colonel Fancy did not try to find it and explain it to Levy. If Coppedge, the father of the aidmen's program, wasn't angry with Levy, if he thought the young Captain more than salvageable, why did General Perez, Colonel Fancy, agent West *et al.* feel differently? This sort of question kept coming back throughout this trial, and the answer on the threshold kept looking suspiciously like a black man.

In any event, the *tu quoque* argument is too feeble to use in a court-martial, and Levy's attorneys didn't try it. But they did try to prove—and came amazingly close to proving—that in fact there had been nothing to disobey.

Captain Ernest P. Porter, ophthalmologist, testified that, for all practical purposes, the medical program Levy was accused of refusing to participate in did not exist. When he (Porter) first entered the program of training Special Forces aidmen, he said, "I had no information as to what they were to be taught." So he just let them "look over my shoulder." He thought that they needn't be taught more than first aid, and he refused to let them use his equipment. Only *after* Levy's court-martial began, he said, did he receive anything that described a program: "I have a sheet which says five diseases that they are to be familiar with. This was received by me a matter of a few months ago, sometime after the Levy court-martial had started." Even so, there was evidence that the program had been thrown together with such speed that it was aimed more at producing results in the court-martial than in the training of aidmen. Said Porter: "It listed conjunctivitis, blepharitis, cataracts, glaucoma, and herpes keratitis. It listed these five entities, with no information as to what they were to know about them, what they had to work with in dealing with these diseases. It only listed them, saying they should know about these diseases, and at this time I was somewhat confused because these are not all emergency problems."

MORGAN: And what did you do with respect to the training of special forces aidmen regarding these medical problems that were not emergency problems?

PORTER: I continued to teach them in the clinic about blepharitis and conjunctivitis and these diseases and entities that I thought they would encounter in the field, again *still having received no information* as to what their duties were and how they were to function. At that time I still had no information. *As of yesterday,* I received information as to how these Special Forces men were to function, what their roles were, how they were trained, what equipment they had available. There was a meeting held yesterday which some of the medical officers were requested to attend, and we were informed by Captain McBride, I believe from Ft. Sam Houston. . . . [Emphasis added.]

MORGAN: You mean—in the middle of this trial, Special Forces flew a man in to tell the doctors in the hospital here what their duty was to have been?

The answer was yes. That was exactly what had happened. Until Levy was put on trial, some doctors—perhaps all the doctors—at Fort Jackson who were supposed to be training Special Forces aidmen had not been told why or to what purpose, and since they did not know that, neither did they know *how* to train them. Levy was on trial for refusing to obey an impossible order because it was without substance. If he had refused an order to teach someone to walk on water, he would have been no more guilty. Or, rather, it would have been no more possible to attribute guilt to him.

In support of the charges both of disobedience and of using insulting language to the Special Forces medics who came around his office (conduct unbecoming), the prosecution trotted out affidavits collected by the counterintelligence agents. But West's proved to be singularly distorted and inaccurate. For instance, he wrote in one of his reports: "In early September 1966 four Special Forces students who had just completed their training, told Source that they had been harassed verbally by Levy . . . and that they were told to leave the dermatology section because Subject would not instruct or train them." The four men who allegedly made these charges were named Hickman, Crane, Hutto and Shimamoto. Hutto's affidavit is not available for quotation. But the others are, and they show how untrustworthy were agent West's reports.

Hickman said in his affidavit: "I had no particular complaint with Levy . . . I have no reason to question Levy's loyalty."

Crane was quoted as saying he considered Levy "a superior dermatologist." Crane said he was trained by Levy's staff, without Levy's objection. Far from being repelled by Levy, Crane was fascinated by him: "I consider Levy to have a very intricate mind and would like the chance to work for him for an extended period just to try to find out why he acts as he does. I do not recall having discussed politics with Levy. . . . I have no reason to question Levy's loyalty."

Shimamoto said he had never heard Levy say anything against the Special Forces "except in a joking manner." Some hubcaps were missing and Levy told Shimamoto jokingly, "I'd better check these Special Forces people." (Not a bad idea, in fact, since they had been the prime suspects in some thefts from Levy's office.)

It is significant that these generally favorable memories of Levy were elicited by a counterintelligence agent other than West. Other agents, for some reason, could find soldiers who liked Levy; West rarely could. One Special Forces aidman who had been assigned to Levy's office during the last of May said Levy never mentioned Vietnam, did not condemn the Special Forces, and "he allowed me to observe his treatment of patients and did not deny any training to me." This young man was searched out and interviewed by counterintelligence agent Robert LeFaiver—not by West.*

At first, in an apparent effort to show that Levy was not being singled out for persecution, Fancy's executive assistant, Colonel Chester Davis, said that he believed one other officer's file was also flagged. Aha, said Morgan, then let us produce that other officer's

---

* It might be well to point out that although an estimated seventeen thousand patients went through Dr. Levy's clinic in the time he was at Fort Jackson, and although the prosecution sent out thousands of questionnaires seeking to find people who had been offended or damaged mentally or misled by Levy's conversation, the prosecution could find only two Negroes who had talked with Levy about Vietnam and could recruit a total of only a dozen witnesses ready to put in a word against him. If a civilian doctor could please his patients one-half so well, he would be ecstatic. But none of the witnesses felt that he had been made to feel even a momentary twinge of disloyalty or disaffection.

file immediately to see *why* he was flagged, *how* the investigation of his case was conducted and how swiftly the case was cleared. The best way to decide whether Levy was being discriminated against, said Morgan, was to compare his case with another's.

At that point Colonel Davis suddenly changed his mind; suddenly he decided he was wrong—there had not been another flagging after all. "I did say that, but it was not correct." No, no, no, nothing like a flag. It was simply a standard security investigation. And, anyway, it had all been "already cleared before he came to this post." But Morgan was not willing to let up quite that easily. He backed through the murk of Colonel Davis' memory to see if he perhaps could not come up with some details. *Why* had this other officer been under investigation?

It was because the officer had belonged to some organization, said Colonel Davis, some suspicious organization. "Friend," said Colonel Davis, in tones anything but friendly, "I could not tell you one of those outfits from the other. But it was an organization which has demonstrated against the war in Vietnam and which has worked with the Negro in the South and ordered demonstrations and marches." No wonder the man was investigated.

But when Morgan persisted, demanding that the other officer's file be produced for comparison, the court refused.

In his summation, the staff judge advocate claimed that even the defense's own witnesses had pinpointed Levy's weakness, to wit: "His own witnesses described him as a volatile, dedicated, hardworking person, devoted to the cause of civil rights. . . . All the evidence in the case, including that introduced by the defense, paints the accused as a man sincerely, perhaps even fanatically concerned with the problems of minority groups and devoted to the advancement of their cause." Then, perhaps to show that he wanted to be fair, the general's attorney added: "This in itself, of course, is not culpable."

It was about the only concession Morgan and the other defense attorneys wrung from the Army—that being devoted to the cause of minority groups is not *in itself* culpable. Joined with an antipathy for war, however, it seems to become very culpable, not to mention unbalanced—"The accused lost his entire sense of perspective in this area and for some obscure and illogical reason related the cause of civil rights to the Vietnam war."

It may very easily have been true that the Army viewed Captain Levy as a bona fide Communist. The Army has its own definition of such things. Judging from his remarks at the court-martial, Colonel Fancy would undoubtedly stand for the true Army position. He did not pretend to a scholarly appraisal of Communism; after all, he had obtained his ideas about Communism, he admitted, solely from "the various news media and magazines and have read about Communism in various military courses that I have taken," but he felt that he had a rather good general idea of what Communism is.

One of the things Communists do, he testified, is excite the downtrodden into a state of "chronic anxiety." He was unable to give any specific examples of what he meant, but he could speak generally: "Well, one example might be a labor union that is infiltrated with communist sympathizers. Certain labor unions ordering or provoking strikes against industries, hospitals or what have you. This would produce anxiety in the people that worked in the industries or hospitals."

Q: What about racial demonstrations?
FANCY: I would feel that this might be a fruitful ground for communist sympathizers to use the techniques of agitation and produce anxiety in the community.
Q: Do you see much evidence of that in the civil rights movement?
FANCY: I have very little to do with the civil rights movement. From what I have read, this seems perfectly possible.

Furthermore, said Fancy, the Communists' disbelief in God bothered him tremendously, for it went against the traditions established by the founding fathers of this country. Asked to be more specific about which founding fathers he had in mind, Fancy said he was thinking especially of Thomas Jefferson and Benjamin Franklin. It was a rather pitiful choice, since both Jefferson and Franklin were notorious freethinkers.

Q: And do you think that much of the agitation about American involvement in Vietnam is—in this country—communist based?
FANCY: I believe so.
Q: How about the people who oppose the bombings in Vietnam, do you believe they are actually sympathetic to the communist line?
FANCY: I believe it is possible.

It was this credo that had prompted Colonel Fancy to address a graduating class of Special Forces aidmen with the remarks that the threat of Communism was as present here as abroad, that the nation was being pestered by "left-wingers" and that the Special Forces troopers should not pay any attention to them but to go into battle with the assurance that "we are behind you."

All of this Morgan dragged from the reluctant and forgetful colonel at the preliminary hearing, scrap by scrap, until the presiding officer came to his brother colonel's rescue.

What, he asked Morgan, did his questions tie into? After all, the colonel had already testified that the charges preferred against Levy had nothing to do with his political beliefs.

MORGAN: That is fine, but I think the Colonel is lying.
OFFICER: Are you trying to relate this to—
MORGAN: I am trying to prove that the Colonel is a liar, yes.

Now that was the kind of civilian talk that cleared the air. Because of the chronology of the action, Morgan was sure that Levy's "politics" were the key to the persecution. It was only after civil rights activities and left-wing reading-and-listening had been translated for Fancy as "Communistic" that he was disturbed, and he was disturbed because it seemed the general was disturbed.

In attempting to rebut the "conduct unbecoming an officer" charge, Morgan found a publication called *The Armed Forces' Officer,* which is put out by the Department of Defense. In this official publication, the hallmarks of a good officer and gentleman were listed: "This is number one. A man has honor if he holds himself to a course of conduct because of a conviction that is in the general interest even though he is well aware that it may lead to inconvenience, personal loss, humiliation, or grave physical risk." Morgan had no trouble finding Fort Jackson officers who said that certainly sounded like Levy.

Likewise he easily won agreement from officer witnesses who knew Levy that the following passage from the DOD booklet sounded much like him: "Secondly, he has veracity if, having studied a question to the limit of his ability, he says and believes what he thinks to be true even though it would be the path of least resistance to deceive others and himself."

The booklet said these Levyesque characteristics were "virtues which provide a firm foundation for patriotism." Morgan's rhetoric on this point seemed to bore the panel.

In the eyes of the military the only practical defense Levy could raise had nothing to do with ethics or conscience—that is, with a man's personal judgment of the facts—but only with the facts themselves. Had he refused to train the Special Services personnel or hadn't he? If he had refused, then he was guilty as charged, and there was no use arguing about whether the training that had been ordered was a virtuous activity. Had he suggested that black soldiers were fools to fight in Vietnam, and, if so, had he made the suggestion in order to discourage such service? If so, then he was guilty as charged, and there was no use arguing about the justice of making oppressed citizens fight for their oppressors. Had he called the Green Berets "thieves" and "killers of peasants" and "murderers of women and children" in order to spread discontent among the troops? If he had, then he was guilty as charged, and there was no use proving that the Green Berets were in fact thieves and killers of peasants and women and children.

He could not plead the truth as a defense against the charge of acting in an ungentlemanly and unofficer-like way; he could not plead the truth in his description of the conduct of the Green Berets as a reason for disobedience. The court would not permit it. The truth had very low status in this court-martial.

MORGAN: Could a man be dishonorable who speaks the truth?
JUDGE BROWN: . . . the dishonor is not only to the individual as a person but to the position as an officer in the United States Army.
MORGAN: Let me carry that further then. Could the question of truth result in dishonor to the position that the man has as a Captain in the United States Army?
BROWN: Oh, yes. I think so. I don't see where truth is really an issue here.

With truth ruled out as being irrelevant, what was left for Morgan to do? There was nothing left to do. With that handicap imposed on the defense, the joust appeared about to come to a halt. The trial was about to die—sending home the sixty reporters who were daily making Judge Brown's name known around the world and who were beating into the consciousness of military officers everywhere the futility of bucking the system.

So, at that critical juncture, Judge Brown astonished the court by proposing that the trial could be channeled down new, dramatic corridors. If Morgan could prove, he said, that the Green Berets were committing war crimes—real war crimes, heinous, infamous war crimes redolent of the Nuremberg Trials—then Levy might be excused for refusing to obey the order to train the perpetrators of those crimes. Yes, that would be an entertaining turn, and Judge Brown offered an out-of-court hearing for Levy's attorneys to bring in evidence to show that the court should consider a Nuremberg defense.

The defense had not asked for this opportunity. In fact, it was flabbergasted by the proposal. To be offered the task of proving that the United States military machine was consciously constructing an apparatus for indulging in war crimes of the Nazi kind, and the further task of proving this to the satisfaction of a panel of colonels who were part of the military machine, hardly seemed like the most promising way to save Levy. Attorney Morgan had, indeed—using Levy's Jewishness as a kind of courtroom gimmick—dabbled already at creating an aura of Nuremberg in the Fort Jackson courtroom. But he had not meant it *that* seriously. Now the choice was no longer his to play with. Judge Brown had decided for him, and it was plain that the judge enjoyed the excitement he was creating. "This is the first time I know of that it [the Nuremberg action] has entered into a domestic court as a defense," he said. "My research discloses the Nuremberg trials involve a rule that a soldier must refuse an order to commit war crimes." And he added that the United States, since World War II, had made the Nuremberg decisions applicable to American courts. He cautioned the defense, needlessly, that "we have to feel our way in regard to making a prima facie case of war crimes and crimes against humanity."

There is no agreement among the experts as to what exactly the Nuremberg decisions mean. Invoked against the Nazi defendants was Article 8 of the London Agreement of 1945 (which, however, was never ratified by the U.S. Senate): "The fact that the defendant acted pursuant to order of his government or of a superior shall not free him from responsibility, but may be considered in mitigation of punishment if the tribunal determines that justice so requires." But how far down the ranks does this go?

Some feel that no serviceman or civilian—at any level—can avoid being held responsible for his acts merely by being able to prove that he was following orders; conscience must be the final arbiter. Others say that only soldiers at the policy-making level can be held accountable. In either event, only in the war-crimes trials after World War II have these questions been more than hypo-

thetical; in the practical day-to-day operation of the world's
armies, it comes down to this, in the words of Detlev Vagts of the
Harvard Law School: "A point can come when an individual says
the system is false and he won't support it. But when a person
takes that stand no one can help him. There is no legal defense."

One keeps coming back to the question of the primacy of discipline, the sanctity of an order. This is what Nuremberg was all
about, and it is one of the things that Fort Jackson was about.

Q: Well, now, if you were running a hospital in Germany in 1943,
and were given orders to perform human experiments and to administer such a program, you know what you would have done
then, don't you?
COLONEL DAVIS: I don't know.

Judge Brown admitted that Levy's impulses were correct and
just; he admitted that "if there is an objectively true . . . directive that these aidmen were to be trained to commit war crimes,
then I think a doctor would be morally bound to refuse to give his
aid and comfort and training to these individuals."

So by Judge Brown's own admission, the question of Levy's
guilt rested *not* on his refusal to obey an order but upon his
judgment of whether or not the order was legal. Levy was on
trial—or, Judge Brown seemed momentarily to agree, should have
been on trial—not for his act (refusing to obey an order) but for his
judgment. That is, did he or did he not have reasonable grounds
for thinking the men he trained would perpetrate war crimes? Or
to approach it a different way, did Colonel Fancy have any
grounds for thinking that the Green Beret medics would *not*
perpetrate war crimes? When Captain Levy informed him as to his
reasons for not wanting to train the Green Berets, wasn't it
Colonel Fancy's duty to find out if Levy was telling the truth, and
thereafter to explain his error to him, if he was in error? One
would suppose that since the Nuremberg Trials the concept of
blind obedience to orders (except perhaps under fire), where there

was a question of possible war crimes, would not be insisted on in behind-the-lines duty.

Only momentarily dismayed by this new "opportunity," Morgan set about his job, announcing through the press his critical need for evidence. "The time has come for those, here and abroad, who charge war crimes to step forward to the witness stand," he was quoted by Homer Bigart of the *New York Times*. The phone calls came in—from England, Japan, Germany, Sweden—giving tips, some sound evidence, much useless advice. In came some written evidence, too, including a massive bundle from Bertrand Russell "big enough," Morgan recalls, "to contain Bertrand Russell himself. From a woman I received half of an antipersonnel bomb. I didn't know what it was—it could have been a chastity belt for all I knew." Morgan would need much more time to get organized. Perhaps a joke would swing it; not too much humor, just a little irony:

MORGAN: Now with respect to the question of war crimes and crimes against humanity . . . It might take an extra day to prove that.

JUDGE BROWN: I'll give you an extra day.

So much for the fate of humor at Fort Jackson. But in the end Brown was more generous; he gave Morgan six days to prepare himself. It was such a mad moment, as Morgan describes it, that "had Sigmund Freud been present, he no doubt would have sought psychiatric assistance from Franz Kafka." There was no time for fresh research, or for verifying some of the new horror tales pouring in, and so in the end Morgan fell back on old, well-known experts: Robin Moore, who spent a considerable time running with the troops to gather information for his book, *The Green Berets;* Donald Duncan, former master sergeant, for eighteen months with the Special Forces in Vietnam and now *Ramparts* magazine's military expert; and Captain Peter Bourne, an Army doctor who won the Bronze Star and the Air Medal during Vietnam service as chief of a Walter Reed Army Medical Center research team studying stress. Bourne had spent four months in the jungles with Special Forces "A" teams.

Even so, relying primarily on these three witnesses, a remarkably complete picture of mini-Nazism in Vietnam came through.

Judge Brown's instructions to Morgan had been that he must show more than isolated incidents of war crimes; he must show that war crimes were being committed "as a general pattern of practice." Brown added, "I think you'll have a difficult time finding anyone to testify to that." But it wasn't so difficult as the colonel had thought. Using as his baffle the Army's manual, *The Law of Land Warfare,* wherein war crimes are defined, attorney Morgan jangled out this contrapuntal tune:

Paragraph 281 of *The Law of Land Warfare* prohibits assigned residence in these terms: "The internment or placing in assigned residence of protected persons [civilians] may be ordered only if the security of the Detaining Power makes it absolutely necessary." It does not say the civilians can be shifted around, their homes destroyed, their lives totally dislocated merely to satisfy a particular warfare technique or because the conquering army feels that it is a good idea. It can be done *only* if there is no other way to wage the war.

Robin Moore testified: "One of the jobs of the Special Forces is to go into a village—a Montagnard village, say, and get all the Montagnards out and bring them into sort of refugee centers where they could be guarded and kept from the Viet Cong and then burn the village so it would be of no more use to the Viet Cong."

Other testimony revealed techniques of burning or poisoning crops. Moore, Duncan and Bourne testified that the destruction of villages and the resettlement of their inhabitants was no freak occurrence but was a *policy* of our government.

Paragraph 504(C) of *The Law of Land Warfare* prohibits the "maltreatment of dead bodies" and calls this maltreatment a war crime.

Moore said that it was commonplace for the local troops, whom the Special Forces supervised, to decapitate the enemy because "the Buddhists believe that if you cut their heads off their souls will wander forever." Vietnamese trained by Special Forces cut the ears off the enemy as a "tally count," Moore explained. "We were paying bounty for the Vietcong dead (10 piastres an ear). We had only a man's word unless we had something to prove it. You know it's very difficult to clip a man's ears unless you have him under complete control."

Putting a price on ears amounts to putting a price on the enemy's head, and that is prohibited by Paragraph 31 of *The Law of Land Warfare.*

Also prohibited by Paragraph 31 are assassinations of the enemy, whether civilian or military. Testimony given at the Levy trial showed that assassination assignments were routine.

Q: Is there any way to fight guerrilla warfare by the rules?
MOORE: Not that I know of. I have never seen it work yet.
Q: Regarding that, as I recall it, you talked about assassination teams. What is an assassination team?
MOORE: Well, it's a team trained to hit targets, a target being the term generally used for an individual to be assassinated *for political reasons or whatever. . . . It is an integral part of guerrilla warfare* just as is medical people trying to help the people of an area to win the hearts and minds of the people. An assassination is also an important aspect. *If you have a political chief, say in Vietnam, and you know that a political—a certain individual very high up in the National Liberation Front, that he is damaging our effort, it only makes sense to assassinate him if possible.*
Q: *Special Forces train them don't they?*
MOORE: *I know of an instance where Special Forces are giving this advice.* Thank God they are, because the Vietnamese do a pretty botched up job of it if left to their own devices. [Emphasis added.]

Paragraphs 29 and 89 forbid mistreatment of prisoners of war; Paragraphs 93, 270 and 271 forbid torture to extract information.

Moore, Duncan and Bourne agreed they had never seen Special
Forces troopers torturing prisoners. The prisoners are, instead,
turned over to the South Vietnamese guerrilla forces, who torture
them.

Captain Bourne acknowledged that the South Vietnamese
guerrilla bands who operate with small teams of Green Berets,
although "technically they are part of the South Vietnamese Army,
in actual practice they are under our control. We pay them. In
actual fact, all command decisions, all policy decisions, are in the
hands of the Special Forces."

As a result of those command and policy decisions, torture takes
place commonly. "I was out on a patrol [with the South Vietnamese guerrillas] where we captured a village in which there
were VC or VC sympathizers. After a while, when the houses were
burning—they had set them on fire—I found a man tied up on the
floor. I yelled, 'Are you planning to burn this man alive?' The
Vietnamese lieutenant laughed and said, 'He's dead.' I untied the
man and got him out of the hut. The Vietnamese lieutenant was
incensed. I knew if I left the prisoner, they'd kill him as soon as
my back was turned. I talked to the American captain who was in
charge but he said, 'Don't rock the boat.' "

Moore said: "I've never seen an example of torture or atrocities
when an American was present. But the only way the American
soldier could express dissent was to walk off. If he tried to protest,
he would be relieved and his career would suffer."

Duncan testified: "The normal practice was that when it [tor-
ture] started you turned around and lit a cigarette."

The Levy defense put together an impressive list of the methods
of torture practiced by the Special Forces' native helpers, including: tearing out fingernails by the roots, cutting off fingers, attach-
ing electric wires to a generator at one end and a man's (or
woman's) breast at the other, squeezing testicles in a vice, wiring a
man's hands to his face by running the wire through the hands and
the cheeks.

Q: Now, regarding the South Vietnamese and prisoners, we do, even with knowledge of what will happen to these prisoners, turn them over to the South Vietnamese, don't we?

MOORE: Well, we have to turn them over. It's the rules.

Earlier he had said that in guerrilla warfare one cannot play by the rules; but when it comes to permitting torture, apparently we try.

Throughout 1970 the Citizens Commission of Inquiry, led by such men as Dick Gregory and Melvin Wulf, obtained new information which greatly broadened the indictment of torture and even murder by our troops.

Among the counterintelligence special agents and prisoner of war interrogators and other personnel who told what they had seen and sometimes had taken part in was Stephen Noetzle, thirty, of Floral Park, N.Y., who served with the Special Forces in 1963 and 1964. He said that Green Beret interrogators had exotic techniques for obtaining information, such as squeezing the victims into tightly-fitting cages of barbed wire. He said he had seen Vietnamese made to wear a steel helmet to which was wired a field telephone; then they were doused with water, and the phone was cranked. The harder the crank, the more painful the shock.

Usually the phone wires were attached directly to sensitive parts of the body before the cranking. John Patton, a former second lieu-tenant with the 11th Brigade of the American Division who now lives in Fort Lauderdale, Florida, and Michael J. Uhl, a former first lieutenant with the same outfit who now lives in Babylon, New York, told of seeing a sixteen-year-old girl's body wired up in this way; when the telephone was cranked "rather hard," she began menstru-ating heavily. Patton (who supervised the torture techniques on some occasions, but says he eventually stopped using the electrical method) tested the phone cranking on himself and admitted he had found it to be "very uncomfortable . . . it's just like sticking your finger in a socket."

From testimony before the Commission, it seemed clear that the torturing of civilian prisoners was especially commonplace. Patton said that the main thing interrogators kept in mind was not to beat and abuse their prisoners in such a way as to leave bruises: "That's the main thing—that's what comes down from command."

Fred Brown, twenty-six, of Anaheim, California, who served in the 172nd Military Intelligence Department, attached to the 173rd Airborne Brigade, said: "When we were under extreme pressure to get information, [our commanding officer] would tell the men that as long as no marks are left on the prisoners, it was all right for us to use force. But we would be held responsible if there were marks."

Brown said that only about one out of every thirty persons subjected to torture supplied any information of tactical value.

The Pentagon has not responded to inquiries about what it intends to do about these tortures, but the spirit of the military has been plainly indicated by the fact that servicemen who had attempted to gather information about other brutalities have been threatened with court-martial.

Paragraph 500 of *The Law of Land Warfare* defines complicity in a war crime as a war crime itself. Article 8 of the charter under which the international military tribunal at Nuremberg operated states that "The fact that the defendant acted pursuant to order of his government or of a superior shall not free him from responsibility." Article 6 of the Nuremberg charter provides that "Leaders, organizers, instigators, and accomplices participating in the formulation or execution of a common plan or conspiracy to commit any of the foregoing crimes are responsible for all acts performed by any persons in execution of such plans."

The Green Berets, everyone concedes, do lead, organize and instigate the civilian guerrilla forces of South Vietnam, who frequently commit war crimes. "The foregoing crimes" of which the Nuremberg charter spoke included the murder of prisoners, the extermination of political commissars, the plunder of occupied territories, the ill treatment of the civilian population and the exploitation of the inhabitants of occupied countries as slave labor—all of which crimes have been committed by the civilian guerrillas of South Vietnam, as testimony showed.

Ira Glasser, one of Morgan's assistants, spelled out the conclusion that is inevitable:

The chilling fact is that the Army does not deny the existence of war crimes. It simply denies its responsibility for such crimes, despite the clear requirements of its own written law. The Army continues to protest that American soldiers do not themselves practice torture or commit murder, as if that fact alone released them from all charges of complicity. Adolf Eichmann lodged a similar protest at his trial in Jerusalem, when he said, "With the killing of Jews I had nothing to do. I never killed a Jew, or a non-Jew for that matter—I never killed any human being. I never gave an order to kill either a Jew or a non-Jew. I just did not do it." And so the Special Forces do not practice torture in Vietnam. Torture just happens, murder just happens, war crimes just happen. No one does it. No one is responsible. It's called complicity.

What, then, is the role of the Special Forces aidmen in all this—the aidmen being the personnel whom Dr. Levy refused to train because he felt that they would not use their training for man's well-being? Did the aidmen participate in these crueler devices? Colonel Roger A. Juel, who was in charge of Special Forces aidmen training, testified:

Q: The nature of a Special Forces mission may require that all twelve members of an A team participate in combat operations?
JUEL: Most surely.
Q: And it may require—well, let me put it this way—at the optimum, all twelve members of the A team would know about all other fields of specialty on the A team?
JUEL: This is an ideal which is never achieved, and everyone is cross-trained, however, to the extent that time permits.
Q: An ordinary medical corpsman could be a conscientious objector, could he not?
JUEL: In the Army, yes.

Q:  And he could not be ordered to kill, could he?
JUEL:  Right.
Q:  But a Special Forces aidman can?
JUEL:  Correct.
Q:  And, consequently, an aidman then finds himself in a position by the government and the program itself, of from time to time having to kill people?
JUEL:  Special Forces trooper is basically a soldier *and an aidman as a secondary occupation.* [Emphasis added.]

In another exchange, Juel spelled out the aidman's tough job more fully:

Q:  Now a statement was made that there is rarely a doctor on patrol, but isn't it often true that Special Forces aidmen are on combat by the nature of the mission of Special Forces?
JUEL:  This is the mission of all of Special Forces.
Q:  Now is not the mission of Special Forces: (a) to plan and conduct unconventional warfare operations in areas not under friendly control; (b) *to organize, equip, train, and direct indigenous forces in the conduct of guerrilla warfare;* (c) *to train, advise, and assist indigenous forces in the conduct of counterinsurgency and counter-guerrilla operations in support of U.S. cold war objectives;* and (d) to perform such other Special Forces missions as may be inherent in or essential to the primary mission of guerrilla warfare? [Emphasis added.]
JUEL:  This sounds to me like it approximates their objectives, yes.

Captain Bourne agreed:

Q:  As I understand medics [meaning the ordinary Army medic], they carry sidearms and are required to stay and protect their patients, are they not?
BOURNE:  This is my understanding, yes.
Q:  As I understand Special Forces aidmen, they leave their patients when the A Team moves out. Is that correct?
BOURNE:  I think so because I think their primary obligation is to the military situation, and I think they are combat soldiers first, and aidmen second.

Moore confirmed this further, with an additional emphasis:

Q:  And there is a difference between an ordinary medic and a

Special Forces aidman?

MOORE: Well, Special Forces—there are certainly conscientious objectors who make good medics [for the regular troops], I am sure, but not Special Forces because they have to be able to fight. That is why they are out there, that is why there is only twelve of them. *Everyone can do everyone else's job.* [Emphasis added.]

In his book *Green Berets,* Moore had written: "A medic, say, can not only efficiently patch up the wounded and care for the sick, but knows how to lay down a deadly accurate mortar barrage and blow up the enemy's rail lines and bridges."

This is what Colonel Juel had meant when he said that everyone in Special Forces, including aidmen, is "cross-trained"—everyone is trained in all aspects of warfare—including the training of assassination teams. In short, Special Forces aidmen are sometimes called upon to violate the laws of land warfare and are therefore sometimes called upon to commit war crimes. This is what Morgan had contended all along.

Morgan also contended that aidmen sometimes use their medical training in intelligence work—and Moore testified that he had seen aidmen giving captives sodium pentothal, the truth drug, before interrogations. Finally, Morgan asserted that, in addition to everything else—in addition to their work as killers and trainers of killers—the aidmen employed their medicine as a political gimmick, almost as political trickery.

Duncan testified: "In many areas in which you will go, you are going to be very unpopular, especially you as a guy carrying a gun, who is coming in there trying to organize them into going out to get themselves shot in some sort of a village defense organization. The one great 'in' that you have is this medic because people are short on doctors and trained medical personnel in there. The one thing to do is sort of push a medic up there in front and let him get the confidence of these people by treating them. Usually it starts off very slow, but the word gets around. Then, of course, this lays the way open now for the rest of the team to come in and organize them in their primary mission . . . it could be civilian guerrilla forces." The political character of the aidman's work was also verified by Colonel Coppedge, formerly Special Forces chief surgeon: "So in this way, we sought to use medicine as a means of approaching the enemy and imposing our will on his. . . . Certainly it is political. This is a political use of medicine; certainly its effects are political. The motives of those who engage in it may differ."

Then the trial shifted gears again. Having himself opened the trial to the consideration of war crimes as a possible excuse for Levy's actions, Judge Brown suddenly and just as unpredictably closed off the flow of evidence. Along with a few days of splashy headlines that kept him and the trial played high in the daily press, the war-crimes diversion had also, through Morgan's adroitness, been made a serious consideration. Perhaps too serious for the comfort of the military.

Mulling over the impact of the war crimes development, Homer Bigart wrote in the *Times:* "Acquittal in the Levy case could conceivably promote disobedience of orders by thousands of enlisted personnel who don't want to go to Vietnam. They might argue that any personal involvement in that war would be criminal." And Nicholas von Hoffman wrote in the Washington *Post:* "There is a tincture of intimidation about the courtroom. And underneath you sense the fear that if Levy gets away, the whole Army will fling down its guns and run back home to watch television and drink beer. 'Well, there is that fear,' says an Army captain. 'That's why after every court-martial they put the findings up on all the post bulletin boards.' "

By the time Morgan had unloaded the first volley of his Green Beret material on the court the Army must have realized that even something short of an acquittal could damage discipline; further exposure of war crimes, even if the exposure did Levy no good, might free the consciences of many soldiers who would—threat of prison or no threat—set out to imitate Levy's stand. The war-crimes portion of the trial had to be cut off. So in the afternoon of May 25, 1967, Judge Brown did it by ruling, "While there have been perhaps instances of needless brutality in this struggle in Vietnam . . . my conclusion is that there is no evidence that would render this order to train aidmen illegal on the grounds that eventually these men would become engaged in war crimes or in some way prostitute their medical training by employing it in crimes against humanity."

And that was the end of that. It came as no surprise to Morgan, and it came as no surprise to anyone else who had listened closely to Judge Brown's remarks at the time he opened the war-crimes hearing. "Basically, as I take the defense's position," Judge Brown had said, "he contends that our involvement in Vietnam is wrong, immoral, and illegal. Now in this regard, I know of no court, civilian or military, that is going to sit in judgment on the President's exercise of his power in disposing the troops of the United States." It was a fair statement that moral judgments of the conduct of the war were going to receive little attention other than in the headlines.

Had Brown played fair with Morgan? The out-of-court hearing, after all, was supposed to give Morgan a chance simply to show whether or not, given a fuller swing, he could develop a war-crimes case worthy of the full court's attention. Morgan had certainly shown that much. It was a rickety case to that point in the trial, but one surely that he had shown himself capable of shoring up if Judge Brown allowed him further time.

But Judge Brown said no. "Brown did not rule that Special Forces were or were not, in fact, engaged in the commission of war crimes," Morgan later observed. "He simply refused to allow the defense to go to the court-martial, he simply closed the door on us."

Morgan had attempted to defend Levy's statements by their truth, and the court refused to permit this. Then, on the court's own suggestion, he attempted to defend his client's disobedience by showing that to have obeyed would have made him guilty of complicity in war crimes. The court also denied him a full opportunity to prove this. But the door was not closed quickly enough to shut out the sight of the Army's operations in Vietnam, and he did go far enough so that he quite justifiably could claim to have proved, as he told a federal District Court, "that by its nature the war in Vietnam is not subject to being fought by yesterday's rules. Consequently, the rules should be changed, the war should be ended or, at least, *this nation should not deceive itself as to the nature of its acts, should not deceive itself as to its own submission to the rule of law or the morality of its position.*" (Emphasis added.)

Judge Brown's implication that a showing of Dachau-type war crimes (something that neither Levy nor Morgan ever suggested they could show) would somehow win the day in court was a totally false—and one might even say teasingly cruel—implication. The Army never surrenders to truth so long as it controls the law. Judge Brown admitted this in perhaps the most revealing exchange of the entire trial; it was an admission that made rather hollow all our protestations that at the Nuremberg Trials we were celebrating right and truth and decency. As Judge Brown interpreted those trials, the Allies were merely celebrating victory. By his interpretation, the Nazis lost the trials because they had lost the war, and by his admission Levy would be judged guilty and remain guilty until and unless the U.S. Army lost the Vietnamese war.

MORGAN: Now, really to just get down to an instance, a position here, and that is that the question of objective truth doesn't matter, and consequently if objective truth were spoken and totally disrupted the Armed Forces, but what was said was true, a person would not be entitled to make these statements.

BROWN: Not as long as that Army won, I suppose.

This was what Eichmann's attorney, Dr. Servatius, had told the court in Israel: "The basic principle of every state is: loyalty to and confidence in the leadership. The deed is dumb and obedience is blind. These are the virtues on which alone a state can build its foundations. Do such virtues merit reward? This depends upon the success of the policy. If it failed, the order would be considered a crime in the eyes of the victor. . . . To fail is abominable crime. To succeed is sanctified action."

It may be only a sentimental hangover from other, less "realistic" ages, but it is still a fairly common assumption that some classes of professionals have loyalties to creeds that justifiably can be placed above loyalty to country. Clergymen are one of these classes; doctors are another.* Although the Oath of Hippocrates is no longer taken by all doctors, those who do not take it swear an oath that is even stricter. This oath sets the physician apart from mere patriotic responsibilities and political loyalties. The doctors who experimented on the inmates of the World War II prison camps were loyal Nazis and patriotic Germans, but elsewhere people have generally taken the attitude that these doctors were unfaithful to a higher loyalty, namely, to humanity and to the particular patient. If they had refused to budge from the Oath of Hippocrates, they might have got in trouble (as Dr. Levy got in trouble), but history would have rated them well, if that were any comfort.

The Oath of Hippocrates says, in part: ". . . I will impart a knowledge of the art to my own sons and to those of my teachers, *and to disciples bound by a stipulation and oath, according to the law of medicine, but to no others.*" (Emphasis added.)

The Special Forces aidmen take no oath that binds them to the law of medicine but rather an oath that reads, "As an American soldier, I have determined ultimately to place above all considerations of self the mission of my team and the cause of my nation." It is a good patriotic oath, but it clashes with a physician's standards of priority.

---

* In a way the Army recognizes this in its combat regulation that provides that if a unit's regular officers are put out of commission, the highest-ranking enlisted man will take command rather than the unit's medical officer.

The Hippocratic Oath continues: "I will follow that method of treatment which . . . I consider for the benefit of my patients, and abstain from whatever is deleterious and mischievous. . . . Into whatever houses I enter I will go into them for the benefit of the sick and will abstain from every voluntary act of mischief and corruption."

Compare that oath with the testimony of Colonel Coppedge, developer of the aidmen's program: "Some people might object to medicine being prostituted to political purposes, but I don't see it that way. I see us in medicine as using the politicians for our purposes, which are purely humanitarian, and why not? At the same time we assume, we in the service assume that we are pursuing the right policy and [it] is the proper one."

MORGAN: You would be the first to state that there are those who disagree with that position?
COPPEDGE: Certainly.
MORGAN: And you also would be the first to state that ethically and based upon their oaths they could come to a different conclusion than yours?
PROSECUTION: Objection.
JUDGE BROWN: Sustained. We are getting too far afield on it.

Although this was the basic assumption of the court—that raising the issue of conflict between humanitarian ethics and Army discipline was drifting dangerously "afield"—Morgan did manage to get into the record statements from Army doctors who agreed that a physician should be left free to interpret the demands of the Hippocratic Oath for himself.

It was a courageous admission for them to make. One captain, Dr. Ivan Mauer, for example, though he had nine and a half months to go before his Army service would end, took this question: "If Special Forces aidmen were trained in how to make incendiary explosives with the delay devices from a chlorate sugar mix, from potassium permanganate and sugar, from sawdust and wax from match heads, to make improvised napalm, improvised thermite grenades, molded brick incendiary, and fire bottles, and were trained in other techniques and were utilized in combat techniques as a primary part of their duties, and if you knew that as a fact, would you train them in medicine?" Without visibly flinching, Mauer replied: "No, I would not."

Immediately after Mauer testified there was a strong rumor around the base that he was being sent to Vietnam. Thereupon, the next Army physician called to the stand testified that the restraints of the Hippocratic Oath should "depend on the individual interpretation of what you assume the role of the Special Forces are," but he made that statement only after trying to avoid an answer by taking the Fifth Amendment. In that court the Fifth had no more status than the First, and he was ordered to answer. Later Judge Brown was quoted as saying, "They see those gangsters on TV taking the Fifth Amendment over and over again, so they do it here in trials where there is no need."

Nonmilitary physicians and medical historians were also called, none of whom was more impressive than Dr. Jean Mayer,* lecturer in the history of public health at Harvard and for five years during World War II in the Free French forces. Although he held a Ph.D. in the medical sciences from Yale and a Doctor of Science from the Sorbonne, he spoke not merely as an intellectual but as one who believed in fighting. To train paramedical personnel who were "required to subordinate their medical judgment to the military and political judgments of their commanders," would, he said, "go against my conscience." And if he were ordered to train them on the grounds that they would do some medical good, he said, he would not buy that argument because "I think the risk to the status of medicine and the independence of medicine from government interference very seldom comes from people who are against medicine. It

* More recently he has been in the news as head of President Nixon's nationwide hunger survey.

is much more likely to come from people who have very good intentions." In short, if he was ordered to train medics who subordinated medicine to warfare, "I would not participate in it."

But he was a non-Army outsider, and a court-martial merely tolerates outsiders. No more influential was Dr. Victor W. Sidel, an honor graduate of the Harvard Medical School and at that time on the Harvard faculty, who testified that "to be a good and ethical physician he must refuse to obey an order which he believes violates his medical ethics" and that in his opinion a soldier trained in "political medicine" would end up "doing neither a good medical job nor a good military job." But, as the prosecution carefully brought out, Dr. Sidel had never served in the Army.

It was hardly the best of defenses—in the Army's eyes—but Morgan attempted to show that the Green Berets didn't know a thing about serious medicine and yet they were sent into the jungles packing along such esoteric and dangerous drugs as chloromycetin. Since the early 1950s the American Medical Association and its *Journal* have repeatedly warned doctors against promiscuous use of the drug, which, improperly administered, can result in aplastic anemia—a condition where the bone marrow has been poisoned and can no longer produce blood cells, resulting in anemia and death. Experienced physicians look upon it as a tricky drug; giving it to Green Beret medics is something no good doctor would tolerate. Morgan also attempted to argue that at least half of Levy's patients were women—WACs, wives of servicemen and dependents—and that it would not have been ethical for him to ask women to strip naked and submit themselves to the stares of eighteen- and nineteen-year-old soldiers who were not medical personnel and were on hand really as official gawkers. Colonel Fancy testified that he would be willing for his own eighteen-year-old daughter to show herself naked to the Special Forces medics "if she gave her permission," but he didn't sound convincing.

In any event, as a regular routine it wouldn't have worked. The Army found that out when Levy's successor exposed the wife of a retired sergeant to the stares of a Special Forces team and all hell broke loose, ending with an apology from the Secretary of the Army himself. As she told the story in court, "When I went in the room, I handed him my records, and all the Special Forces were in the room. He asked me where my trouble was. I told him below the waist, below my belt, and on my legs. He then asked me in front of all these young men could I show him without going to the examination room. I guess he wanted me to pull up my dress and down my pants in front of all the audience in his office. I did not make an answer whatsoever; I gave him a dirty look. So he sent for the sergeant to get a nurse." Whereupon the patient undressed, lay on a table under a sheet, expecting only the doctor and nurse would view her, but no—in came two doctors "and eight or ten Special Forces men and gathered around the foot of the table. He pulled the sheet down, looked at it, showed those men the private part of my body . . . even to the point of pulling my thighs apart so all could see."

When her husband complained to Colonel Fancy, he replied, "She will just have to accept that if she accepts treatment."

It was this sort of continuous rhubarb, in which the doctor is expected to violate the confidences of his patient, that Levy was trying to avoid—among other things—by refusing to train the young medics in how to ogle horrified wives. Or so Morgan argued. But such delicacies escaped the Army panel entirely.

In the early summer of 1967, one month before his hitch in the Army would have ended, Dr. Levy was judged guilty and sentenced to three years. Colonel Davis, Fancy's caterpillar-mustachioed assistant, probably reached the high point of his life when, following the trial, he stepped forward and roughly slapped handcuffs on the slender physician and hauled him from the court-room as one might have dragged a felon to the gallows in the days of Hogarth.

The trial record filled nineteen volumes, mostly random, dis-

jointed, bizarre testimony. Yet there was one thing of utmost
significance in the record that did make sense and that will remain
a chilling memento for the men who run this country—that is, for
the first time in our history, the question of war crimes was made
an official part of a federal trial.

On the morning the Army flew Levy away from Fort Jackson to
begin his term in Leavenworth Penitentiary, there was a gathering
around the small plane—Levy, Morgan, some other friends, a few
soldiers to guard the prisoner—and the atmosphere was neither
cheerful nor sad, but stoical and wry. He had known he would be
shafted by the Army; they had all known it; so there was nothing
they could say that would add to or take away from that truth, the
kind of truth that is irrelevant in courts-martial. It was one of
those early, strange, Army hours of the morning that provokes
unusual remarks. And the colonel in the group of guards must
have felt it, because he turned to Levy and said, "You know,
Captain, I may not agree with you but that's why I'm in the
Army—to protect your right to say what you want to say." And he
doubtless meant it. After all, the Army *had* let Levy speak out; it
was sending him to prison for doing so, but it had *let* him. "Well,
I'll be goddamned," said Levy, which, after all, was about the only
thing left to him to say as he climbed aboard the plane, forgetting,
as always, to salute the colonel.

*Epilogue:* At midnight on January 20, 1969, Levy became a
plain doctor again: he was dismissed from the service. Eight days
later he was transferred from Leavenworth to the civilian prison at
Lewisburg, Pennsylvania. Once again Morgan appealed to the
courts to release Levy on bond until his court fights were ended.
This time the government's attorneys admitted they did not think
Levy would flee the country. (Fort Jackson's officials had refused to
let him out on bond because they said they had it on "good
authority"—another of the many nameless, faceless accusers Levy
had to contend with—that Levy intended to go to a Communist

country.) This time they argued that to release Levy would be bad for military morale.

More than a year after he had been imprisoned, the Court of Military Appeals refused to review his case—perhaps, in terms of legal questions, the most important military case of our generation.

On August 4, 1969, one week before he would have been freed on parole, Dr. Levy was released from prison on bail. The order had come from Justice William O. Douglas.

On August 6 the Pentagon announced that one noncommissioned officer and six officers, including the commandant of the Green Berets in Vietnam, had been arrested on suspicion of the murder of a Vietnam national. Reporters for several major newspapers revealed that it was widely suspected the victim had been tortured before he was assassinated. Activities that Levy's defense attorneys had been able to strike at only obliquely two years earlier were now common material for the daily press.

When Levy arrived in Atlanta on the first leg of a vacation with attorney Morgan, he noticed the big Green Beret headlines on the Atlanta *Journal*. Morgan commented on it; so did the newsmen with them. But Levy had the last word: "As I was saying before I was so rudely interrupted."

# 5. Putting Down Dissent

MOST OF THE NATION'S three and a half million men in uniform go about their lives with only the usual amount of grumbling, and their commanders don't worry about that. To the career officers on their verandas, the traditional GI griping that wafts out of the barracks and across the drill fields registers only as one note in the distant, comforting drone of regimentation. But other kinds of complaints are being made today, in a fashion that shatters tradition. A startling number of servicemen have decided not only to do their own thinking—even to the point of candidly appraising the war policies that ask them to take considerable risk—but also to act upon their convictions. Together their efforts constitute an unprecedented movement within the armed forces, in opposition to military autocracy. Not unexpectedly, the movement has produced a reaction in which the military, feeling threatened, is using its faithful old weapon, its system of justice, to put down dissent.

Judgments vary enormously as to how big the GI dissent movement really is. One of the better-known dissent organizations, the American Servicemen's Union, claims a membership of seven thousand. The ASU demands: an end to the saluting and sirring of officers; the election of officers by vote of the men; racial equality in the armed forces; rank-and-file control of court-martial boards; the federal minimum wage; the right of collective bargaining; the right of free political association; and the right to disobey illegal orders. (In fact, every serviceman already has this latter right, but the ASU means the right not to fight in an illegal war.) Some of those who support these young men make it sound as though every other serviceman is about to rise up. The Reverend Richard Weston, for example, in whose Unitarian church in Whittier, California, several runaway Marines have received sanctuary, said that when he visits nearby Camp Pendleton, he flashes the peace signal and "fully fifty percent of the soldiers I pass flash it back, and it's quite clear by their expressions what they mean. I'm surprised at how large the underground in the Marines is."

Comedian Bob Hope was doubtless also surprised at the size of the Army underground. Cracking his predictable jokes to a crowd of ten thousand troops in Vietnam shortly before Christmas, 1969, he made a remark indicating support for the Administration's war policies and was greeted by boos and gestures—hands raised in the peace sign—from at least one-third of the servicemen, newsmen estimated. It was such an awesome show of protest that Hope dropped that pro-war remark from his act.

More and more servicemen seem to be turning out for antiwar parades—given the proper occasion, several thousand will show up—and at the November, 1969, peace march in Washington at least a dozen *military policemen* were wearing peace buttons. In the same month, servicemen and ex-servicemen interested in GI rights took the customary step for a group of Americans who want influence: they held a national convention in Washington and discussed the possibility of establishing a lobby. Dissident servicemen have already promoted their own cadre of lawyers, several hundred of them, drawn mostly from the American Civil Liberties Union and the National Emergency Civil Liberties Union—old stand-bys decked out for this fight in new titles such as the GI Civil Liberties Defense Committee of New York and the New York

Draft and Military Law Panel. Ex-GIs are setting up counseling offices to help servicemen apply for conscientious-objector status, and sometimes to assist them in deserting and escaping to Canada.

Of course not everyone who cries "peace" should be counted as a rebel by the military authorities, but on the other hand the official count is ridiculously low. An officer in the Pentagon assigned to keep a list of the leading troublemakers says their number shifts between thirty-five and a hundred. If the Pentagon takes its own count seriously, however, it is all the more puzzling why the military commanders are so furiously determined to silence dissent by any means, legal and humane or otherwise. Panicking, they have engaged in the clumsiest—and most easily publicized—kind of oppression. The estimate of between thirty-five and a hundred applies to *leaders*. The entire body of dissenters in the armed services is estimated by the Pentagon to be about one-tenth of one percent of the men in uniform—which would come to about three thousand. This is such a trivial number as to underscore again the military's curious panic.

It is always done in the name of patriotism, of course. Often it is done specifically in the cause of antisubversion, as in the case of the "coffeehouses" near military bases at which small, informal GI groups meet regularly to discuss ways to challenge military authority and undercut the Vietnam war. A retired Pentagon officer who now serves as the public information director for Fort Jackson, South Carolina, expressing himself perhaps more candidly than most officials in a similar position, passed around to newsmen a leaflet he had received in the mail which he thought "pretty well gets to the crux of the matter." The leaflet, sent to him by Mothers of Servicemen, an organization based in South Pasadena, California, was entitled "GI Coffee Houses for Peace—Communist Tactic." It explained that the coffeehouses near Army bases were part of what Earl Browder, former secretary of the Communist Party U.S.A., thirty years ago called ideological "transmission belts."

If that were the end of it, one could dismiss this as the reaction of the celebrated little old ladies in tennis shoes with whom Southern California supposedly abounds, abetted by the gullible reaction of a single PR man. Unfortunately, however, this is also the official position of the military, and it is encouraged by FBI Director J. Edgar Hoover. Testifying on behalf of the FBI's 1970 budget before the House Subcommittee on Appropriations, Hoover warned that a group "which includes representatives of various subversive organizations, such as the Communist Party-USA and the Socialist Workers Party among its members [is developing] a program to establish coffeehouses near military installations throughout the United States for the purpose of attracting military personnel and to serve as alternatives to the 'militaristic, drab, occasionally violent Army town environment.' " Elsewhere he describes it as a project "to establish 'GI drop-in centers' near military facilities in order to offer a political program to aid servicemen in their organizing efforts within the military." Except for the labeling of coffeehouses as a Red plot, it was a very accurate description.

Hoover indicated that he considered keeping an eye on such establishments as being part of his most important internal security work. The average person, however, would probably be unable to detect the subversive character of the conversation and other activities in the coffeehouses. While it is true that they offer a different kind of entertainment from that found in most military-town establishments—there is no boozing permitted in the coffeehouses, no solicitation by prostitutes, no shill games—much of what goes on seems rather ordinary. The oldest house in the "transmission belt" was the UFO in Columbia, South Carolina, and its appearance gave no clue as to the reasons the FBI, the "mothers" of Pasadena and the military were so afraid of it. Decorations consisted mostly of posters, and the most subversive poster in the house (not counting the one for Al Smith's 1928 presidential campaign, which UFO workers found when they moved into the building) was one with the put-on legend, "Uncle Tom says—Only YOU can prevent ghetto fires!" There was rock music and sometimes dancing. But for the most part there was only coffee drinking and talk.

The UFO opened its doors in January, 1968, and existed rather placidly for the next two years, except on such occasions as when MPs came in to beat up a worker or a patron for no apparent reason. To be sure, the UFO staff did not go out of its way to placate the citizens of Columbia. Once the UFO displayed in its window a picture of what purported to be U.S. Special Forces soldiers holding up heads cut from Vietcong bodies, complete with some vulgar expressions which Columbians are not accustomed to seeing in the window of buildings across from the City Hall, which is where the UFO is situated. The photo created hard feelings around town, especially because it was undraped the day Columbia put on a parade for the town's favorite son, General William Westmoreland. And, in addition to the decapitation photo, UFO added to the festivities with a large sign, "Welcome Home, Westy, the War's Over," which some townsfolk took to be unduly sarcastic.

"We put up with the place," an editor of the local newspaper said in the spring of 1969, "but we don't like it." But by November the people who run Columbia decided they would no longer put up with the place, even if they had to frame the young people to get rid of them. UFO activities were innocent and were conducted in a restrained way. If they hadn't been, the police who visited the establishment several times a night and the Army intelligence agents who hung around would doubtless have shut it months earlier. Though having no evidence of misconduct, downtown merchants presented a petition to the county prosecutor asking that the coffee-house be closed. The prosecutor obliged by charging the UFO operators with running an establishment where "marijuana and other narcotic drugs" were sold (no proof of that), an establishment where minors were corrupted by peace placards and obscene posters (such as Raquel Welch wearing a furry bikini), and where fighting, cursing and loud noises made it a public nuisance. Many non-Southern newsmen have visited the UFO and written stories about it, and none of them have described it in the language of the indictment. By recruiting from the local riffraff and promising immunity for the "right" testimony, the prosecution concocted a case that ended in six-year sentences for the coffeehouse operators.

So for now, the UFO is closed. And the same fate hangs over other coffeehouses near other bases. Most have come under extreme pressure and harassment, directly from the military and indirectly through city officials, who of course—viewing the military paychecks as necessary to the economy of the community—go out of their way to make existence uncomfortable for the sponsors of off-base meeting places. This has happened in Texas, New Jersey, Kentucky and the State of Washington. MPs try to bar the door at some coffeehouses; some servicemen who ignore them and go in anyway claim they have received "punitive reassignment" of duties.

In mid-1970, the Internal Revenue Service came to the rescue of the Army in a potent way by notifying the United States Servicemen's Fund—which has scraped together much of the operating funds for the coffeehouses and many of the underground newspapers—that its tax-exempt status was being withdrawn retroactively to the time of its founding a couple of years ago. Unless the USSF wins its appeal in court, this verdict will burden it with a debt far beyond its means to pay.

The most alarming thing about the coffeehouse chain is that the military is so concerned about it. The same might be said about the more than four dozen antiwar underground GI newspapers (some of them mischievously published on Army mimeograph machines). The oldest of the GI papers is *FTA,* established at Fort Knox in July, 1968. (The longer title of this newspaper is *Fun, Travel & Adventure,* but the initials title is more popular because "FTA" is also the abbreviation for what most GIs think should be done to the Army.) Some of the other underground newspapers also sport saucy titles: *The Short Times, Open Sights, Fatigue Press, Last Harass, Rough Draft,* etc. The best of them are gabby, colorfully gripy, intelligently critical and entertainingly scurrilous—written in a tone somewhere between those of an old Wobbly broadside and a Dick Gregory peacenik gag. The worst of them are merely dull.

Whatever their quality, the underground newspapers fill a function not filled by the authorized base newspapers, whose orthodox rigidity is described in an issue of the *Columbia Journalism Review* by Jeffrey D. Alderman, former editor of the *Armored Sentinel,* the approved newspaper at Ford Hood. When it was discovered that the *Sentinel* contained an advertisement for a writing contest sponsored by a radical organization, says Alderman, twelve thousand copies of the newspaper were burned by the authorities.

One of the best of the underground papers, at least the most notorious, is *Last Harass,* published at Fort Gordon, Georgia, by the successors to Private First Class Dennis Davis of New York City, a member of the Progressive Labor Party who was its first editor. Davis was handed an administrative undesirable discharge sixteen days before he would have completed his two-year hitch with an honorable record. Except for editing a newspaper which the Fort Gordon commandant, Colonel Lester D. Royalty, believed to be fomenting "unrest and disloyalty" among the troops, Davis had a spotless Army career. Colonel Royalty said that in his judgment the mimeographed newsletter "would have little effect on seasoned officers and NCOs, but would be dangerous in the case of trainees or men in the Army against their will."

There is some question whether what the Army saw as subversion in *Last Harass* would also seem subversive to the intelligent reader. A typical issue under Davis' editorship featured on its front page a statement by Abraham Lincoln to the effect that the people have a "revolutionary right to dismember or overthrow" the government, since it belongs to them. Inside, the reporting was mostly about battles around the country between antiwar GIs and their commanders. There was an abbreviated history of how the Army has been used to scab in labor disputes. The newspaper supplements its own steady anti-Vietnam barrage with supporting quotes from such revolutionaries as Dwight Eisenhower, John Kenneth Galbraith and Senator Richard Russell. One article, which Army intelligence agents must have had a hard time rating, urged soldiers to give up marijuana for politics. It is likely that anyone who could be made disloyal by *Last Harass*—presumably looked upon by the Army as the most revolutionary of the underground papers—is much too unstable to be issued firearms anyway.

In an earlier chapter it was mentioned how Private Bruce Petersen, editor of *Fatigue Press* at Fort Hood, learned about freedom of the press: he got eight years for possession of marijuana, although the amount of the drug found in the lint of his pocket was so minuscule that it was all destroyed while being tested, the Army said. Army officials claim that they didn't know he was editor of the underground newspaper when they filed charges.* At Fort Dix, Specialist 4 Allen Myers, editor of the newspaper *The Ultimate Weapon,* was court-martialed for distributing antiwar literature "in bad taste" and "prejudicial to good order." He was not convicted. But Specialist 4 Harold Muskat was later sentenced by a Fort Dix court to serve six months at hard labor for distributing an underground paper. A number of soldiers have been punished at various camps for the same reason, and there have been many search-and-seize raids on soldiers' lockers to discover hidden caches of the papers.†

Of all the hysteria that has arisen from this area, none can match the Navy's response to Roger Priest. As usual when the military works itself into a dither of anxiety, the case had its

---

* In December, 1969, thirteen months after Petersen was sent to prison, the Army Court of Military Review threw out the conviction on the grounds that the Army CID agents had no legal basis for searching the soldier. This judicial reversal hardly lessened the atmosphere of intimidation in which forthright soldiers must exist.

† Once again, however, it must be said that the Army is not uniformly obdurate. At Fort Eustis, Virginia, the commandant permitted distribution of *Rough Draft* during specified hours.

hilarious moments.

A twenty-five-year-old journalist seaman apprentice from Houston, Priest was assigned to the Pentagon. His first trouble with authority came when he named as the beneficiary of his service-connected life insurance policy none other than the War Resisters League of New York. There was nothing illegal about it; the rules say that a serviceman can leave his insurance to "any person, firm, corporation or legal entity, individually or as trustee." When the Pentagon wrote that rule, it apparently had in mind a serviceman leaving his death benefits to the Boy Scouts or IBM unless it went to the home folks. The War Resisters League, however, was surely not what it had in mind. Priest was called in and scolded for forty-five minutes by his division officer, who threatened him with an investigation, talked about the possibility of a five-year prison term "if we find you belong to any subversive group," and topped it off by saying the Navy had a good mind to write his parents and tell on him.

Instead of altering his life insurance policy to please the Pentagon, Priest started putting out his own mimeographed newsletter for servicemen. The title was *OM*, with the "O" designed to look like a peace symbol. The first issue proposed that other servicemen who didn't believe in the dogma of the military and who found the Vietnam war repugnant should change *their* life insurance policies, too. Otherwise, it was a rather tame issue, with only a touch of black humor here and there (as in a "Famous Quote" from General Westmoreland, to wit: "I bet that Russian army is jealous as hell. Our troops are here getting all this experience, we're learning about guerrilla warfare, helicopters, vertical envelopment, close artillery support. Those Russian generals would love to be here. . . . Any true professional wants to march to the sound of gunfire").

Priest was quickly transferred to a hole-in-the-wall job at the Navy Yard, and Navy investigators began to tail him. Later the Navy disclosed that it had assigned *twenty-five investigators* to keep tabs on Priest, and that at one peace movement meeting he attended in Cleveland six of the fifteen people present were Navy investigators. They did their lowly work with a will, even digging through the garbage and trash of the apartment house where Priest lived to see if he had thrown out anything subversive. (He never did, apparently, for the most that they could produce from the trash at his preliminary hearing was a letter he had received from one of their agents.) They also employed some good-looking Waves in an effort to soften him up and catch him saying unpatriotic things.

They needn't have bothered. Everything Priest had on his mind he was pouring quite openly into his newsletter, which, by the third issue, was bubbling with low comedy and high outrage. The cover featured a picture of Defense Secretary Melvin Laird, identified as "People's Enemy Number One" and the legend, "A pig, by any other name, is still a pig." On inside pages General Earle Wheeler, Chairman of the Joint Chiefs of Staff, was also identified as a pig. There were several suggestions such as "Smash the Pig Army!" and "Today's Pigs Are Tomorrow's Bacon." FBI Director J. Edgar Hoover was told, "When the revolution comes, you will be the grass, and we will be the lawnmower, so take care." A three-paragraph outburst against capitalism, imperialism and an economy based on militarism ended with the admonition: "BOMB AMERICA, MAKE COCA-COLA SOMEPLACE ELSE."

The outstanding item was titled "Bobby Seale's Parable" (Seale is a Black Panther) and it told how a man was trying to get a drink of water from a stream but "he noticed that the stream was full of muck and filth." He tried to clean the filth from the stream but it kept on coming. Finally another man happened by and informed the thirsty one that "the stream was full of muck and filth because a huge hog was standing in the middle of the stream at the top of the mountain pissing and shitting in the stream, and that is why it is so dirty." To clean up the stream, the two men climbed the mountain to move the hog, and when they got there, they shouted in unison: "L. MENDEL RIVERS! GET YOUR ASS OUT OF THAT STREAM! YOU HEAR, BOY?"

This is a young man's rage; quite overdone. But it was also quite obviously directed at improving his country. One could say that Priest offers a scurrilous version of the Fulbright–McGovern–Stephen Young–Hatfield–Goodell line, which no responsible person has yet called disloyal. If the intention of the Navy had been to show reason and balance, the newsletters would have been ignored. But the purpose of the Navy was to suppress opposition, and the next thing Priest knew, he was scheduled for court-martial. The grounds were that he had shown disrespect to General Wheeler, had used contemptuous words toward Rivers, chairman of the Armed Services Committee of the House, had been equally contemptuous of Secretary Laird, had made disloyal remarks about the United States and had promoted disloyalty by, among other things, writing, "Be Free Go Canada—Deserters from the U.S. military can still find refuge in Canada contrary to recent misleading reports in the Establishment press," and listing the addresses of organizations that work with deserters. So dull-witted was the Navy that in its charge sheet it reproduced all the juicier remarks, including the Rivers parable, thus making what would have been transient journalism at best, a permanent and very readable part of the public record.

The clash between Roger Priest and the Navy raises a constitutional issue, as well as what might be called a territorial issue.

The constitutional issue relates not merely to free speech but to a seeming conflict within the Constitution itself—"seeming" because the conflict really isn't there. Article I, Section 8, Clause 14, of the Constitution states that "The Congress shall have power . . . to make rules for the government and regulation of the land and naval forces." From this clause have come all efforts, including the present Uniform Code of Military Justice, to keep servicemen from the ordinary protections of the civilian courts and of the

Bill of Rights. The powers poured upon the military through this chink have been much more elaborate than the writers of the Constitution ever envisioned. As Justice Hugo Black pointed out, this clause was slipped, not hammered, into the Constitution; it was included only in the final draft and was never discussed or debated. The clause did not appear in either the original draft presented to the Constitutional Convention or in the draft submitted by the Committee of Debate.

A reading of the *Federalist Papers* will show that the purpose of the clause was not to remove the military from coverage by the Bill of Rights but simply to establish national armed forces. Seven of the *Federalist Papers* were written by Alexander Hamilton in an effort to soothe the fears of many people of that day who thought that a central standing army might lead to a dictatorship and who felt, instead, that each state should furnish whatever militia it might need. The quarrel was not over whether men in uniform should or should not be treated as citizens—everyone agreed that they should—but only over whether they should be mustered by the states or by the central government. Article I, Section 8, Clause 14, gives the power to the central government. That's all.

On the other hand, the First Amendment flatly orders that "Congress shall make no law . . . abridging the freedom of speech or of the press." Does the "no law" prohibition cover the Military Code, which Congress passed in 1950 as a substitute for constitutional law? It is exceedingly difficult to read "no law" to mean anything but "no law," yet modern military courts have consistently ruled that, on this point, the Bill of Rights does not mean what it says.*

* The farcical quality of the conflict was seen at the court-martial of two young soldiers at Fort Ord in 1968. For writing and distributing a leaflet recruiting other GIs to join their union "to voice our opposition to this war," the two were sentenced to four years in prison and dishonorable discharges. During cross-examination of a prosecution witness by the defendants' ACLU attorney, this dialogue took place:

Q: Have you heard of the First Amendment?
A: Yes, I have.

Irving Brant, in his *The Bill of Rights: Its Origins and Meaning,*
deals with this blind spot:

Strangely enough, the greatest uncertainty about the meaning of the
amendments has developed where the wording seems most clear and
definite: in the command that "Congress shall make no law . . .
abridging the freedom of speech or of the press." These were the protections most vociferously demanded by the people. Nobody in Congress challenged them and they were approved without discussion.
   This absence of clarifying debate has been interpreted in two ways.
To one set of judges and like-minded commentators, it has meant that
freedom of speech and press cannot be abridged, *except*—and what a
mammoth exception this is—except by punishing such speech and
writings as were punishable under the common law of England. . . .
For hundreds of years, Englishmen had been fined, whipped, pilloried,
imprisoned and had their ears cut off for speech and writings offensive
to government or society. Surely, say those who believe that *"no*
abridgment" means "abridgment only when, on balance, it is thought
necessary," the framers of the First Amendment could not have intended to wipe out abridgments of speech and press so thoroughly and
respectably established. If they had such an intention they would have
not used so ambiguous a term as "Congress shall *make no law.*" They
would have said "no law *whatsoever.*" . . .
   What the framers should have done, perhaps, was add a second section to the First Amendment, saying: "The preceding section means
what it says." But that might require a third section with the same

---

Q: Do you believe that these two men are protected under it?
A: Yes, but there are limitations as to its scope. Soldiers, for instance, are
   subject to all the rules and regulations of the United States Army.
Q: Can you think of any rule or regulation which says that these two boys
   shouldn't have been passing out leaflets such as this?
A: No—well, in effect, yes, I can; I do know that every soldier, whether
   he enlists or is drafted, takes the oath of induction and swears to be loyal
   to the United States Army.
Q: Do you know the oath of induction?
A: Yes.
Q: Would you please repeat it?
A: I swear to defend the Constitution of the United States. . . .

Spectators say that at that point there was so much laughter—including some
irrepressible snickers among the court officers—that the judge had to call
a recess.

wording, and perhaps a fourth and a fifth, to prove that "no" means "no." . . .

The guarantees are not worded as admonitions. They are unqualified commands. They sank to the level of admonitions because that was the way Congress and the judges treated them. It is the rejection of the mandate that has created the problem and made it look insoluble. When "no abridgment" becomes abridgment at the discretion of Congress and the courts, *freedom* becomes a *degree of freedom,* and the degree varies with the temper of the times. . . .*

From time to time the U.S. Court of Military Appeals hands down some buttery opinion that sounds almost in harmony with the above. In 1960 it ruled, "It is apparent that the protections in the Bill of Rights, except those expressly or by necessary implication inapplicable, are available to members of our Armed Forces." But this proclamation is ruined by the breezy sweep of its "except those" clause. The Court of Military Appeals knows that in practice the serviceman has no rights but those given to him on a day-to-day basis by his commander. His life is putty, newly shaped by every hand of authority that picks it up.

One of the most famous of the misleading statements issued by a justice of COMA was Judge Robert E. Quinn's ruling in the Voorhees case, a freedom-of-the-press case, in 1954. "I think I should make it clear," Quinn said, "that, in my opinion, every individual in the military service is entitled to the same constitutional rights, privileges, and guarantees as every other American citizen, except where specifically denied or limited by the Constitution itself." A more honest statement of the court's position was made during that same case by Judge George W. Latimer: "I believe it ill-advised and unwise to apply the civilian concepts of freedom of speech and press to the military service unless they are compressed within limits so narrow they become almost unrecognizable." Fitting the Quinn and Latimer statements together, Detlev F. Vagts observed in the *Columbia Law Review:* "The consensus

* Bobbs-Merrill Co., 1965, pp. 71 and 224–25.

then appears to be that the freedom of speech guarantee does apply in theory to the military but that in practice the protection it affords will be narrowly construed." In other words, our soldiers and sailors are treated as citizens in theory but as noncitizens in practice.

As for the territorial issue raised by the Roger Priest case, it is whether or not the military has, or should have, any control over the conduct of servicemen in their off hours, off base. The startling thing about this question is that only a few weeks before Priest was brought to heel the U.S. Supreme Court had ruled the military does *not* have such control. Then how dare the Navy try to take such a step? It dared because, as already observed, if the Constitution carries little weight with the military, the U.S. Supreme Court has even less influence.

The military was unusually candid in its refusal to accept this decision of the Supreme Court. The Pentagon, in fact, sent out word to its commanders to disregard the ruling and continue to operate as always. This challenge was made not to an ordinary decision of the Court but to perhaps the most important decision on a military case in two generations. A law review weekly described the upcoming case in January, 1969, in this dramatic fashion: "The entire system of military criminal law, except in the narrowly defined area of peculiarly military offenses, is being challenged."

As with so many of the great criminal decisions handed down in recent years—*Gideon* and *Miranda,* for example—this one evolved from the seediest of origins. There was little that was appealing about the man for whom justice was advanced.

On July 20, 1956, while stationed at Fort Shafter, Oahu, Army Sergeant James F. O'Callahan dressed in civilian clothes and went on an evening pass to Honolulu. After too many beers in a Waikiki Beach hotel bar, he entered the residential part of the hotel and broke into a room and tried to rape a fourteen-year-old girl. The hotel detective caught O'Callahan before he could get out of the building; he was turned over to city police, who turned him over to the MPs, and O'Callahan was charged with violating three articles of the UCMJ: Article 80 (attempted rape), Article 130 (house-breaking) and Article 134. This latter is the notorious catchall article—British soldiers used to call it "The Devil's Article" because it was so invidious—and its words are a meandering web: "Though not specifically mentioned in this chapter, all disorders and neglects to the prejudice of good order and discipline in the armed forces, all conduct of a nature to bring discredit upon the armed forces, and crimes and offenses not capital . . ." In other words, *any* charges not specifically permitted under one of the other articles can be plucked from this grab bag.

O'Callahan was legitimately off duty, legitimately off the base and out of uniform, but the military courts claimed that Article 134 gave them jurisdiction anyway. He was sentenced to ten years at hard labor. Later he was paroled. But his parole was revoked when he was convicted of another rape in Massachusetts. From his cell at the federal penitentiary in Lewisburg, Pennsylvania, O'Callahan filed a petition for habeas corpus. He argued that the revocation was illegal because the military had no power in the first place to try him for rape, since rape is a civilian crime.

History supported his argument. The Declaration of Independence says one of the reasons for considering King George's rule "an absolute tyranny" was that he had tried "to render the Military independent of and superior to the Civil Power" and that one way he had attempted this was by *giving his troops courts-martial for crimes which properly were under the jurisdiction of the civilian courts.* The 1776 Articles of War declared that an officer who refused to surrender a soldier to a civilian court, if accused of a civilian crime, would be cashiered from the service.

The civilian government's distrust of the military in such matters continued right up to 1916 (except for one brief interlude during the Civil War), when, on the eve of our entry into World War I, the military was granted jurisdiction over some civilian crimes. At first rejecting the change, Congress finally gave in, but only after President Wilson, who was very fond of the military, angrily appended it as an amendment to the fiscal 1917 military appropriations bill.

The most important change in the general catchall article made by the 1917 amendment was the addition of the phrase "conduct of a nature to bring discredit upon the armed forces." Before that time the military had to rely on the other phrases which forbade action that was prejudicial to good order and discipline; and for many years it had been conceded that for an action to be prejudicial to good order and discipline, it had to be committed either on the military base or against a military person or military institution. "Conduct of a nature to bring discredit upon the armed forces" rescued the military commanders from their previous restrictions and permitted them to intrude into a serviceman's life anywhere and for any misconduct. If a soldier off base, off duty and dressed in civilian clothes were to rob a hen house or get drunk in his girlfriend's parlor, he could (after 1917) find himself before a court-martial. In fact, he might be court-martialed even for failure to pay his income tax (the military has prosecuted such cases).

The extension of military jurisdiction had been slyly achieved. Actually, when the addition of the phrase "conduct . . . to bring discredit" was first suggested, in 1912, the military assured Congress that "The new language introduced in the article is for the purpose of covering the cases of *retired* enlisted men who are guilty of conduct (not crimes) which is discreditable and yet not directly prejudicial to discipline; such as refusing to make proper provision for the support of their families, or the disgraceful nonpayment of a debt for the necessaries of life." (Emphasis added.) Just for retired enlisted men, they said. It wasn't even needed for retired officers, they said, because retired officers could be kept in line with the admonition against "conduct unbecoming an officer and a gentleman."

No sooner was the catchall phrase added to military law, however, than the Army began to cheat on it. The 1917 *Manual for Courts-Martial* acknowledged that the "principal" purpose for adding the phrase was to deal with retirees; however, now the Army insisted that there was at least "a *limited* field for the application of this part of the general article to soldiers on the *active* list in cases where their discreditable conduct is not made punishable by any specific article." (Emphasis added.) So the door had been opened. By 1928 the *Manual* was mentioning only obliquely that retired personnel were covered by the article, and by 1949 the *Manual for Courts-Martial* did not mention retirees at all. Thus, between World War I and the end of World War II, the military had inched its jurisdiction over all civilian crimes committed by men who are on active duty—including such crimes as O'Callahan's attempted rape.

This was the history that O'Callahan and his attorney, Victor Rabinowitz, one of New York's best-known and most controversial lawyers, had to work against when they went before the Supreme Court in 1969. Rabinowitz had one powerful argument: rape is not a federal crime. It is a state crime. And simply because rape may, in the impossibly vague words of the Military Code, "bring discredit" on the armed services, this does not magically transform it into a federal crime.

A five-to-three majority of the Court accepted Rabinowitz' arguments, and Justice Douglas handed down the opinion. "Courts-martial as an institution are singularly inept in dealing with the nice subtleties of constitutional law," he wrote. "History teaches that expansion of military discipline beyond its proper domain carries with it a threat to liberty." Therefore, unless a crime is "service-connected," a serviceman who commits his crimes off the base and off duty must be tried in civilian courts.

The heart of the Court's decision was this:

We have concluded that the crime to be under military jurisdiction must be service connected. . . . In the present case petitioner was properly absent from his military base when he committed the crime with which he is charged. There is no connection—not even the remotest one—between his military duties and the crimes in question. The crimes were not committed on a military post or enclave; nor was the person whom he attacked performing any duties relating to the military. Moreover, Hawaii, the situs of the crime, is not an armed camp under military control, as are some of our far-flung outposts.

Finally, we deal with peacetime offenses, not with authority stemming from the war power. Civil courts were open. The offenses were committed within our territorial limits, not in the occupied zone of a foreign country. The offense did not involve any question of the flouting of military authority, the security of a military post, or the integrity of military property.

The first outraged reaction came from some of the Pentagon's conservative friends in the press corps, who produced remarkable explanations of why they thought the Supreme Court had done grievously wrong. Of these journalists, none was so imaginative as Lyle Denniston of the Washington *Star,* who fretted about what he called a grand old tradition dating back to the time of George Washington: "Men were tried by courts-martial for killing a cow, stealing poultry, or helping themselves to shirts and blankets at the town store. Their trials, recorded in Washington's order book, helped establish an Army tradition: *acting as the stern parent* watching over the behavior of its own." Denniston became so carried away in his defense of judicial militarism that he even wound up with the dizzying conclusion that the court-martial system is nothing so crude as a criminal-law process but is, in fact, "a form of internal *personnel management."* (Emphasis added.)

The Army didn't waste its time arguing in public, however. The Supreme Court's decision was handed down on June 3, 1969; on June 5, 1969, Major General Kenneth J. Hodson, Army Judge Advocate General, notified commanders throughout the world (almost identical messages were dispatched by the top law officers in the other services) that the Supreme Court decision did not apply to any cases except those "unequivocally not service connected." And he meant unequivocally. Or, approaching the problem from the opposite direction, *only* those specific cases that fit "squarely within the rule of the decision in O'Callahan" were to be spared court-martial proceedings.

Clarifying his position, the general stated that an off-duty soldier smoking marijuana in a civilian bedroom could be fairly tried by court-martial for "unfitting oneself for military duty." Or if soldiers were caught fighting in a bar, they could be tried for behavior "prejudicial of good order and military discipline—especially if difference in rank were involved," such as between private and corporal.

In fact, said the general, where the military authorities felt they should take action and there was no visible excuse for their doing so legally, "we would try to find *some* military significance" in the arrested serviceman's behavior. Wouldn't that be fudging? Well, yes, perhaps; but the general made it clear that if the serviceman didn't like being railroaded this way, he could always seek remedy in civilian court. Of course, few servicemen have the funds or the sophistication to fight the Army. General Hodson said that since the Military Code went into effect in 1951, the Army alone had held 1.3 million courts-martial; by his estimate, at least one-third of these might be affected by the Supreme Court ruling, which is retroactive. But the burden of proving injury is on the GI or ex-GI, for where the Army and the individual disagree (which will be most of the time) it will be up to the wronged person to take legal action to clear his record.

In other words, the Army intends to thwart the Supreme Court ruling by throwing up a wall of inertia between its actions and the Court. And if the fellow from Weed, Arkansas, now earning $78 a week as a filling station attendant feels that he was illegally court-martialed and unjustly given a bad-conduct discharge back in 1962, he can always spend several thousand dollars and several years of his life trying to fight it out with the Army in court.

As Fred P. Graham, the *New York Times* reporter at the Supreme Court, noted, "[General Hodson's] directive served as a reminder that almost any disreputable—and therefore controversial—act by a member of the military can be said to be 'service-connected.' Rape has now been designated a nonmilitary act, but beyond that persuasive arguments can still be made that virtually any other reprehensible act by a serviceman harms his service—or at least his usefulness to it."

In a two-to-one ruling on March 6, 1970 (Judge Homer Ferguson dissented) the Court of Military Appeals refused to apply the Supreme Court's O'Callahan decision retroactively on the grounds that it would bring chaos to the military court system. (Once again it is clear that the only criterion is order and neatness, not justice.) If retroactivity were permitted, COMA wrote, "it is an understatement that thousands of courts-martial would still be subject to review . . . involving such actions as retroactive entitlement to pay, retired pay and veterans benefits." The implication is that justice that costs money is especially to be avoided.

The case in which the Court refused to apply the opinion retroactively was, significantly, another in which an Army sergeant (Joseph P. Mercer) was convicted for an off-base rape in Hawaii. The essentials of the case were exactly the same as in O'Callahan.

Undermining the Supreme Court's O'Callahan decision has become almost a game with the military courts. As Arthur John Keeffe wrote in the June, 1970, issue of *Current Legal Literature,* "One can see that O'Callahan has produced a legal revolution in the services. By hook or crook every judge advocate is doing his best to establish that every crime is 'service-connected.' " And COMA is playing along. For example, COMA confirmed the conviction of a Marine Corps private for forgery. He had cashed a stolen check at a Greyhound bus station in New York to get money for bus fare back to his base in North Carolina. Judge William H. Darden wrote: "Where the accused's military standing facilitates the deception of his intended victim and permits him to obtain his desired goal, the offense is 'service-connected.' " In another case COMA upheld the conviction of a soldier who took a used car out for a test, and never brought it back. His uniform, COMA ruled, had helped him convince the used car dealer that he was trustworthy and therefore the theft was "service-connected." The Court of Military Appeals also upheld the conviction of a serviceman who was court-martialed for burglarizing another serviceman's off-base home.

All of which may one day be seen as no more significant than rhetorical wrestling, for, as Keeffe has pointed out, "With the retirement of Chief Justice Warren, the majority in O'Callahan is a minority." Keeffe notes that the new Chief Justice, Warren E. Burger, has described the Uniform Code of Military Justice as "universally" recognized as "the most enlightened military code in history and as one affording the basic elements of fairness." If Burger's judgment prevails, and if the opportunity presents itself in a comparable case, the Supreme Court may junk O'Callahan. This was the prediction of Judge Advocate General Hodson in a report to the Judge Advocates Association in Dallas, Texas, on August 11, 1969.

If the generals merely wanted to retain jurisdiction over servicemen involved in off-duty brawling and raping, that would be a jurisdictional quarrel that could be leisurely dragged out over the next few years to nobody's great harm. Under certain circumstances, there are reasonable and practical arguments to support military jurisdiction; that is, where a rural civilian community near an enormous military base does not have the police and judicial machinery to cope with Saturday night busts, at least a temporary reliance on the military to prevent off-duty anarchy may make sense. But the truth is, the generals and admirals want to go much further than policing the sin strips of Bogalusa and Abilene. They want also to control Roger Priest's mimeograph machine.

The most notorious illustration of what, at the extremity, this can lead to occurred one hot Saturday afternoon in 1965 in El

Paso, Texas, when a dozen college students were led by a history professor on a march around San Jacinto Square to protest the war in Vietnam. Also in the group was Second Lieutenant Henry H. Howe, Jr., twenty-four, a graduate of the University of Colorado stationed at Fort Bliss with the 31st Engineers. Lieutenant Howe was off duty, and he was wearing civilian clothes.

He was to become the first soldier punished for public opposition to our foreign policy in Vietnam. He was also to become the first since the Uniform Code of Military Justice was enacted in 1950 to be tried and convicted for criticizing a politician—convicted under Article 88, a three-hundred-year-old hangover from the days when British kings first decided that servicemen who criticized the Royal Family should be punished. We cannot blame Howe's trial on the British, however, for they discarded that worthless historical relic from their military code in 1955—ten years before his downfall.

To understand what happened to Howe, one must understand a little about El Paso. Because of its location on the Mexican border and because it has for so many years depended on military payrolls for a large share of its income, El Paso is probably as trashy and as characterless a major city as any in this country. It is a way station for prostitutes, dope smugglers and other border types. Its Chamber of Commerce, with an eye on the nearby military bases, is driven by a kind of hyper-patriotism. So when the little band of war protesters sought a permit to march, the response from the community was pronounced. The Junior Chamber of Commerce suggested that El Pasoans fly the American flag prominently to show their united "stand against Communism." The Civitans Club adopted a resolution demanding that professors at the local college who sympathized with the students be "silenced." Letters poured in to both of the city's newspapers damning "Communist-inspired beatniks."

That was El Paso's mood on the Saturday afternoon of the protest. The signs the protesters carried were mostly bland: "End the Bombing"; "Would Jesus Carry a Draft Card?"; "Tell the Truth About Vietnam." Lieutenant Howe's sign was somewhat stormier. It read: "End Johnson's Fascist Aggression in Viet-Nam," and on the other side: "Let's Have More Than a Choice Between Petty, Ignorant Fascists in 1968."

What reason could Howe possibly have had for doing such a thing? Perhaps he took his theme from retired Marine Corps Commandant David M. Shoup, who, without being court-martialed, has urged us to "keep our dirty, bloody, dollar-crooked fingers" out of depressed countries. If that sounds like an acceptable definition of fascism in foreign policy, then Howe was simply echoing a distinguished general—a former member of the Joint Chiefs and Medal of Honor winner—but more bluntly. (Webster's unabridged dictionary defines fascism as "any program for setting up a centralized autocratic national regime with severely nationalistic policies, exercising regimentation of industry, commerce, and finance, rigid censorship, and forcible suppression of opposition"—and in light of what was about to happen to him, Howe was at least fractionally correct in his choice of words.)

The demonstration lasted only half an hour. Of the two thousand or so people who watched it, only four were in uniform. From the shouts that were heard from the crowd ("Yellow Reds!," etc.), one might surmise that the demonstrators won few recruits. And, since nobody in the crowd was aware of Howe's connection with the military, nobody could have concluded that he was speaking for the military. In fact, the only reason he was detained as a member of the Army was that en route to the demonstration he had stopped at a filling station to ask directions, and the attendant, who saw the Army sticker on his car and noticed the anti-Johnson sign in the back seat, called officials at the base and reported the "suspect." Military Police were so unsure of themselves that they asked the local police to rig up some excuse to arrest Howe and frisk him to see if he was carrying an ID card.

As the march broke up, Lieutenant Howe was edged aside by

several El Paso plain-clothes detectives who, they admitted later, had no grounds for apprehending him and did not look upon him as a lawbreaker. He had acted properly in every way. Police, who admitted that nothing about him suggested he was under the influence of either drugs or alcohol, said they were only doing a favor for the Military Police. City police took his placard from him, removed a small American flag from his pocket and hustled him off to the city jail. There they prepared to book him for vagrancy, a charge which, as one El Paso detective admitted under oath, "could apply to everyone" in that city. The detectives also questioned him about whether or not any of the demonstrators were homosexuals—a curiosity they never explained. It was a bogus arrest in every way, and the more the detectives explained their action, the more obviously oppressive it seemed. This was part of the cross-examination of one detective during Howe's trial:

Q: Did you suspect Lt. Howe of any offense?
A: Well, under the conditions he was certainly in suspicious condition.
Q: What did you suspect him of?
A: Well, it was hard to say who he was. We like to check the people out we don't know in town. [All strangers in a city of 300,000? All strangers in one of the most transient cities on the continent?]

Later the military admitted that the charge by which they had obtained Howe's arrest was illegal. They also conceded at Howe's trial that if he had been a civilian, the charges leveled at him by the Army would have been considered unconstitutional on their face. Howe, in short, was getting some very special treatment.

Having been thrown into the Fort Bliss stockade, rather than, as was customary for officers, allowed to remain free or restricted to quarters (Major General George T. Powers III explained that

Howe "was not fit to be an officer" or be treated like one),* Howe
was charged three days later with three offenses: using contemptuous words against the President (Article 88); conduct unbecoming
an officer and a gentleman (Article 133); and (under catchall
Article 134) with conduct of a nature to bring discredit upon the
armed forces. The last charge, however, was dropped because the
*Manual for Courts-Martial,* in giving guidance for those who conduct military trials, gives as examples of the kind of prohibited
statements covered by Article 134: "public utterances designed to
promote disloyalty or disaffection among troops, as praising the
enemy, attacking the war aims of the United States, or denouncing
our form of government." The officer who conducted Howe's
pretrial hearing decided that this did not apply since to praise the
enemy and attack the war aims would necessitate our being
formally at war, which we were not.

Of the remaining two articles, Article 133 is of no interest.
Either you believe or do not believe that "conduct unbecoming an
officer and a gentleman" is far too vague to meet the constitutional
requirement that a defendant must be permitted to know what he
is charged with. It is such a soggy bag of semantics that there is
hardly anything in it that one can get hold of to argue about; it is
mostly a matter of faith, as countless defense attorneys have discovered when they attacked this article on constitutional grounds
without making the slightest impact on the military judges.

Article 88, however, is overflowing with potential. It reads:
"Any commissioned officer who uses contemptuous words against
the President, the Vice President, Congress, the Secretary of Defense, the Secretary of a military department, the Secretary of the
Treasury, or the governor or legislature of any state, territory,

---

* By way of contrast, First Lieutenant William L. Calley, Jr., charged
with one of the most notorious crimes of the Vietnam war—overseeing the
massacre of more than one hundred natives—was not even restricted to the
base, much less imprisoned while awaiting court-martial.

commonwealth, or possession in which he is on duty or present shall be punished as a court-martial may direct."

This means that servicemen stationed in places like Georgia, Alabama, Mississippi and Louisiana can be punished with several years' hard labor and a dishonorable discharge for calling the governors or legislators of those states racist crackpots; that servicemen anywhere can be punished for calling House Armed Services Committee Chairman Mendel Rivers a drunk—as Drew Pearson called him many times in his column with impunity; or Senator Thomas Dodd and Congressman Adam Clayton Powell cheats—as evidence shows them to be.

In the early days of our new nation the rationale behind Article 88 was an imminent fear—one which modern Americans should be able to sympathize with—that the generals might pull a coup. The prohibition was meant to keep them in line. As John G. Kester wrote not long ago in the *Harvard Law Review,* explaining the beginnings and meanderings of Article 88 over the years:

During the Revolution the civilian authorities had seemed at times to fear their own army as much as that of the British and not without some cause. Mutinies had been frequent, and a military coup might well have taken place had a lesser man than George Washington been at the head of the Continental forces. Washington had at all times been exceedingly deferential to civilian officials, but the officers of his army had not always followed his example. Perceiving the danger in such outspokenness the Continental Congress for its part had tolerated no disparagement of civil authority.

Emergency protections of the civilian government suitable for a new nation might logically be expected to decline as the civilian government grew stronger and less vulnerable to the impact of criticism. Instead, because the prohibition against criticizing the government was found to be much more useful in maintaining military discipline in the ranks and among junior officers than in silencing pushy generals, the military establishment prevailed upon Congress to keep *expanding* the prohibitions. When first made a part of the military code, in 1776, the prohibition was simply against criticizing Congress and the state legislatures. In 1806 this was made to include the President, the Vice President and the state governors as well. In 1916 it was again expanded to include the Secretary of War and the governors of territories as well as of states. And finally in 1950 it was further expanded to protect from criticism every Secretary under the roof of the Pentagon and the Secretary of the Treasury (because he had something to do with the Coast Guard—he doesn't any more, but the law still includes him) and the ruling politicians of *any* "state, territory, commonwealth, or possession."

A few members of Congress were disquieted when this latter provision moved through in 1950. The late Senator Estes Kefauver, for example, said he knew of no reason why politicians should be immune from criticism, and he suggested that "we ought to be able to criticize, and in the second place our greatest reservoir of men who may take part in public life, or should take part, would come from men who are officers, retired officers, or Reserve, or what not."

But there are officers and then there are officers. Since the founding of the Republic something over one hundred military men have been given general courts-martial for criticizing the civilian leadership. There is no record that any officer above the rank of major was ever tried under this prohibition. The records do show, however, that enlisted men, noncommissioned officers and junior officers have received sentences ranging up to thirty years in prison for insulting politicians. Many of the convictions were for insights that history would not totally repudiate. For instance, a private was convicted in 1925 for telling a buddy that President Coolidge "may be all right as an individual, but as an institution he is a disgrace to the whole Goddamned country." Also convicted was a lieutenant who, overhearing someone mention President Franklin Roosevelt, inquired, "What has that son-of-a-bitch done now?"

As a method for guiding military personnel, the speak-no-evil article is asinine. Kester appraised it with complete accuracy:

> Those in the military with sufficient power and authority to make statements causing serious concern to civilian officials usually either are themselves too strong politically to be attacked through criminal charges, or can be dealt with more conveniently in quiet and less formal administrative ways. Instead of chastising insubordinate generals, the article has usually served as an extra prop to the Army's already formidable system of internal discipline, and a rather superfluous prop at that.

On December 22, 1965, Lieutenant Henry Howe was convicted of both charges and sentenced to two years at hard labor; later the sentence was cut to one year. On November 9, 1967, all his appeals having failed in military courts, he was expelled from the Army. One may draw whatever conclusions one wishes from the fact that in the previous two years not one officer who received a general court-martial for an offense that was strictly military (as was Howe's) was punished with a prison sentence.

In judging this case, one should not forget that Lieutenant Howe's loyalty to his country and to the Army was never questioned. He was willing to do everything he was told to do and to do it with good grace. But, as he told a Denver *Post* reporter in a telephone interview from the stockade: "One of the hallmarks of fascism is the suppression of free speech. There is a clear distinction between responsibility to the military and the rights of a citizen. I have never refused to obey an Army order. I would go to Vietnam if ordered to do so. On the other hand, I believe I have the right to express my opinions as a citizen. . . . I believe it is my responsibility, as a citizen, to protest against something I think is wrong." (At that point an Army officer eavesdropping on the conversation broke in and would not allow the interview to continue.)

One should also remember that Lieutenant Howe was acting in obedience to Army Regulation 600–20, 46.1, which warns that since "participation in picket lines or any other public demonstrations, including those pertaining to civil rights, may imply Army sanction of the cause," soldiers cannot participate during duty hours, when in uniform, on a military base, in a foreign country, when the activity is against a civil law, or when violence might result. Lieutenant Howe had carefully avoided all these risks.

Then why had the Army come down on him? It seems rather fair to speculate that the reason lay in the fact that at that time the antiwar ferment was reaching its first great crest in the nation. In the same month that Howe protested in El Paso, the first massive antiwar march hit Washington—to the distress and outrage of President Johnson. Demonstrations of this sort in his home state must have irritated him even more, or perhaps the commanding officers in Texas may have only been trying to anticipate Johnson's irritation. In any event, several high officials in the government, in and out of the Pentagon, made it quite clear that the treatment being inflicted upon Howe was the treatment they would have liked to inflict upon all dissidents everywhere. Howe was just a scapegoat.

An Army lieutenant who picketed the White House in 1968 carrying a sign that read "120,000 American Casualties—Why?" was not court-martialed, although, by being in uniform, he was clearly violating Army regulations. One discernible difference between this and the Howe case was that Howe committed his "offense" in the President's home state, in a community where the daily press and community feeling encouraged a crimping of dissent, and in a year when the Administration still hoped to sweep the public along with the Vietnam build-up; whereas Second Lieutenant Dennis Morrisseau, the officer who picketed the White House, was protesting at a site where almost daily somebody protested ("I can't even go to the gate without the dogs barking," President Johnson complained in his earthy fashion), in a community normally tolerant of dissent, and in the very month, March,

when President Johnson himself finally decided that the war had
killed him politically and that he would surrender the office without fighting public opinion further.*

Throughout Howe's trial, and throughout his appeal, the military
authorities revealed that they were completely insulated from the
growing (but still weak) concern for servicemen that has been
noticed in recent years in the U.S. Supreme Court. This is understandable; the Supreme Court has never demanded the respect or
attention of the military. Indeed, like the military establishment itself, the Court for most of its life has failed to recognize any difference in the need for justice between a small professional army and
a large conscript army. But in this failing there is more excuse for
the military authorities than for the Supreme Court, whose perspective is not narrowed by the necessities of a specialized community.

In 1866, even though the nation had just gone through the
experience, during the Civil War, of having an enormous conscript
army, the Court tossed away the serviceman's right to the protection of the Bill of Rights. "The power of Congress, in the government of the land and naval forces and the militia," it ruled, "is not
at all affected by the Fifth or any other amendment." In other
words, the Articles of War as approved by Congress could not
legally be tested against the Bill of Rights. That ruling has prevailed for more than a century. And this was not the Court's first
surrender to the military—or its last. In his often-quoted lecture at

---

* Apparently to avoid the stench of a First Amendment case, Major General K. B. Lemmon, commanding general of Morrisseau's base at Fort
Devens, Massachusetts, decided instead to ship him off to Vietnam immediately. The general offered his own aircraft for the first lap of the
ferrying job, and when Morrisseau wouldn't climb aboard, he was charged
with refusal to obey an order. But he wasn't even brought to trial on that
charge, because Lieutenant Colonel Luther C. West, head of military justice
at First Army headquarters, spotted so much command influence in Morrisseau's preliminary hearing—and the Army was so worried about this command influence being disclosed if the case should ever come to trial—that
the commanders decided to forgo their vengeance. Thus Morrisseau pulled
off the singular rebellion of not only picketing the White House in uniform
but refusing to go to war—and went unpunished.

the New York University Law Center on February 1, 1962, Chief
Justice Earl Warren noted:

> So far as the relationship of the military to its own personnel is
> concerned, the basic attitude of the Court has been that the latter's
> jurisdiction is most limited. Thus, the Supreme Court has adhered con-
> sistently to the 1863 holding of *Ex parte Vallandigham* that it lacks
> jurisdiction to review by certiorari the decisions of military courts. The
> cases in which the Court has ordered the release of persons convicted
> by courts-martial have, to date, been limited to instances in which it
> found lack of military jurisdiction over the person so tried, using the
> term "jurisdiction" in its narrowest sense. That is, they were all cases in
> which the defendant was found to be such that he was not constitu-
> tionally, or statutorily, amenable to military justice. . . .
> This "hands off" attitude has strong historical support, of course.
> . . . It is indisputable that the tradition of our country, from the time
> of the Revolution until now, has supported the military establishment's
> broad power to deal with its own personnel. The most obvious reason is
> that courts are ill-equipped to determine the impact upon discipline
> that any particular intrusion upon military authority might have. Many
> of the problems of the military society are, in a sense, alien to the
> problems with which the judiciary is trained to deal.

This, one must submit, is a truly pathetic explanation of why the
Supreme Court has deserted the conscript citizens' army. The very
fact that one of the most courageous and humane Chief Justices in
the nation's history would take the position that civilian courts are
"ill-equipped" to oversee the rights of more than three million
citizens shows how difficult is the fight that confronts those who
would reform military justice by making it subordinate to the civil
courts.

Although Warren accurately conveys the traditional feeling of
his predecessors and his colleagues, there have been times, nevertheless, when the entire Court has seemed tormented by its neglect
of the serviceman, and times when a minority of the Court became
outraged by the unwillingness of the other justices to spread the
protection of the Bill of Rights to men in uniform. In 1953, for

example, the Supreme Court ruled (in *Burns* v. *Wilson*) that "The military courts, like the state courts, have the same responsibilities as do the federal courts to protect a person from a violation of his Constitutional rights." Since the Court didn't say otherwise, it must have meant *all* constitutional rights, including free speech. But could it possibly have meant during times of war, declared or otherwise? Doesn't the Supreme Court recognize the need for special restrictions during war? If it does feel that way, the Court has certainly taken pains to hide its feeling. In fact, from the things it has been saying in recent years, it seems to feel that basic freedoms take no holiday (though it has yet to assure basic freedoms *specifically* to the armed forces). In 1968 Justice Warren wrote: "The phrase 'war power' cannot be invoked as a talismanic incantation" to destroy the First Amendment.

To be sure, Warren's opinion came after the unlucky Lieutenant Howe had ended his appeals tour through the military courts. But the justices had ample sentiments to follow, if they wished, from previous Supreme Courts. In 1951, for example, Justice Frankfurter had written: "The First Amendment . . . exacts obedience even during periods of war; it is applicable when war clouds are not figments of the imagination no less than when they are."

The Court of Military Appeals, to which Howe's case ultimately rose, is legally and structurally independent of the Supreme Court and does not feel bound by Supreme Court opinions, even for guidance. COMA considers itself an equal to the Supreme Court, and so it ignored the highest Court's sentiments and went dutifully about its rite of condemning Howe on the basis that he had spoken out during time of war. "We need not determine," the military court ruled, "whether a state of war presently exists. We do judicially know that hundreds of thousands of members of our military forces are committed to combat in Vietnam, casualties among our forces are heavy, and thousands are being recruited, or drafted, into our armed forces. That in the present times and circumstances such conduct by an officer constitutes a clear and present danger to discipline within our armed services, under the precedents established by the Supreme Court, seems to require no argument."

But more amazing still, COMA based this passionate portion of its ruling on those aspects of Howe's conduct which would have applied to neither of the articles he was charged with violating but solely to Article 134, which the original trial law officer had thrown out in preliminary hearing because, by his sound reasoning, we were not at war and therefore it did not apply. In other words, the Court of Military Appeals was *retrying the case on a charge that had been dismissed*.

In the spring of 1970, two and a half years after Howe had lost his appeal before the Court of Military Appeals, partly as a result of that court's feeling that he had committed his offense in time of war, COMA ruled in favor of a defendant by reversing itself and taking the position that we are *not* clearly at war. In the later case it was a U. S. civilian who had been convicted at a court-martial in Vietnam for attempting to steal 36,000 government batteries. Civilians accompanying our armed forces overseas in time of war are covered by military law, but, wrote Judge Darden in this case:

We emphasize our awareness that the fighting in Vietnam qualifies as war as that word is generally used and understood. By almost any standard of comparison—the number of persons involved, the level of casualties, the ferocity of the combat, the extent of the suffering, and the impact on our nation, the Vietnamese armed conflict is a major military action. But such a recognition should not serve as a shortcut for a formal declaration of war, at least in the sensitive area of subjecting civilians in military jurisdiction.

Thus COMA confronts us with these confusing standards: Although he is ten thousand miles from the front line a soldier may be deprived of his off-hours free speech by an undeclared war, but it takes a declared war to deprive a camp-follower in the fighting sector of his right to a civilian trial.

In its pained efforts to appear fair, COMA entangled itself in the strangest of reasoning. It acknowledged that "no one can quarrel with the general proposition that 'freedom of expression upon public questions is secured by the First Amendment.'" It even cited the binding decision in such matters—*New York Times* v. *Sullivan,* 1964. But having made this acknowledgment, it thereupon ignored the fact that the *New York Times* ruling included protection of debate of the very kind charged to Howe, debate so rigorous as to include (in the words of the *Times* ruling) "vilification of men . . . prominent in church or state" and personal attacks on public officials however "vehement, caustic, or unpleasantly sharp."

Didn't this cover Howe's remarks about President Johnson? Quite clearly it did, but in an effort to get around this, the Court of Military Appeals decided to ignore Johnson the politician and treat him strictly as Johnson the Commander in Chief, a military man and not the top politician in the country. It treated Howe as though he had only one relationship to Johnson—that of a junior officer. Although admittedly in 1967, the year that this case finally reached the Appeals Court, there were many in the country who suspected Johnson of parading the darkened hallways of the White House at night in the uniform of a generalissimo, the fact remained that he was only another tub-thumping politician and indisputably covered by the *New York Times* decision about vilification.

In his article in the *Harvard Law Review,* John Kester summarized the shame of the Howe trial and imprisonment:

To dust off a virtually obsolete law in order to heap upon a young second lieutenant just off the college campus the greatest disgrace the Army can impose, as well as a penitentiary sentence, for expression of political opinion which was ineffective, isolated from any military audience, and probably not even very embarrassing until the Army made it a cause célèbre, demeans the Army more than the lieutenant.

Yet after making a splendid delineation of the issues in this case, Kester could not resist the orthodoxy that the military has demanded of the nation for so long:

While a civilian charged with an offense such as inciting desertion in the armed forces might legitimately demand that the government prove his words created a real and immediate possibility that troops would defect, for Howe to claim immunity from punishment simply because he did not obviously endanger the discipline of troops at Ft. Bliss or their willingness to obey their commander-in-chief may be asking too much.

Why? If the "clear and present danger" test works for civilians, why can't it work for military men? Kester continues: "Otherwise it would be difficult to explain the unquestioned application of traditional limitations imposed across-the-board to preserve military efficiency and discipline."

That's just the trouble. The military has reveled in the sweet bullying luxuries arising from "unquestioned application of traditional limitations" long enough.

# 6. The Final Degradation

Periodically some bloody account of mistreatment in a military prison catches the attention of the national press, and briefly there is outcry and concern. Each instance, however, is treated as if it were an aberration in an otherwise satisfactory system. Actually, of course, no such instance is an aberration. There is nothing unusual about military prison brutality. It crops up almost everywhere (except, by and large, in Air Force prisons, which either are very good at covering up their mischief or are singularly humane). It should not be considered the perversion of military justice but rather the logical extension of a system in which the debasement of the accused is the first objective and the last.

Dachau, Germany, is best known as the site of the concentration camp where thousands of Jews were tortured, killed and burned by the Nazis. Some of these Nazis futilely pleaded at the postwar Nuremberg Trials that they had done their evil not from evil hearts but because they had been ordered to. The United States Army now maintains a prison near the former extermination camp, and it was here in August, 1968, that Sergeant Wesley A. Williams, acting on orders from his superiors, severely beat five jailed soldiers with a rubber hose wrapped in green tape. The stockade commander, Major William B. Moore, later told a court-martial that the victims were "known troublemakers" transferred from another prison, and he justified the beatings with the argument that it was good preventive discipline. "Give them a welcoming party— but don't leave any marks," Sergeant Williams said he was told, and he did bludgeon the five men. His explanation that he was "only following orders" was apparently enough to satisfy the military tribunal. It acquitted him of any wrongdoing.

The Williams case raises thoughts that the responsible civilian, desiring to be proud of his government, will want to reject. The obvious historical parallels are too unpleasant. Without further evidence, he will shrink from the notion that his, too, is a government that could condone brutality and rig justice to protect a corrupt system.

For evidence of condoned brutality, however, there is no shortage of places to seek. In this country and overseas the Pentagon supervises 138 Army, Air Force, Navy and Marine brigs and stockades with an overflow population of fifteen thousand prisoners. From these establishments comes an endless stream of grotesque reports: of the homosexual at the brig on Treasure Island, San Francisco, who was forced to suck on a flashlight for the amusement of his Marine guards; of the Army officers at Fort Riley, Kansas, who panicked when they discovered one of their soldiers was only twelve years old and "hid" him for three months in solitary confinement; of the Marines forced to strip to the waist and roll in fresh feces; of the inmate in the Great Lakes Naval Training Center brig who was punished by wrapping his throat in a wet towel, clamping a bucket over his head and making him smoke cigarettes under it until he passed out; of the three hundred suicide "gestures" at Fort Dix in one year, and of the soldiers at Fort Dix who were sprayed with water and then pushed out into wintry weather, naked, for varying lengths of time (one of them for three hours); of Fort Dix soldiers seeking conscientious-objector discharges who were imprisoned "for their protection" in a special cell with known homosexuals; of the Fort Leonard Wood inmate whose body was covered with gray paint and who was made to stand at attention until the paint was dry; of the Marine at Treasure Island who was picked up by his guards like a battering ram and run, head first, against the wall; of the several sailors and Marines who, according to reports from different bases, were made to do such strenuous exercises right after eating that they threw up, after which the guards pushed their faces in the vomit or made them roll in it or (in two instances reported) made them eat it.

The unhappy enlisted man, who on any given day can be numbered in the many hundreds of thousands, and the resentful ex-serviceman, who is even easier to find, pour out these stories in such abundance as to challenge credulity. Some of the stories can be checked and verified; many cannot be. The normal reaction to such stories is skepticism. The great value of the Presidio trials was that they threw open the doors, for a moment, on the nastiness within one stockade and proved that such things were going on with the knowledge of high-ranking officers. The Presidio affair wrenched the nation away from skepticism and forced it to face up to the possibility that the military often treats its prisoners with calculated cruelty.

After the Presidio troubles were debated in Washington, Congressmen received dozens of letters from former prisoners. Typical of these was the letter from a former inmate of the Fort Ord stockade who told of how the guards made him kiss the wall, crawl on the floor and then hurled him against the wall and pounded on him. Another said that at Fort Riley, Kansas, "we had lettuce, beans, potatoes, bread and water which they sometimes *threw* at us. Most of the time we weren't allowed to leave our cells to go to the bathroom so we relieved ourselves on the floor." The guards wouldn't hit prisoners in the head because the bruises and cuts would show there, he said; "Instead, they punched us in the stomach." A group of concerned citizens in the St. Louis area organized under the title Committee for the Defense of Military Prisoners and investigated Fort Leonard Wood, where they found conditions similar to those at the Presidio. They reported that 380 prisoners occupied space for 200; that the prisoners were some-times allowed only five minutes to eat; that letters from the men's families were sometimes returned; that mentally disturbed prison-ers were thrown in with others, resulting in serious beatings and razor slashings; that suicidal prisoners were put in segregation on diminished rations, and that, just as they did at the Presidio, the guards sometimes taunted those with suicidal tendencies by giving them razor blades and encouraging them to "go ahead." One GI, beaten by guards, had his eyes gouged on the way to the hospital. Another prisoner, dragged from a top bunk by a guard, struck his back against a footlocker in such a way that he was permanently paralyzed.

Although the Army can usually suppress news of its stockade brutality for a time, eventually word gets out. More than three months after the riot at Fort Bragg, North Carolina, in the summer of 1968, when 238 inmates seized the stockade and held it for three days, Andy Stapp, head of the American Servicemen's Union, was able to learn details of the incident that provoked it.

"A certain Private Johnson," Stapp said, "of the black prison-ers, was beginning his seventy-eighth day in solitary confinement on that morning of July 23. Johnson faced almost twenty years' imprisonment because he had dared to fight back when the com-mandant of the prison, a major, had spit in his face and taunted him. For this he was charged with assault on a superior officer and put in solitary for close to three months. And three months is a hell of a long time to sit in a room seven by eleven feet.

"Well, it seems that on this particular day Johnson had just about had it with that little room, and after he had been taken to use the latrine, he asked permission to stay out in the hallway for a while to get some exercise. When the guards tried to hustle him back into the rat hole, he physically resisted, knocking the MPs down and climbing to the top of the prison bars. The major, a real sadist, ordered him blasted off by a fire hose. The impact from these hoses will rip the bark off a tree at a hundred yards, and when they turned it on the desperate prisoner, he was immediately knocked to the ground, the force of the water breaking his fingers.

"The guards then rushed in and spread-eagled Johnson on the floor. After they had got him securely pinned down (which wasn't hard for them to do considering his dazed condition), a lifer E-6, his fist wrapped in a pistol belt, began to methodically beat in Johnson's teeth.

"And that's where their little game ended. Because Mike O'Connor and about six other prisoners who had been watching this horror from behind a fence on the other side of the compound went right over that fence and rushed the bastards who were mauling Johnson. And behind them came several dozen other prisoners, for by now the fence had been completely torn down."

After that, one thing led to another, until a full-blown riot was under way.

On June 5, 1969, more than 150 soldiers in the Fort Dix, New Jersey, stockade rioted. Later, word came out through the grapevine that nineteen of the rioters had been kept in solitary confinement for three weeks and forbidden contact with their lawyers. One man was held without food for three days. Prisoners said the reason for the rebellion (during which inmates burned a few louse-ridden mattresses to call attention to conditions) was that 800 prisoners were squeezed into quarters built for 350 and that food was so scarce they were constantly hungry. Reportedly the riot was touched off when the inmates were made to stand in formation five hours through the hottest part of a sweltering day, after which they stood in line three hours for dinner, only to find that there weren't enough water bowls for half the men. (One of the reasons the inmates call the Fort Dix prison "The Pound" is that they drink from bowls.) Prisoners said one method of punishment used by guards is to strap a prisoner's ankles and wrists together and keep him immobile for hours. Prisoners are sometimes served water from toilets.

Congressman Mario Biaggi, a Democrat-Conservative of the Bronx, actually got out and investigated conditions at Fort Dix. (So far as could be discovered, Biaggi was the *only* member of either house of Congress to go to the trouble of personally investigating the brutality rumors; others, such as Senators Goodell and Cranston, simply issued press releases of protest.) Biaggi found that at Dix prisoners were fed what he called the "most inhuman" diet he had ever heard of—lacking meat, dairy products and condiments. Biaggi verified the reports of beatings and the failure to give medical care for the injured and sick.

In its 133-page survey released in May, 1970, the Special Civilian Committee for the Study of the United States Confinement System throws some additional light on the subject. This is its description of what it found at Fort Dix: "At the time of the Committee's visit, the maintenance and sanitation of the kitchen and mess hall were below standard, and the latter had a drab appearance in contrast with those in other stockades. Mice were observed in the dishwashing area. However, the worst condition was found in the center of the mess hall. Workmen from the post engineers, in the process of clearing clogged sewer lines, had dug three holes in the mess hall floor. One was 6 feet long and about 3 feet deep. All three holes were filled with dirty water. The stockade commander stated that they had been there since the workmen left the job 3 weeks before and did not return. The generally bad condition of the kitchen and mess hall were attributed in part to the fact that a replacement for an incompetent mess sergeant had been requested, and that the replacement had not yet arrived." Note the bland acceptance by the committee of this excuse. We are expected to believe that with more than a million men in uniform, the Army couldn't find a mess sergeant to take over, and so for three weeks kitchen life just naturally revolved around three ditches filled with filthy water.

Stockades and brigs are frequently turned over to the control of the most thuggish guards that can be recruited, men who are real troublemakers in their own right. Jim Niles, who once worked in the Fort Hood, Texas, stockade, says that a riot was provoked there not by the inmates but by the guards. This is his account:

"In the stockade there is no method of channeling frustrations in a constructive way, so most prisoners are inclined to channel this frustration onto one another. The guards took advantage of this. They like for the prisoners to fight among each other, because that gives them an excuse to crack down with stiffer regulations. So several of the guards began to organize the whites, dropping whispers here and there that the blacks were going to revolt and take their vengeance out on the whites. Two of the more prejudiced guards, who had convinced the whites that the blacks were out to get them, showed the whites how to make razor-blade knives. The whites then organized and decided to get the blacks before the blacks got them. The blacks, of course, heard about it and decided the same thing. There were twenty-one casualties altogether, three critical, more than were reported for Vietnam in the same day."

A young deserter from Rockport, Missouri, had been AWOL thirty-one times, had been put in five stockades—at Fort Leonard Wood, Fort Riley, Fort Sill, Fort Ord and the Presidio—and had escaped a total of seven times from three of these places. He came away with these memories of his two months in the Fort Ord prison:

"I was thrown in the box for having contraband—a cigarette lighter. I slept on the floor because the mattress had crabs. There were no bunks. We were put on rabbit chow—lettuce, bread, potatoes. The corners of the floor were painted red, and if I stepped on that red part, the guard would come in and knock me around. I don't know why—maybe he just liked red. One boy in there, having convulsions, asked to go to the hospital. The guards called him a troublemaker for that. Once he stopped breathing and another inmate had to give him artificial respiration. After that they threw him in maximum security and held him for several weeks with no hospitalization. One fellow, because he was beaten every day, tried to hang himself. They threw him in the box for that.

"The first day I was there five guards came into my cell and started beating me and trying to get me to swing back, but if I would have swung back, I would have been killed. So I hung onto my belt and just let them do their thing. The next day one of the guards brought me a pair of boots, size 7, and ordered me to wear them and break them in for him. I couldn't even get them on. I wear a size 9 boot. When I told him this, he came in the cell with two other guards and proceeded to beat me up again, so I let them. I was in the box for fourteen days and was beat up five days straight, three times a day.

"After five days another prisoner was brought in. He had refused to do physical training because of his heart. He had a profile [a medical record showing heart trouble], but this didn't really seem to matter to the guards. After doing some exercises he wouldn't do any more, and he told the guards to beat on him if they wanted to, and they did the same thing to him a few days they had done to me, until he finally wound up in the hospital. One time this other fellow was beat up by a civilian that used to be a guard at the stockade but got discharged and just happened to be on hand because he was there to visit and take another look at the stockade.

"I really do believe these guards are insane. They actually try to find a reason to beat people up, and of course they only pick on the ones they know won't strike back—prisoners that are the nonviolent type such as me. I once saw a prisoner sitting down reading a Bible when in walks a guard, takes the Bible out of the prisoner's hand and throws it down and then asks, 'Do you believe in this shit?' The prisoner says, yes, he does, and the guard beats

him up. These things go on all the time. The prisoners go to the
CO and the CO laughs. One prisoner who was beaten wrote to his
Congressman and his Congressman wrote back saying he was
going to do something about it. The prisoner took this letter to his
court-martial, and he was discharged right then, I guess because
the Army didn't want any publicity about it."

In the spring of 1969 about three hundred prisoners at the Fort
Ord stockade held a sit-down protest against the brutalities of the
guards, the bad living conditions and short rations. So desperate
were they that they made their protest despite the fact that they
knew they could be charged with mutiny; in fact, they made their
protest while the mutiny trials of fourteen men from the Presidio
(who had held the same kind of demonstration for the same
purpose) were under way at Fort Ord itself.

As indicated by the Dachau incident mentioned at the beginning
of this chapter, the Army takes its shameful penal philosophy with
it wherever it goes in the world. Twelve miles north of Saigon, for
example, is the infamous Long Binh Jail, dubbed "LBJ" by
soldiers in Vietnam in honor of the recent President. Almost
monthly there are riots at LBJ to protest conditions. The most
spectacular occurred in 1968, when several hundred black soldiers
actually took over a section of the stockade area. A month later,
according to some reports, a handful of them were still holding out
against MPs in one part of the prison.

Like most stockades, LBJ is usually packed about 75 percent
above its regulation capacity. Several men who have spent time in
LBJ said the following experience, that of a black soldier who
cannot be identified since he is still in the Army, is not at all
atypical:

"We got one meal a day, usually, and that was canned rations.
They would punch a hole in the cans about a week before they
gave us the food, so it would be dried up. That was part of the
punishment. I got beat about twice a day for a month. Everyone

knew why I was there [he had refused to fight any more after having taken part in a sortie in which, he says, about three thousand of the enemy were killed]. I was in minimum security for two weeks, and then they stuck me in maximum security for three months because they heard me telling the other fellows why I wouldn't pick up a rifle and why they shouldn't. They have about thirty maximum-security holes. You sleep on dirt floors. You can't see out, but they have a hole where they can see in on you. It's total dark, day and night. If you were lucky enough to have a guard who had a heart, he'd take you out for a crap. Otherwise, you crapped in the hole. The room was about five by eight. One black GI who raised a fist salute was accused of trying to incite a riot and about ten guys jumped on him, stomped him, kicked him. About 60 percent of the prisoners are black. Racial tension couldn't have been higher. Fights every day. The blacks had one barracks, and the whites couldn't go in there. If they did, we'd beat them. The Vietnamese people would give us marijuana and all kinds of stuff. If you had a stockade arm band on, they'd do anything for you. We'd go to the fence and they would throw us over bundles of grass. It was really great. The guards used the drugs, too. I'd smoke with some of the guards, but they'd turn right around and beat me the next day anyway."

One young ex-sergeant, Robert Lucas, better known later as a coordinator of the 1969 Vietnam Moratorium, recalled having to escort a black soldier to LBJ. The prisoner had not been convicted of any crime, and he had only been charged with being AWOL. This, says Lucas, was the way they processed his prisoner:

"When we got there, they put the black fellow inside a large cage just inside the gate. They took his belt, cap and shoelaces. From there he was escorted to the incoming building. I explained that he was a pretrial prisoner, that he wasn't hostile. But they treated him just as though he had committed first-degree murder. They stripped him, made him bend over so they could inspect his butt to see if he was hiding anything; they checked his groin, looked in his mouth for contraband. This was just done to humiliate him; they knew any serious smuggling around a prison is done by the Vietnamese workers. There were three clerks watching. One of the clerks grins at him and says, 'Sit down and I'll give you my first haircut.' So he shaved him bald. Then they led the prisoner to a military shipping box—a steel box about six feet high, about seven feet deep, about five feet across; it's usually used for shipping heavy things like typewriters or ammunition. That's where he stayed his first night in LBJ. He had a bucket to piss in and some water to drink. He was in that steel crate from four o'clock that afternoon to seven the next morning. That's standard procedure."

The Marines have a prison in Vietnam that rivals LBJ. It is the Danang brig, and prisoners there testified to its miseries by burning down a whole cell block. Garret Gianninoto of New York City, an ex-GI who spent three months in the Danang brig, gives this report on its solitary-confinement cells (in which he spent eight days): "The cells were six by eight feet. The only furniture was a square box covering one-half of a twenty-five-gallon drum—this was your toilet. The drum was taken out once a day and the stuff was burned. Some fellows who had been in other prisons' solitary-confinement cells complained because they didn't have any place to go to the toilet, but I would rather not have had. Those toilets got pretty awful when the temperature inside the cells got up to 130 degrees. And you had to sit on the toilet all day. That was an order. You couldn't sit or lie on the floor. . . . The food was lettuce and rice and, in the morning, two boxes of Kellogg's corn flakes and water. Stuff like that, and in the food it was commonplace to find slugs and flies and weevils." Gianninoto said he had seen no physical brutality.

Most of the men in the Danang and Long Binh prisons, as is true of most military jails, are guilty only of having been AWOL.

Down the California coast five hundred miles from the Presidio is a U.S. Marine base, Camp Pendleton. Spread over twenty acres, its prison—which the Marines identify, in Navy parlance, as the "brig"—is a conglomeration of temporary wood-frame buildings thrown up during World War II to house prisoners of war, and temporary prefabricated metal buildings and tents erected in the intervening years as the requirements for prisoners grew. Under normal conditions there is space in the brig for 400 prisoners (the Marine Bureau of Personnel rates the capacity at 612), but these days the population is always above 800 men and often it passes 900.

In April of 1969 a group of about forty Pendleton prisoners came upon a fellow inmate hanging from the cyclone fence, spread-eagled. His feet were off the ground. A guard had made him stand on a stool while he was being handcuffed to the fence; then the stool had been kicked away. The men sat down and said they would stay there until something was done. The situation might have developed into a Presidio-type "mutiny," but in this instance coolheaded officers intervened.

Father Alban Rosen, a Catholic priest who has done volunteer chaplain work at Pendleton, said that the official brig chaplain told him of seeing men forced to run in a circle until they fell from exhaustion, at which point "the guard would just come over and kick them until they got up and started trotting again. This stuff goes on all day."

The Marines have a punishment called Correctional Custody Platoon. It is not for criminals but only for men who violate simple regulations—haven't tied their tie correctly, perhaps, or have given a sloppy salute. CCP punishment does not even go on a man's record, so one might suppose the punishment would not be very severe.

A Marine who has been in a CCP at Pendleton twice and has observed its operations many times gave this account:

"I've seen guys go in there weighing 180 pounds and come out weighing around 100. They make you carry a double-head sledge hammer—a head at each end—with a bucket of sand on each end of the hammer. Then they make you carry that over your shoulder while you run across the base to the place where you are going to break rocks all day. And you are there *all* day, except for dinner. And if you don't crack rocks like they think you should, they'll make you stop and do a few hundred squat-thrusts.

"And if you don't do either thing like they want, they've got other treatment for you, like the room with mirrors. They make you stand naked in front of the mirrors all day, every day, until something happens—either you crack up or you agree to do things the way they want. When I was in CCP, there was a guy who stood in front of the mirror for twenty-one days. Or, if you collapse on them and refuse to stand in front of the mirrors, they'll beat you up and then lay you out on the floor spread-eagled—your arms out and legs spread apart, naked. You lay there and they'll drop rifle casings beside your ears—ping, ping, ping, ping—they'll just keep doing this all day long.

"Oh, they've got all sorts of routines for you. Some of them they do to you even if you haven't done anything wrong. Like sometimes they'll put a bucket over your head and make you dry-shave underneath the bucket, double-timing in place while shaving. If you're not double-timing fast enough, they'll pound on the bucket with a stick."*

Jack Eugene Lunsford, twenty, who was a guard in a Correctional Custody Platoon at the Marine Corps Recruit Depot in San Diego until he couldn't take it any longer and deserted, described one of the more memorable techniques:

"They have this hook on the wall, seven feet or so off the floor. The hook sticks out about four inches and is big around as your

---

* This and many of the other quotes in this chapter come mostly from men interviewed on the West Coast—in Whittier, Los Angeles, San Francisco —and in South Carolina, Georgia and New York City. Some were still in uniform, some were deserters, some had been honorably discharged, some had been removed with dishonor. Though they were an extremely varied lot—and the reader should bear this in mind as he weighs their credibility —still, their accounts were impressively alike.

thumb. If a prisoner doesn't cooperate, they'll put him in a strait jacket that has a ring in the back, and they'll hang this ring to the hook in the wall. It's painful and a lot of the men pass out.

"There's an interview that all the prisoners go through. I've seen twenty or thirty. You walk in with your seabag that weighs between 75 pounds and 115 pounds. You hold this above your head full arm's distance. While you hold it like that, they make you turn in a circle fast as you can go, screaming 'Yes, sir!' and 'No, sir!' Once I saw a sergeant climb up on top of two footlockers and jump on the bag one fellow was holding. The bag fell on his head and he was knocked flat to the floor. It broke his nose and knocked out a couple of teeth."

Terry Chambers, nineteen, a former Marine who is now a deserter, said that when he was a prisoner in the Marine Correctional Custody Platoon, "they hung me between two bunk beds, hung me by my thumbs and toes to the top posts of the beds. I still don't have feeling in my thumbs."

Father Alban, among others, counseled against doubting these reports. "No matter how bad it is," he said, "you can believe just about anything the Marines tell you about the punishment routines. I really don't doubt any of the stories, because of the things I've seen and heard. I've seen faces beaten in. I know about the room of mirrors."

Reports like these might well be met with skepticism, coming as they do from an outsider, even though the outsider is an unusually responsible one. But we do not need to rely solely on Father Alban. Many of his accounts have been verified by the most unimpeachable of insiders. Dr. Larry McNamee, now doing his residency in Cleveland, Ohio, was the Pendleton brig physician for more than a year, until July, 1969. He was the first, and reportedly the last, doctor to hold that job on a full-time basis. He was a full lieutenant in the Navy Medical Corps.

Dr. McNamee told of one young Marine in maximum security who "was screaming all the time and the guards didn't like that, so they taped up his whole face except for his nose. They left a hole for his nose. The only problem was, the kid had sinus and bronchial trouble. That night he had a real bad attack, but since he was taped up, he couldn't say anything. All he could do was keep banging his head against the door. They had to hospitalize him."

Dr. McNamee's appraisal of the Correctional Custody Platoon was much the same as that of the men who had experienced it. "It is impossible," said McNamee. "When men first check into the correctional custody unit, the guards are especially tough on them. I've seen fractured noses, bruises all over the body. One day I saw two or three guys who said they had been clubbed—the guards had some kind of wooden thing with tape around it and the men were banged with this club. They had bruises all over their chests and backs. I brought this up to the CO, who had an investigation like always. Of course the guard-instructors said they knew nothing about it—no, no, they wouldn't treat anyone like that. Well, the investigators walked into the instructors' shack and found the club. It was exactly the way these prisoners described it.

"One of the guys who was responsible for this was seen by a psychiatrist and deemed to be sadistic and should not be working in a correctional facility. But he continued to work there until he was discharged from the service. None of the guards are screened. The guy who manacled the prisoner to the fence had been seen earlier for psychiatric difficulties, and he's still working there."

After a time, Dr. McNamee began keeping a catalogue of atrocities. Here one finds a record of the private who came to the doctor with a black-and-blue scrotum, kicked by a guard when the prisoner refused to eat his food off the floor. Here is a record of broken noses, of back pains caused by guards jumping on prisoners lying on the floor; of men who were kicked, beaten in the face with wet towels, made to lie prone while guards kicked them in the back, in the head, in the neck.

Dr. McNamee told about the "Ice Box," a special punishment facility of six cages set on a concrete slab in the open. The cages were covered with canvas that was lowered during the sunny hours to parboil the prisoners and raised at night so they would freeze. Sometimes, the doctor said, prisoners would be held for up to eight hours in the "Bull Pen," a fenced area with neither toilets nor water fountains.

When Dr. McNamee exposed these conditions in the September 15, 1969, issue of *The Nation,* the Marine Corps hurriedly decided that the Ice Box and the Bull Pen were no longer in use. At least that is what Marine spokesmen told reporters. But the inmates felt that conditions were not yet perfect, apparently, because within hours after Pendleton officials declared that they had put an end to the more brutal aspects of their penal care, about two hundred enraged prisoners drove their guards into a hut and pelted it with stones. One thing Pendleton officials do not pretend is that the maximum-security building is out of service. It still thrives—all forty-eight dungeons. The interior of this building is in virtual darkness, so few are the light bulbs. Prisoners are required to sit on the cement floor up to twenty hours each day. Exercise is limited to ten minutes. There are two toilets and two washbasins for the forty-eight men.

What, beyond simple sadism, could explain such apparently senseless and random brutality? Part of the answer is to be found in the military's philosophy of punishment—not an official, public philosophy but a pragmatic, cultural understanding that is the psychic heritage of every military professional. According to it, imprisonment is intended not to rehabilitate an offender but to make an example of him. It is meant to show that, no matter what the Uniform Code of Military Justice says, once a man steps outside the perimeter of approved behavior, he has lost all authority over his own mind and body. At the wish of his keepers, he may be broken—literally. They recognize no obligation to maintain his health; on the contrary, health is merely another privilege to take from him in the course of his necessary degradation.

Thus the officers who ran the Pendleton brig often refused to let the prisoners receive treatment they needed for even serious ailments. For eight consecutive Mondays Dr. McNamee made appointments for one of the prisoners to visit a chest specialist for treatment of bronchitis. But brig officers never permitted the prisoner to be taken for treatment. Men with broken bones sometimes had to wait two days before they were escorted to an X-ray clinic. A man with gonorrhea was scheduled for bacteriological studies on October 23, 1968; in January, 1969, when he got out of the brig, he still had the gonorrhea and he still hadn't received the study. Men with hernias missed hospital surgery appointments; men scheduled for psychiatric appointments, or blood tests, weren't permitted to keep them. Dr. McNamee said that 53 percent of the prisoners who needed treatment in special clinics or surgery at the base hospital were never taken, because there were no guards to escort them, "although there always seemed to be enough guards to escort prisoners to cut the commandant's lawn." Of the drugs he prescribed for prisoners, only 15 percent ever reached them.

Prisoners at Pendleton were deprived not only of their physical health but of their mental health as well. The means, in addition to filth and brutality and overcrowding, was boredom. To break the grim monotony, prisoners resorted first to fights and regular rioting; one riot in the spring of 1969 sent twenty men to the hospital. Then came drugs, illegal but available. Prisoners who could not afford drugs injected themselves with almost anything—coffee, Kool-Aid, various medications—and as a result, one to two cases of serum hepatitis appeared in the brig each month. Prisoners would catch wild mice and try to keep them as pets; several prisoners were treated each day for bites. Bored inmates also threw razor blades at one another, for excitement, and lacerations were common. Another desperate diversion was a contest in which two prisoners would place lighted cigarettes in the crooks of their arms to see which man could stand the pain longer.

It would be wrong to conclude that the military establishment has a higher percentage of sadists than any other element of the population, or that the military establishment would not prefer to bend and break its personnel under polished and sanitary conditions. Nor should one conclude that most military commanders knowingly encourage brig and stockade officers and noncoms to engage in the downright cruel bullying that goes on. Just as the American Telephone & Telegraph Company would prefer to give perfect service to its customers while strengthening its monopolistic hold on the industry, the highest military officers, eager to perpetuate their own monopoly over the lives of more than three million men and over 80 percent of the federal budget, would doubtless prefer to achieve total discipline with a minimum of blood and abuse. The military corporation is no less devoted to good public relations than are its civilian counterparts.

After the rotten conditions of Fort Dix's kitchen were publicized, the Army filled and cemented over the trenches in the floor and placed a potted plant where the largest hole had been. For the military, that's reform on a majestic scale.

When the above conditions at Camp Pendleton were first disclosed, for example, the brig officer was hastily replaced and, as already mentioned, the Ice Box and the Bull Pen were, at least temporarily, closed down. Few other changes were made, however. Living conditions in the brig are about the same as they have been for years, and the attitude of the guards toward the prisoners is reportedly unchanged. Military penal reforms and reforms of justice come in small ripples, not in waves, for military authorities have what they consider to be bigger things, more central missions, to worry about.

In a harried, off-and-on, vague fashion the Marine Corps had been worrying about the brig conditions for several years, and the conditions were known at the highest level of the Corps. A confidential memorandum from Quartermaster General Wallace H. Robinson, Jr., to Chief of Staff W. J. Van Ryzin, dated March 17, 1969, acknowledged that

the Marine Corps has recognized that a truly explosive situation exists.

. . . The Senatorial investigation of conditions at the Presidio could serve to assist the Marine Corps in obtaining authorization and funding of this line item [a new barracks for the brig], because recognition of a need for more adequate service brigs would helṗ us. However, a public disclosure of existing conditions at the Camp Pendleton Brig could tend to place the Commandant in an embarrassing defensive position.

Accompanying this confidential memorandum was a summary of conditions, which opened candidly with the acknowledgment:

It is clear that the Armed Services are presently in a position where we must make some rather dramatic changes in our corrections program. This fact is re-emphasized daily by the press in support of a growing popular concern about many of the DOD corrections facilities. A case in point is the recent Presidio imbroglio. The Marine Corps has been included in some of the peripheral discussions and accusations surrounding this incident.

The survey admitted that facilities at Pendleton were "grossly inadequate"; that the guards were untrained and overworked; that "oil heating used in the tents and metal buildings is considered a fire hazard and represents a serious threat in the event of a prisoner disturbance"; that the toilet facilities—most of which sit out in the open with no protection from the weather and no privacy—"are inadequate for the number of prisoners"; that there are not enough showers and sinks and that the ones on hand are often broken or inoperable; that the Ice Box was "an inhumane and indefensible practice"; that security was terrible—166 prisoners had escaped during the previous year (which means conditions were such that 166 men, practically all of whom had committed no crime worse than being AWOL, were willing to risk getting shot for the chance to flee the place); that during the same year the commanding officer had made only six recommendations for clemency; that the prisoners were bored beyond endurance; and that the buildings sometimes seemed ready to collapse.

On this last point the report read:

The 1942 vintage building being utilized for all newly confined prisoners undergoing indoctrination and/or awaiting classification is a fire and safety hazard. . . . It was reported that if the prisoner load on the second deck was past a certain level the doors to the cells on the first deck would not open. There is only one escape hatch on each deck, all the windows and doors being either barred or secured to prevent escape. . . . Even the new building is inadequate; there are 48 cells in this building and only two commodes, the heating is poor and food must be carried from the mess hall and served in the individual's cell which routinely, during the winter, results in cold, greasy food.

Bearing in mind that this report is now a year old, one must wonder why the Marine Corps hasn't done more to correct the situation. The answer (aside from the low priority given penal and legal reforms) lies, first of all, in the fact that the military is generically sluggish and, second, in the fact that it must peddle such reforms as it desires to Congressional committees, which are even more callous than the military itself; after all, there is very little pork in the barrel of penal reforms.

The sluggishness was illustrated specifically by the fact that on October 10, 1968, *five months* before the Quartermaster General's investigating team discovered the horrors of the Bull Pen, Dr. McNamee had sent a memo to the commanding officer of the headquarters regiment complaining about the situation; when Dr. McNamee was discharged in July, 1969, four months after the Quartermaster General's survey was sent to the commandant, nothing had been done to improve conditions. Nothing done in nine months, despite formal acknowledgment of the problem.

As for the Congressional drag, an insider's view of that was supplied by Dr. McNamee's wife. One day three Congressmen showed up and toured the camp. The colonel in charge of the brig facilities heard they were there and found them just as they were leaving. By coincidence, Mrs. McNamee was in the parking lot when the colonel and the Congressmen met. "The colonel begged them to come see the brig," she recalls. " 'Just give me five minutes,' he said. 'Let me show you how horrible it is here.' They laughingly and politely refused. They said, 'Everyone has his problems, everyone needs money. We've got other things on our agenda. It was nice talking to you.' The colonel kept pleading with them. He said, 'I really want to show you how bad it is,' and they said, 'Well, that's how it is. We can't stay.' And they went on to their car, waving back at him. The colonel was not the most sensitive officer, to say the least, but even he recognized the problems of the brig."

As Dr. McNamee not only acknowledged but insisted, many of the problems of the brig were not always caused by deliberate sadism on the part of the staff. Often it was the sadism of a situation, an environment: a volatile stew of humanity, overcrowding and understaffing, everyone tired and frustrated, no privacy for the inmates and no rest for the guards, a situation in which everyone snapped and yelled, and where impossible human relations were the only ones. The Marines who ran the place needed help, and knew it. But their one effort to get relief from three Congressmen was spurned. It was a small episode, perhaps, this vignette of the parking lot, but it brings us to the crucial question in the whole problem of military justice: Should the military be forced to be the petitioner of reform?

# 7. After Flogging, What?

UNDOUBTEDLY WE SHOULD NOT DENY servicemen any right that can be given reasonably," Judge George W. Latimer of the Court of Military Appeals said fifteen years ago in a freedom-of-speech case. "But in measuring reasonableness, we should bear in mind that military units have one major purpose justifying their existence: to prepare themselves for war and to wage it successfully. . . . If every member of the service was, during a time of conflict or preparation therefore, permitted to ridicule, deride, deprecate, and destroy the character of those chosen to lead the armed forces, and the cause for which this country was fighting, then the war effort would most assuredly fail. . . . If it is necessary for survival that this country maintain a sizable military establishment . . . then I have a great deal of difficulty in following an argument that those who serve should be entitled to express their views, even though by so doing they may destroy the spirit and morale of others which are vital to military preparedness and success."

Although voiced by a civilian judge, this is the military's old, old argument. Over the years, however, the argument has been couched in other terms. The military used to argue that if the power to flog a man or to put him in irons were ever taken away, the ranks would disintegrate into pure anarchy. Today the objections are much more refined, but they still are based on grim predictions of "an undisciplined mob that will fail on the field of battle" unless the normal rights of citizenship are shed, by the cadence, somewhere between the recruiting depot and the training field and unless the men are held in iron harness from then on. It is an argument-of-catastrophe by which the military seeks, and has always sought, to hang onto the established system.

Often the argument is sincere, as when uttered by a man like Colonel Thomas Maertens. Maertens commanded the brigade that produced the troublesome Fort Jackson Eight. "I'm all Army," he likes to say. He was born on a small Army post in Alaska. He has never lived one minute of his forty-six years in any environment but the military. His father was an Army colonel who was killed in World War II. His stepfather is a retired Army colonel with thirty years' service. Both brothers are Army colonels. He has a son in West Point. He himself is a graduate of West Point, class of '45.

Maertens is a handsome, jut-jawed, friendly fellow who is plainly baffled and hurt by what is going on. "I really never gave this whole proposition [of constitutional rights for soldiers] much thought, and it never reared its head until I found we had an element here, in my own brigade, which began to scream out that the Army was violating its constitutional rights, began to scream out, 'We have a right to dissent, we have a right to arbitrate, we have a right to defy, if necessary'—all of this is completely incompatible to the Army."

Jittery, naïve, suspicious in matters relating in any way to "rights," the military professionals do the best they can. But their training has left them pitifully limited; they wear blinders that shut out the beauty of the liberties of the civil landscape and hold their eyes to the old, rutted military road. They fight very well. But they are not much good, either by training or instinct, for anything else. And since fighting alone is enormous enough a responsibility in a world full of fighters, the military should not be given the extra burden of reforming its justice.

Justice is too important to be left to the military. If military justice is corrupt—and it is—sooner or later it will corrupt civilian justice. Perhaps this already has begun. The Supreme Court was wrong when it said that "the military constitutes a specialized community governed by a separate discipline from that of the civilian." When one-fifth of all adults have had military experience, the two ways of life cannot be separated so distinctly. There is inevitable seepage, by means of the movement of civilians in and out of the military and of the indoctrinization that lingers a lifetime. Whether or not he was thinking of military justice, the point was made by General David M. Shoup (Ret.), former commandant of the Marine Corps: "Today most middle-aged men, most business, government, civic and professional leaders, have served some time in uniform. Whether they liked it or not, their military training and experience have affected them, for the creeds and attitudes of the armed forces are powerful medicine, and can become habit-forming. . . . For many veterans the military's efforts to train and indoctrinate them may well be the most impressive and influential experience they have ever had—especially so for the young and less educated."

Military justice, in fact, is an experience in totalitarian expediency, a persuasive experience from which the insecure America of today emphatically does not benefit.

But does it make sense to speak of "reforming" military justice? Previous attempts at reform have largely failed. A good example is the Court of Military Appeals, generally viewed as the finest and most progressive thing to come out of the 1950 reform of military justice. The court is composed of three men, appointed by the President to fifteen-year terms. Because the Code stipulated that all three must be civilians, it was supposed that this highest court in the military system would thus establish civilian control over the military.

This has turned out to be not true at all. In fact, the philosophy of the Court of Military Appeals is rarely distinguishable from the military's. The latest to join the court was William H. Darden, appointed at the request of Senator Richard Russell, a famous partisan of the military who was then chairman of the Senate Armed Services Committee. Darden had been Russell's secretary for three years, then served as chief clerk and chief of staff of the Armed Services Committee for seventeen years before becoming a military appellate judge in 1968. He took the place of a man who had been equally partial in military matters, Paul J. Kilday of Texas, who for twenty-two years had served on the House Armed Services Committee. His honors included several citations from military organizations for "tireless efforts to build national armed strength." Kilday, however, was considered a moderate compared with Chief Judge Robert E. Quinn, a former Governor of Rhode Island who has been a captain in the Naval Reserve for the past twenty-eight years. Generally considered the most liberal member of COMA is Homer Ferguson, who, as head of the permanent Senate Investigating Committee in the 1940s and early 1950s, ran some useful graft probes but also dabbled in the Elizabeth Bentley–type ("Queen of the Communist Spies") witch-hunting of the era.

If nonconformist servicemen fear that such judges may have a hard time adjusting to the perspective of the coffeehouse, they can stop worrying because the Court of Military Appeals probably won't accept their cases anyway. It is required to hear only appeals involving the death penalty or cases in which generals or admirals are imperiled. Otherwise, the court has no obligation to listen, and it usually doesn't; it refused, for example, to listen to Howard Levy's appeal. Of the 109,656 men given courts-martial of all kinds in 1969, only 164 cases were accepted by the Court of Military Appeals—which means that far fewer than one percent of the men convicted got a full review. Although the court claims to have the power to issue extraordinary writs, when servicemen come to the court for injunctions and writs to protect what they consider to be their constitutional rights, the court is seldom willing to hear them.

An even less useful aspect of the 1950 "reforms" is the boards of review that were set up as the intermediate appellate stage. These boards have jurisdiction only over cases in which bad-conduct discharges and/or one-year sentences, or worse, have been handed down. The members of these boards, all of them military officers, are under the thumb of the Judge Advocate General of their particular branch of the armed forces, being appointed by him to sit just so long as their decisions please him. Frederick Bernays Wiener, once a colonel in the JAG office, was a great defender of the system when he was wearing a uniform, but after he went into civilian practice, he began to suspect that the review boards were almost fraudulent. He told a Congressional committee, "The existence of the board of review does not help an accused substantially, and I feel so strongly about that that I no longer take retainers before boards of review because it is a waste of my time and of my client's money." The best way to reform the boards of review, he said, would be to "abolish them altogether and shorten the process" because all they offer are "built-in delay, and built-in expense."

The Military Justice Act of 1968 (in effect as of August, 1969) is typical of the trivial patchwork by which the Pentagon and its allies in Congress hope to keep the UCMJ in force. This act brought about the first alterations in the UCMJ since it was written in 1950, and the alterations are hardly impressive as eighteen years of progress. The boards of review will operate about the same as always, but they have been prettied up with a new title—Courts of Military Review. The act's most highly touted change is the supposed "independence" of the courts-martial law officers, who have been given the title of "judge" for the first time. The Pentagon claims that under the new policy these military judges are free of command influence because they are responsible only to the Judge Advocate General's office; free at last of pressures from unit commanders, the military judges can finally begin to act like men of high integrity.

Or can they? Less than four months after the new judging policy was to have gone into effect, significant doubt about the reform was raised by the case of Roger Priest, who will be remembered as the seaman whose newsletter offended Representative Rivers and Defense Secretary Laird. On November 19, 1969, the military judge in this case, Captain Raymond Perkins, dismissed two charges against Priest. But Rear Admiral George P. Koch, commandant of the Washington Naval District, ordered the charges reinstated, and six days later Captain Perkins bowed to command.

Whatever the appellate outcome of such quarrels, it is plain to see that periodic "reforms" cannot remove command influence, and it is plain that if command influence cannot be removed, the Uniform Code of Military Justice should be junked. Even Edmund M. Morgan, chairman of the committee that drafted the Code, conceded in 1953 that if command control persisted, a new system would have to be established.

Ironically, the most dramatic admission that command control does exist was prompted by a case that came not from the troubles of a dissident group but from those most ardent of warriors, the Green Berets—specifically from the colonel, two majors, three captains and one enlisted man who, briefly in the Indian summer of 1969, were accused of murdering a suspected Vietnamese double agent. Before the charges were dropped by an order from the White House, the Green Berets' continual complaint was that they could not receive a fair court-martial, could not receive a court-martial untainted by the vengeance of their commandant, General Creighton Abrams, whom they accused of wanting to railroad them. They argued that a feud existed between Abrams and one of the accused, Colonel Robert Rheault, head of the Green Berets. They begged that their case be transferred to a civilian court. Whether or not they were accurate in their appraisal of General Abrams' desire for a particular conclusion to the trial, the Green Berets made the public aware of the issue of command control as never before. At last the issue was pegged to the fate of men who were not accused of being disloyal or lukewarm to the cause of war but were fanatically zealous in the pursuit of it. If command control could do an injustice to *that* kind of warrior, what terrors must it hold for the afternoon soldier and sailor?

The same question arose from the case of Lieutenant William L. Calley, Jr., charged with the murder of one hundred or so Vietnamese civilians in My Lai. His attorney is George Latimer, who, when he was on the Court of Military Appeals, was slow to see command influence even when commanders were known to have instructed court-martial panels to crack down for the sake of discipline. But now that Latimer is again on the other side of the bench, he sees command influence more easily; in Calley's case, he saw it coming all the way down from the Commander in Chief himself, Mr. Richard Nixon, who told a press conference that the massacre was "abhorrent" to all Americans—a declaration which Latimer understandably suspects may have influenced Army Chief of Staff Westmoreland and all underling officers and deprived Calley of any possibility of a fair trial.

Because the military has been so singularly unconscious of its defects and so inept at correcting those it does recognize, countless attorneys, millions of servicemen and ex-GIs, some civilian jurists and even some politicians are now convinced that there is no use to wait longer for internal reforms and that the best thing to do is simply to take away the judicial process and return jurisdiction to the civilian courts.

Some critics, such as Senator George McGovern, would "put the *serious* legal and criminal questions in the hands of the civilians." Others, like Charles Morgan, Jr., who was Captain Levy's defense counsel, would go all the way. "There's just no point of having any sort of trials conducted within the military," Morgan says. "The military is incapable of understanding the Constitution." Morgan begins his argument from the context of the Levy affair. "Several things are going to have to happen if we're going to have a decent Army in the future. First of all, there's absolutely no need to have

Army physicians. You can get physicians for the Army who don't
have to run around in khaki green, saluting. Let the Army hire
civilian doctors. Secondly, you don't need chaplains in the Army.
Let the various churches pay for them and send them to accom-
pany the Army, if they want to. And the third thing is, the Army
should be made to give up its lawyers and its courts. The handling
of folks who've got good sense is a great problem, and the Army
doesn't know how. People with good sense expect to be covered by
the Bill of Rights, and Army justice doesn't permit this. There's
absolutely no argument against giving Army personnel the protection of civilian juries."

A reasonable man will ask if it is possible to take away the
military courts without leaving the services in a state of chaos.
Many practical questions immediately come to mind. Without the
authority to court-martial a man in the ranks, how would his
officer keep him from going back to bed when he should be at the
rifle range? Or walking off the base and never coming back? Or, at
the very least, destroying order by stepping out of ranks and loudly
denouncing the officer as, perhaps, a warmongering, capitalistic,
racist pig?

These worries are not unreasonable, but they are easily dispelled.
In the first place, the commonest trouble in the military comes
from surrendering to the desire to get away from the military.
More than 90 percent of all punishment in the military is handed
out for being absent without leave. *And there is no evidence that
the threat of punishment discourages anybody from going AWOL.*
There is evidence to the contrary. When General David Shoup
became commandant of the 1st Marine Division at Camp Pendleton in 1957, he found the brig clogged with men who had been
AWOL. He ordered everyone in the brig released except the
felons. It almost cleared the brig. To those who had been AWOL,
he said in effect, "Now go back to work. That's what you're here
for, not to sit around going stir-crazy. If you want to skip out again,
go ahead; we'll find you and bring you back and put you to work
again. And we'll do it as often as we have to, until you serve your

enlistment time, so you might as well settle down and serve it out now." The policy did not end AWOLs, but it did reduce their number and it did ease tensions. Discipline was not hurt in the slightest.

If there is any one compelling reason for returning all Americans in uniform to the jurisdiction of the civilian courts, it is that the military courts make no allowance for the types and backgrounds of the people who come before them. No sounder logic was voiced in the Presidio trials than that of attorney Hallinan when he argued that if blame is to be assigned in such cases, then, "Blame the Congress, blame the recruiting system, blame the draft boards which allow the strong and intelligent to stay out of service and force the weak and the sick to serve." Many of the young men who wind up in military courts and then in stockades are the victims of the Pentagon's "benevolence"; specifically they are the victims of a plan started by Defense Secretary Robert McNamara. "Project 100,000" lowered the recruiting standards to permit the services to take in that many "underprivileged" men each year who otherwise could not have qualified. McNamara said he was doing it so they could get an education and learn a trade; the U.S. Department of Education said it was a grand idea.

As it turned out, many of the men who enter the services through Project 100,000 get in trouble immediately and never get out of trouble while they are in uniform. Some of those taken into the service today are not only unschooled but incapable of learning, because of instability or lack of mental capacity. Yet the Army expects them to perform normally, and the result is, inevitably, tragic. A report of the fate of the first quarter-million enlistees under Project 100,000 was released by the Pentagon in late January, 1970. It showed that those who wound up in the Army were court-martialed more than twice as often as the normal soldier—3.7 percent compared to 1.5 percent. The Army prefers to hang on to these young men for combat use if at all possible (37 percent see combat compared with 23 percent of other enlistees). The Navy and the Air Force give them undesirable or unsuitable discharges at a rate two and three times higher than for their normal recruits. The Army's Lieutenant General Albert O. Connor explained that the soaring desertion and AWOL rates could be accounted for by the fact that "we are getting more kooks." But the officers who hand down justice make no allowance for the kooks. When one officer at Amarillo Air Force Base did make such an allowance—he suspended a bad-conduct discharge handed down in a special court-martial so that the Air Force could give the young man rehabilitation training—the officer's commander disallowed this action with the explanation that rehabilitation of felons was "contrary to 12th Air Force policy."

In passing it should be noted that a number of major armies are moving toward looser discipline and decorum—if not always democracy—without falling apart. In Great Britain, the Judge Advocate General is a civilian office. Not since the end of World War II have West German soldiers been subject to military courts; recently they were freed of the obligation to say "sir" to superior officers. The East German Army did away with sirring long ago. France, shocked by the obedience of junior officers to rebellious generals in Algeria, has rewritten its code of justice to permit much more independence of thought and action. And in some respects the Israeli Army is almost a classless society.

Leaving aside these encouraging examples, those who fear chaos can take comfort in the existence of Article 15 of the Uniform Code of Military Justice, which gives commanders all the "housekeeping" disciplinary powers they need. Article 15 allows military commanders to administer nonjudicial punishment for minor infractions of discipline without resorting to the regular criminal-court process. It's a slap-on-the-wrist or kick-in-the-pants kind of punishment, but, most importantly, it does not go on a man's record as a federal conviction. Men can be given extra duties, such as KP, or they can have certain privileges withheld for set periods. Officers can be put under quarters arrest for up to a month and can lose up to one-half of two months' pay; enlisted men can be knocked down in rank, can lose half-pay up to two months and can be put in correctional custody for a month if the sentencing is done by an officer higher in rank than a major. "Correctional custody" can include hard labor. Sailors can be confined for a week and can be put on three consecutive days of bread and water.

Article 15 punishments, then, are not always light. They are even severe when one considers that they are handed down by the authority of a single officer sitting in splendid *souveraineté absolue,* untouchable by any appeal to a higher officer or court. But this system of punishment has the great virtue of not being considered in any way the conviction of a crime. The Article 15 process is not a part of the court-martial system, so let the military have it.

And let it have nothing else. Deserters can be tried in civilian courts just as easily as draft evaders are today. Servicemen whose disturbance of base operations is too serious to be adequately punished by an Article 15 can be taken care of in civilian courts just as easily as are those civilians today who disrupt church services or create a public nuisance or disturb the peace. Civilian courts can handle servicemen who rape, murder, rob, gamble, get drunk, fornicate in public, abuse animals, expose themselves, fight, steal cars or commit any other notable mischief just as easily as they can handle civilians who do these things.

But how will the change be made and who will make it? This is the question that freezes those who would liberate the serviceman. The chances for changes can be easily measured by the fact that modifications in the Military Code of Justice must be agreed upon *not* by the Senate Judiciary Committee, which, though reactionary enough (being the fief of Senator James Eastland of Mississippi), at least has some general interest in law, but by the Senate Armed Services Committee, dominated by John Stennis of Mississippi and Richard B. Russell of Georgia, a group whose alliances with the Pentagon managers are notorious and whose defense of the Pentagon's way of doing things—including the dispensing of justice—is usually total.

The odds against change via the House Armed Services Committee are much heavier. Even when the Pentagon has made timid gestures in the direction of more libertarian regulations, the House Armed Services Committee, scandalously chaired by Mendel Rivers of South Carolina, has protested the liberalization and has demanded, and gotten, a return to the old ways.

Over the signature of Major General Kenneth G. Wickham, Adjutant General, Secretary of the Army Stanley Resor sent out a memorandum on May 27, 1969, titled "Guidance on Dissent." The memo counseled field commanders to take a more relaxed view of the coffeehouses, the GI underground newspapers, on-post demonstrations by civilians and dissent in general. Principles that are taken for granted by civilians must be spelled out for the military, so Resor pointed out that dissent is legitimate in this country. He warned that "a commander may not prevent distribution of a publication simply because he does not like its contents," that "mere possession of a publication may not be prohibited," and that "the Army should not use its off-limits power to restrict soldiers in the exercise of their Constitutional rights of freedom of speech and freedom of association by barring attendance at coffeehouses." He warned against viewing complaining soldiers as "enemies of the system."

Commanders were also instructed that "a specific request for a permit to conduct an on-post demonstration [by civilians] in an area to which the public has generally been granted access should not be denied on an arbitrary basis." (However, the memo assured commanders that they need not allow demonstrations if they presented a "clear danger to loyalty, discipline, and morale of the troops.")

It would not be accurate to suppose that this order resulted in massive antiwar demonstrations on countless posts across the nation. In fact, as a result of the order, only one commander allowed a demonstration: At Fort Meade, Maryland, almost within earshot of Resor's office, forty antiwar protesters were permitted to demonstrate for ninety minutes, and one of them quietly passed out fliers to soldiers.

Under the heading "Tired of the War? Tired of the Army's Pushing You Around?" this is what the flier said:

### G.I.'s

We are a group of people from all walks of life—students, workers, teachers, vets, and even some active G.I.'s—who are seeking an end to the lousy war in Viet Nam and a solution to America's problems at home.

We are aware, as no doubt you are, of the increasing antiwar sentiment among active G.I.'s. We are also aware of the movement inside the armed forces for more rights for G.I.'s, something we whole-heartedly support since G.I.'s are the people who risk their lives on the front lines.

We are not a group which seeks to preach to you and tell you what to do. You get enough of that from the brass. Rather, we see ourselves as providing an opportunity for you to get together with us, and with each other, to talk about the war and other things you may have on your mind. If you feel strongly enough to try to solve some of the problems you're concerned about, we'll provide any assistance we can. But we respect your right to solve these problems in your way.

For more information contact the Baltimore Defense Committee.

Everything was under control; there was one MP for each demonstrator, including the children. There was no violence, no confrontations, no harsh words; all went off very well.

That is, all went off well until the House Armed Services Committee heard of the Resor memorandum and of the subsequent demonstration at Fort Meade. The Army Secretary was called on the carpet and scolded like a stupid child. He was told that the memorandum he had issued was "most repugnant," was "nauseating," was "one of the most damaging documents ever put out by the Army." He was instructed that instead of thinking up ways to permit "entirely unconstitutional demonstrations," he should be plotting ways to catch spies who infiltrate military bases.

Resor kept trying to calm the legislators by stressing the Constitution: "I think it is very important to the Army that we adopt a position that appears to the public as a wholly reasonable position and not an arbitrary one. The military is under attack from many elements, and if we are going to survive, we must show that we are acting in a reasonable way and show we are standing up for the Constitutution. That is all we are doing."

Chairman Rivers, unresponsive to Resor's soothing, rolled over him, jeering at him for "making a great case for that First Amendment," and thundering a warning that "the committee is going to spend a lot of time trying to find some constitutional amendment whereby we can assist you in stopping this kind of thing. We recognize the Supreme Court's decision as a pretty sorry opinion." On he went, increasingly angry, increasingly loud, turning finally on a quiet witness, Army Chief of Staff William C. Westmoreland, and shouting, "General Westmoreland, I will bet my hat you don't agree with it. Now, if you have got one drop of South Carolina blood left in your veins, you don't agree with it. This is an awful thing to come to pass." He paused, swallowing hard. "It is very difficult for me to compose myself and I am stopping myself right now." He adjourned the meeting.

On September 12, 1969, new guidelines on dissent were issued by the Department of Defense. They wiped out the mellowness of the May 27 guidelines and incorporated virtually every hard-line recommendation made by Rivers' committee. Gone from the new guidelines, for example, was the admonition "to impose only such minimum restraints as are necessary to enable the Army to perform its mission."

The initiative for the reform of military justice—which is to say, the dismembering of it—will no more originate in the Congressional military committees than it will in the military itself, and the accommodation of those bodies to reform will be equally painful. What progressive ideas can one hope for from a Congress which, before 1969, had never in its history made a complete investigation of the military penal system?

Movement, if it comes, must come from an outraged and fearful public—outraged by the things the military has done to its young men in the name of "disciplinary necessity," fearful because of the national tolerance of injustice that can result over a long period of time. It may seem too simple to suggest that the only remedy lies with public pressure, but that is, in fact, the only source of remedy. Public pressure after World War II, because of the massive injustices in that war, for the first time forced the military to write a significantly new code of justice. Public opinion, exerted again, can force the military to surrender its claim to any judicial supervision of what are essentially, in the ranks, a civilian army and navy.

Meanwhile, since the exclusion of the military man from the protections of the Bill of Rights appears to be a *fait accompli,* it may seem a waste of time to argue over whether or not he is covered; it may be, under these circumstances, a purely academic exercise to debate whether or not the founding fathers originally intended to treat their virtually nonexistent Army and actually nonexistent Navy with the same care guaranteed to all other Americans. But even if historical debate is superfluous, the practicalities of the present have convinced even many constitutional scholars who take the negative in this debate that the time has come when servicemen *should* be covered, whatever the tradition has been. No less a luminary negative authority on military law than Frederick Bernays Wiener has written (in the *Harvard Law Review*): "When in the years to come, the serviceman shall be recognized as having constitutional rights, such recognition will be, not a reflection of original understanding, but a part of the continuing and continuous process of making law, insuring that, in Maitland's phrase, 'every age should be the mistress of its own law.' Just as every generation makes its own law, so every generation can and must make its own constitutional law." His advice was given twelve years ago; the time for this generation to write its own constitutional law is slipping away.

# Index